ur

ome

brilliantideas

one good idea can change your life...

Create your dream home

Secrets of home makeovers

Lizzie O'Prey

Copyright © The Infinite Ideas Company Limited, 2008

The right of Lizzie O'Prey, Jem Cook, Mark Hillsdon and Anna Marsden to be identified as the authors of this book has been asserted in accordance with the Copyright, Designs and Patents Act 1988

First published in 2008 by
The Infinite Ideas Company Limited
36 St Giles
Oxford
OX1 3LD
United Kingdom
www.infideas.com

A CIP catalogue record for this book is available from the British Library.

ISBN 978-1-905940-33-2

Previously published as *Create your dream garden* (978-1-904902-24-9) and *Create your dream home* (978-1-904902-03-4).

Brand and product names are trademarks or registered trademarks of their respective owners.

Text designed and typeset by Baseline Arts Ltd, Oxford
Cover designed by Cylinder
Printed and bound in India

Brilliant ideas

Brilliant features

Each chapter of this book is designed to provide you with an inspirational idea that you can read quickly and put into practice straight away.

Throughout you'll find four features that will help you to get right to the heart of the idea:

- *Try another idea* If this idea looks like a life-changer then there's no time to lose. *Try another idea* will point you straight to a related tip to expand and enhance the first.

- *Here's an idea for you* Give it a go – right here, right now – and get an idea of how well you're doing so far.

- *Defining ideas* Words of wisdom from masters and mistresses of the art, plus some interesting hangers-on.

- *How did it go?* If at first you do succeed try to hide your amazement. If, on the other hand, you don't this is where you'll find a Q and A that highlights common problems and how to get over them.

Introduction

Set aside all the practical reasons why you have a home – a roof over your head, a place to sleep, somewhere to eat, storage for all your possessions – and consider just one thing: *do you love being there?*

Does the combination of colours, the choice of furniture, the use of materials and the way it's been laid out fit perfectly with your tastes and lifestyle?

If you find yourself thinking that this is not entirely the case, then maybe it's time to make some changes. Here's where this book steps in.

There are guidelines that you can follow and advice that makes great sense and while I am not a fan of rules, some can be applied to tackling the design of your home (but don't feel that you always have to stick to them rigidly). Interpret them in your own way and for your specific situation.

You can seek the advice of a professional interior designer and they will do a magnificent job on decorating your home. But wouldn't it be more fun and give you greater satisfaction if you knew that the inspiration and execution were all your own?

This book will help you make the best decisions in design terms about every room. You may agree with some of the ideas and you may find others just don't fit with

your own perception of what makes a house a home. This has been written from one person's understanding and experience in choosing and using colours, fabrics, furniture and the space in which they will sit. It sets out to inspire rather than lay down the law, so please use it as a guide and not a set of rules.

It sets out to inform and instruct you how to approach certain activities and will hopefully result in you understanding much more about the space in which you live.

It's intended to be enjoyable. Designing and decorating may be hard work but it should be a labour of love. I hope this book helps you to create your perfect space be it the bedroom, bathroom, kitchen, lounge or hallway.

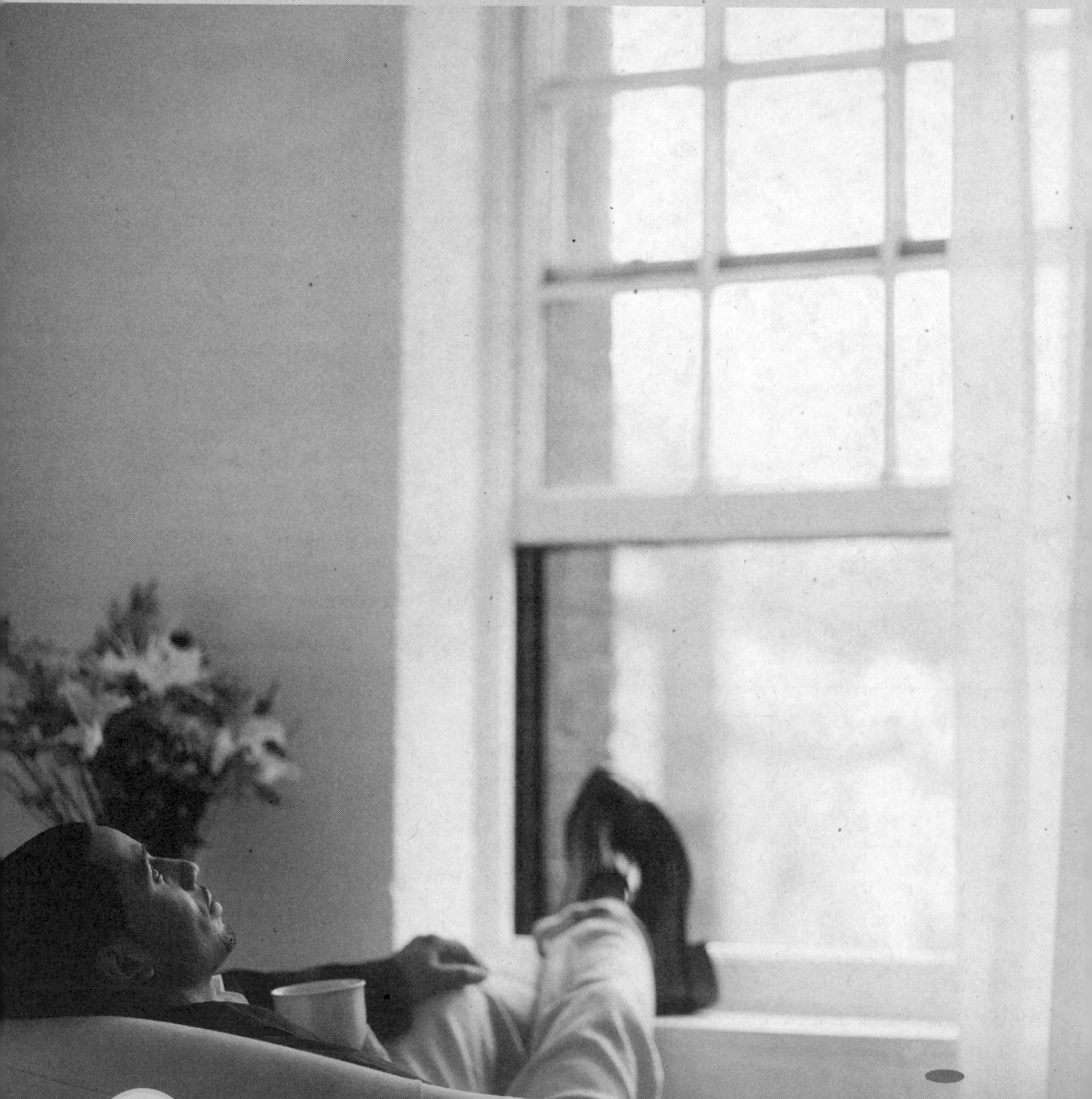

1

Home sweet home

Learn everything there is to know about your home before you begin your design and decoration.

There's a saying 'to know me is to love me', and in the case of my home it's a love that's grown over time. Getting used to a sloping floor and living with uneven walls seemed at first a little annoying, but now I love the charm of my slightly unusual rooms.

I've come to accept, for example, that there is no way that I can open up the chimney without incurring excessive costs. But I can still make a feature of it with a shelf above to simulate a mantelpiece and a pile of lovely logs to decorate the hearth. It's an illusion but it generates a cosy mood – even without the flames. Let's be honest. When we buy a property we rarely give it a thorough going over. Well, it's a bit embarrassing to get caught out with the spirit level by the owner of the house. And you are not going to be able to open every window, close every internal door, look at the construction of every cupboard (to see if the hideous DIY job can be ripped out), run every tap and move furniture around (to get a better idea of how to use the space) even during a second viewing.

Here's an
idea for
you...

Walk around the rooms in your new home. Look at where light fittings are positioned – both ceiling and wall mounted – as this will affect where you position your lamps. Measure up recesses because a piece of storage that was in your old dining room may fit perfectly in the lounge. Consider the flooring. With nothing cluttering up a room is there a spot where you would love to put down a designer rug so that it is seen in the best light? Why not position the furniture around it rather than vice versa, which is more usually the case? Is there a wall space that would be the perfect place for a piece of art or a monumental mirror? You don't want to waste the area by putting a tall cupboard or bookcase there.

Defining
idea...

'A man builds a fine house; and now he has a master, and a task for life: he is to furnish, watch, show it, and keep it in repair, the rest of his days.'
RALPH WALDO EMERSON

2

Which means that the day you move in is a bit like going out on a date arranged by a dating agency. You've seen the picture of the person (house). You've read the biography of the individual concerned (estate agent's details). And you've realised you have no idea what you are going to do next because you don't know their preferences for food, their taste in film or their political leanings.

In 'house' terms these queries could translate into any of the following:

- Does the heating system really warm every room or will you have to redecorate in colours that will help raise the temperature in specific spaces?

- Will your minimalist interior preferences realistically work in a Victorian conversion or are you going to have to rethink your ideas to cope with small rooms rather than loft-style expanses?

- How much natural light does each room enjoy through the day and through the seasons, and are you going to have to invest in task lighting for a study or wall lamps for a living room in order to be able to use the space efficiently?

So how do you proceed in getting to know your home?

I would urge you initially to leave the unpacking (apart from kettle, teabags and mugs) and to go through the house with a large notepad and make notes. Do this before you empty all the boxes and clutter up the space. And if it means that you sleep on your mattress on the floor that night, then so be it. You may think this is unrealistic given the pressures of co-ordinating moving out and in with your purchasers and your vendor but at the very least give yourself an hour or two in the empty property. This is a time that you and the house will never have again because once the furniture is in place and you've put out your collection of china, the room has already been given a 'look'.

Consider these three things:

- **Light:** If you are going to need to maximise the light in a room but need privacy maybe you need to forget curtains but put in blinds that roll from the bottom of the window up rather than vice versa. Or choose designs that have a filtered panel as part of their make-up.

- **Colour:** Redecorating may be the last thing on your mind but could painting just one wall white in a green room make it seem bigger?

You can get the best use of any space by planning the layout of the room. See IDEA 34, *That hits the spot*, for more ideas.

Try another idea...

'I have always felt that one of the greatest compliments anyone visiting your home can pay you is to sit down and take off their jacket unprompted, to be as easy and comfortable in your surroundings as you are. Although serendipity may come into it, such ease isn't accidental: on the contrary, comfort, simplicity, pleasure and practicality are the natural by-products of good design, a combination of intelligent planning, informed choice and creative application.'
SIR TERENCE CONRAN

Defining idea...

3

■ **Balance:** Positioning furniture can create a formal, structured look to the room if everything is aligned, or a more casual relaxed look if pieces are set at angles or left 'floating' in open spaces.

By getting to know your space you'll have a much better chance of a creating a happy and harmonious home.

How did it go?

Q **I've considered all this careful planning but I know that by the time I get into the house, I will have to get the kids settled and two bedrooms and the lounge will need to be unpacked so they can at least watch TV while I tackle the rest of the house.**

A   *Be prepared to be flexible. For starters, ask your agent before moving in if pictures were taken of every room, or if the owner will let you go in and do this. That way you can at least begin to work with existing colour schemes. Decide which rooms are a priority and leave them empty. Stack as many boxes as possible in the guest room so that you can plan the main bedroom, or load up the lounge but leave the kitchen clear for example.*

Q **OK, but there's only so much time that I can survive without the essentials for everyday living.**

A   *Now this is a real pain but I have to advise you to plan your packing. It's so easy just to go round the rooms and pack everything available in the least time possible. I would advise you to assess each room before you start packing and label a box 'Essentials' for things that you know you won't be able to live without. You can put all of these boxes in one place when you arrive in your new home, so that at least you can access the more important things that you need.*

You've got the look

Settle on your style to create a room that's pleasing to the eye.

There is no way that you could or even should stick to every single rigid design rule when putting together your home. However, if you're happy to work with some guidelines in place, you'll reap the rewards in terms of creating an appealing and desirable space.

It's all about putting together the furniture, soft furnishings and accessories that match a certain mood.

I'm a minimalist, modernist, neutral colours kind of person and that means I have certain requirements in setting my style. There has to be plenty of storage in a room to keep it free from clutter. (I have serious storage issues but I do try to keep them behind closed doors.) The window treatments have to be simple. I have never contemplated curtains at any of my windows – it's always Roman blinds because of their clean lines. Fabrics are, in the main, natural: linen, wool, cotton and canvas. My vases are plain, clear glass and my flowers arrangements are always uncomplicated. And that's how to set a style.

Sit down and make a list of all the elements that you need. Break it down into the following: furniture, soft furnishings, flooring, window treatments, lighting and accessories. Now estimate a price beside each item on your list. It doesn't have to be exact, just a ballpark figure. Total this up and consider whether you can spend more or need to cut back. You can take away a chair and save some money or add an elaborate chandelier if you have the cash. Once you have a list that matches your budget, go to work on that room.

'To me style is just the outside of content, and content the inside of style, like the outside and inside of the human body – both go together, they can't be separated.'
JEAN-LUC GODARD

Think about spaces that you are drawn to. These could be a good indication of your personal style. (I loved the old Saatchi gallery in London's Westbourne Grove because it was just a vast, open, clutter-free space.) If you find yourself drawn to grand stately homes or always book a cosy country cottage for your holidays, these could be a starting point for tailoring a room to suit. Use a mood board to help you put together the look, incorporating a picture of your ideal room to inspire you as you work.

SO WHAT ELSE INFLUENCES YOUR STYLE?

Taste in music? You might worship at the feet of Elvis and so employ a retro approach to your interior.

Love of gardening? Cultivate a collection of floral prints that will give a theme for your scheme.

An historical period? Look for reproduction – or if you have the bank balance original – antique furniture.

Another country? Source sumptuous silks from the Orient, porcelain painted in China or hand-carved accessories from Indonesia.

This should be polarising your thoughts. So now consider the practicalities of putting your plan into action.

Give yourself a budget: some looks are less expensive to achieve than others. What about structural alterations? Will knocking two rooms into one give you the space you need to make a dramatic statement? You might also give some thought to the future. If you are planning to stay in the house for only a couple of years, should you tone down the colour scheme so that you won't have to redecorate when you want to sell? Last but not least, will your style work in the space that you have? Light-drenched loft style is difficult to achieve in a basement flat.

If you set a style and get all the elements right, then you'll be happy to live with the look for years.

Here's an idea for you...

It's the lavish use of fabrics and ornate detailing that set a stately home style. Think long draping curtains complete with decorative pelmets and tasselled tiebacks. In the lounge you can look for a sofa that includes piles of cushions in its design. For the bedroom choose a four-poster bed or a design with a scrolling iron headboard and decorative posts finished with balls or finials. If you are drawn to this kind of place you'll be happy to fill the room with lots of extra furniture and accessories. Bring in a pouffe or covered footstool, a nest of tables and a writing desk complete with matching chair. Include one or two rugs on the floor to augment the 'soft' look of the room.

Try another idea...

If you are thinking about changing the lighting in one or two rooms, see IDEA 19, _An illuminating experience_, for some helpful hints.

How did
it go?

Q **I've designed my dining room around my love of English country gardens. I have used floral prints on the walls and a petal patterned fabric at the window, and put down some rugs with rose designs woven into the borders. We entertain regularly so there are always flowers on the table. During the summer there is a lot of natural light and I'm quite happy with the busy design, but how can I lighten it up a bit in the winter months?**

A *It sounds like you have embraced the principles of planning a look, but it's also good to give rooms a mini facelift from time to time. Try the following. Take down one of the floral prints and replace it with a mirror. A gold frame might be a good choice to add a little touch of glitz. Have some slip covers made for the dining chairs in plain white cotton – this will lighten the room. Do you have a pendant light or wall lights? You may want to change the shades to a lighter fabric or even glass designs. Take the rugs away and see if that alters the mood. It might be a good opportunity to have them professionally cleaned and you can view the room without them.*

Q **I have realised that the different items that I own suit a whole different range of styles. I don't want to get rid of some pieces. What do I do?**

A *There are certain key items that do set a style. The sofa in the lounge and the bed in the bedroom would be two such pieces. Now it would be silly to suggest that everything that isn't modern, antique, blue or green, depending on your scheme, should be dumped. Remember that you're creating a home, not a museum or a show house, and allow yourself a few pieces in any space that are there just because you like them rather than because they are a perfect fit. That's part of what makes a house a home.*

3

Work that colour

Find the shades and tones that suit your home. The pick 'n' mix approach is all very well at the cinema sweetie counter but. . .

Colour scheming your whole house may sound like a huge challenge but by breaking it down room by room it is simply a matter of application. And in order to create a harmonious environment, it's really the only sensible approach.

OH GOOD GRIEF, DO I HAVE TO BE SENSIBLE?

Well yes, if you want to end up without colour clashes and disharmony as you move from room to room. Imagine when all the doors in the house are open being able to see a little bit of purple to the left (lounge), some green to the right (dining room), and walking through yellow (hallway), as you head for the blue kitchen. It's a quite a prospect isn't it?

(On a very practical level, if your room colours complement each other, then furniture, furnishings and accessories should work in a number of different places.

Here's an idea for you...

You may already have a room that is wallpapered and it can be fag or just a downright waste of time to strip the room in order to match your overall scheme. Choose a colour from the paper, it may be a touch of blue in the print, for example, and then use that in an adjacent room to link the two together.

This means that you can move pieces around your home when you want a change of scene, or to swap dining room for living room or guest room for master bedroom for example.)

I'm not the colour police. This approach doesn't mean that you have to be all white at every turn (apart from woodwork on which I would very rarely use any other paint). My advice is to stick with colours from the same broad family spectrum across most of your home or at least introduce the same colour in some form or another in each room. But there are three alternatives for successful colour scheming so take your pick from the list below. And if you decide to break the law in the odd space (hopefully just the box room) then you can live with your own guilt.

Take a look at a colour wheel and consider adopting the red and orangey siblings. Move around the wheel and introduce yourself to the yellow and greens or opt for the blues and purples. Each of these groups can affect your mood and effect changes of perception of the shape and size of the room. At the most basic level, for example, a red dining room will stimulate, a yellow dining room will cheer you up, and a blue room will engender a sense of calm.

The size of rooms should have an influence on your colour choices. If you have a series of small rooms you'll need to stick to a lighter palette. Where there's the luxury of generous proportions you can afford to move to the darker colours in the spectrum.

Here are your choices:

- **A tonal scheme:** This is where you pick just one colour but use it in varying tones. With purples, for example, you might combine the palest lavender and lilac, magenta, plum and wine. For greens, you might use eau de nil, olive, sage and pine.

- **A harmonious scheme:** Choose colours that are closely associated. The best way to do this is to look at a rack of paint charts and take three or four adjacent to each other. Start with red, next to it you'll find terracotta, copper and then chestnut.

- **A complementary scheme:** This uses colours that are opposites of each other. Orange versus blue, green versus purple, yellow versus scarlet. You will need to decide which one of the two colours will be more dominant in a room; indecision here can cause infighting that will wreck the scheme.

Whichever of the above you choose, one simple way to unify the rooms in a house is to stick with the same colour for your woodwork throughout.

YOU MAY HAVE HEARD THIS A THOUSAND TIMES BUT LISTEN AGAIN!

Start out by buying tester pots. Then paint large pieces of white paper in your chosen colours and pin them up around your home. Leave them for several days. Watch how the light affects them in different rooms and swap them around to see how they may

Try another idea...

If you like the idea of using neutral and natural colours for your scheme see IDEA 5, *Natural stimulation.* For an all-white approach, turn to IDEA 11, *When white is right.*

Defining idea...

'Colour possesses me. I don't have to pursue it. It will possess me always, I know it.'
PAUL KLEE

11

alter the perspective of a space. Make notes. Let someone else have an opinion (within reason). But do not paint a wall until you have lived with them for a least a week.

'Fools rush in' when it comes to making colour choices, so take time and take care and you won't 'fear to tread' in any of your rooms.

How did it go?

Q I've used a complementary scheme of lilac and green in the dining room but the purple on every wall seems to dominate the room.

A *You can create balance by including a neutral colour in the space. A grey will work with green and purple. Use the tester pot experiment and paint a piece of paper in a soft grey. Something subtle like mink. Stick it on one or two walls at different times of the day to see which best helps it balance the scheme. For other complementary schemes, a taupe will work with both blue and orange, and white is just right for yellow and scarlet.*

Q OK, but what if I can't face repainting a wall?

A *This is where you can use furniture, flowers and accessories – basically any tool in the designer's repertoire to make it work. Position a set of shelves in a neutral colour against one of the main walls to break up the expanse of purple. Or find a print or picture that you can hang on one wall that, again, will break up the block of colour. A huge bunch of beautiful white lilies placed in the middle of a table will always draw the eye to that particular spot.*

4

Welcome to my world

Seen first and frequently passed through, your hallway deserves more attention than you may think.

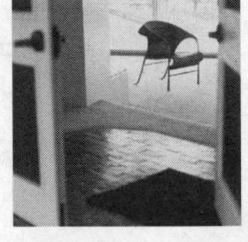

There are certain spaces that we often neglect. It is lack of thought more than a deliberate disregard, and the hall all too often falls into this list. In fact it could well be at the top.

Which is ludicrous when you think that this is the first space that you see when you get home and the last area that you pass through when you leave. Think about all the trips that you make through this space. You probably go through it in the morning to get tea from the kitchen and then you traverse it again on your way back upstairs to have a shower. Later on, you retrace your steps downstairs to make breakfast and then you nip into the hall to pick up the post. Are you getting the idea? You spend more time in the hall than you think. So it should, above all other rooms, deserve careful attention and a loving touch.

- **Make it welcoming:** A chair or reclaimed church pew that is tucked against the wall allows people to rest for a minute after they walk through the door.

Here's an idea for you... **A decorative chimney pot or length of earthenware pipe, placed in a stylish bowl, makes an alternative umbrella stand.**

- **Keep it useful:** Coat hooks, umbrella stands, a mat to wipe feet on and a table to dump the post on make it a functional space

- **Light it right:** Make sure that you have switches at the bottom and top of the staircase. If it's very dark, consider replacing a solid wood front door with a design that has glass panels.

- **Make your home secure:** Add as many devices as you want: bolts, chains and a spy hole are all advisable.

It's more than likely that this area leads into other spaces so choose a colour scheme that won't clash with adjacent rooms. It is also probable that there is a lot of empty wall space and you could easily use it to hang a collection of prints. Are there areas that you could use to create extra storage space or redefine for another purpose? The space under the stairs, for example, might be used to house a desk or utilised as a laundry. These are all details that will enhance the look and functionality of your hall.

STEP BY STEP

Give plenty of thought to your staircase. What seems to be an immovable feature can be replaced or dressed up according to your budget. Accepting that wood is the material that most of us will inherit when we move into our home, it's a revelation when you think about the other materials that can be used to construct a staircase: glass, concrete and steel are all utilised in new builds and conversions to fit in with the overall scheme of an interior.

Consider one of the following options:

- If you need to bring more light into the space, then choose a glass balustrade and beechwood treads.

- Should you want to continue an open plan theme, commission a hanging wire system where the treads are seemingly suspended in space.

- Do you live in an industrial-style loft? Add rubber treads to the edge of each step.

- Want to be decorative but can't afford a runner (and they can be pricey)? Then leave the central half of each step in natural wood and paint the quarter each side to match the balustrade.

- Modernising an old building? Cover the steps with flexible zinc sheeting.

If you take the time to pay attention to your hallway you'll be rewarded with a welcome every time.

'I have heard that stiff people lose something of their awkwardness under high ceilings, and in spacious halls.'
RALPH WALDO EMERSON

Defining idea...

There are plenty of options when you come to choose the flooring for your hall. IDEA 28, *A tough decision*, may give you some ideas.

Try another idea...

'There is room in the halls of pleasure
For a large and lordly train,
But one by one we must all file on
Through the narrow aisles of pain.'
ELLA WHEELER WILCOX,
American poet

Defining idea...

15

How did it go?

Q **I realise that I've neglected the staircase and I'm thinking about painting the wood so that it matches the walls. What do you think?**

A *In theory this sounds lovely. But can I just tell you that there is no worse job in the decorating arena than painting or stripping the spindles, so unless you can pay someone to do the job, you might want to consider living with what you have. I know from experience the pain, anguish, tears and monumental boredom that are involved in tackling this job. My observation is that you have to be having the love affair of your life – the one – the only – the 'never felt like this before and don't believe I ever will again' relationship with your home if you are prepared to go through this.*

If you still want to go ahead, then make sure you prepare the woodwork for paint, set aside a month of Sundays and good luck to you.

Q **I have a dark hallway so I chose a light-coloured carpet for the flooring, however, it's now getting very grubby, particularly by the front door. If I put a mat down it's going to obstruct the doorway, so what should I do?**

A *Make yourself a mat well. Measure up an area roughly 1 metre long from the door and remove the carpet using a heavy-duty craft knife. Take this along to a carpet specialist and find a coir or seagrass that is of the same thickness as your carpet. Order a mat to be made up to the dimensions of the space that you have cut and drop it into place. Fix a threshold strip between the two types of flooring to neaten the join.*

5

Natural stimulation

**Sand and stone, woodlands and heather strewn hillsides...
nature provides inspiration for stunning interiors.**

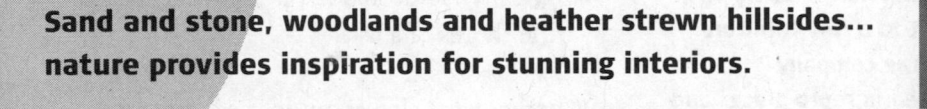

Whether you choose whitewashed walls
reminiscent of crumbling cliffs or a smoky
grey grass flooring that reminds you of walks on
the moors, there is endless stimulation for the
jaded designer when you look outside.

Using natural materials in a room makes for a relaxed and comfortable space. And
small pieces from the great outdoors – a rough length of driftwood in the
bathroom, a vase of smooth pebbles in the lounge, a bowl of sea-worn iridescent
seashells beside the bed – all offer a way of introducing interesting texture into
your home.

I like to sit down and list the looks and finishes I want to mimic when creating a
naturally inspired interior:

- The roughened texture of yellowy grass on a sand dune

- The silvery brown of a worn tree trunk

The most fun you can have with furniture is to copy a technique that I saw, and got to try out, on a visit to a fine furniture factory. The company specialised in repro pieces and part of the process of turning new into old involved repeatedly beating a cabinet. The tool used was a collection of nuts and bolts (I added a couple of keys when I did this at home) on a chain. Repeatedly flog the surface until you have knicks, scratches and dents to suit. It's fine therapy too.

- The fluffy, curly, creamy wool from a sheep

- The myriad of smooth greys on pebbles by the shores of a lake

Whether your closest outdoor escape is a forest, a field or a beach, use that environment as a starting point for planning a room. (If you feel it's time for a break, take a walk in the country now! Take snapshots of the things you see as you stroll with your fabulous mobile phone or digital camera and you can download these images and use them in your mood board for the room.)

All these colours are in some way slightly bleached out. They are subtle and no one shade stands out as dominant. This means you can mix and match them to your heart's content without creating colour clashes in a space.

Imagine a grey flannel-covered sofa or chair, a mellow seagrass flooring, a chunky beechwood table. Put these in the midst of a room where the backdrop is a limestone-coloured wall and the windows are draped with unbleached linen curtains and you are beginning to commune with nature.

There's one collection of paints you must look at: Kelly Hoppen's Perfect Neutrals from Fired Earth. Choose from Shell, Bone, Pebble, Linen, Orchid, Tusk, Clotted Cream, etc., etc., etc. – all gloriously evocative names (though how you visualise In

Love With Taupe without seeing it bears some thought). These are colours that you'll come back to time and time again. You'll reuse them when you move from one home to the next because they are just perfect examples of the best of the natural palette.

But aren't they a bit bland? I here the colour cravers cry . . .

Here's where you rely on texture to bring that interest into the space. I love natural fibre for floors. There's something refreshing about the thought that you are walking on grass (yes a refined type I know). But if that option is a little bit too rough for your tastes (and I would avoid it in bedrooms), then I would suggest a loop pile carpet. In flecked wool this is both practical and pretty much perfect for a natural scheme. And you'll see the texture.

Next fabrics. No smooth silks or flat cottons. For blinds, use hessian and wicker weaves. For curtains choose one of the 'new' suedes. They look like the real thing but are a fraction of the cost. You are looking for anything that has a 'touchy-feely' quality, so a rough linen or a robust corduroy also fit the bill. Knitted cushion covers or throws with bobbles and fringes are just what you need.

If you let a love of nature inspire your interiors you'll find it easy to create a mellow and relaxing home.

'*Nature does nothing in vain.*'
ARISTOTLE

Defining idea...

If you like the idea of natural flooring take a look at IDEA 41, *The soft side*, for some materials that might suit.

Try another idea...

'*The unreal is natural, so natural that it makes of unreality the most natural of anything natural.*'
· GERTRUDE STEIN

Defining idea...

19

How did it go?

Q **I understand the point of introducing texture but all my walls are new plaster, so beautifully smooth, and my furniture is mostly pine.**

A *The quickest solution is to think about using paint effects. (No, I'm not going to begin a lesson in stencilling so don't turn the page just yet.) You can use them for maximum impact with a natural colour palette. Texturing, ageing or crackle-glazing are perfect for these rooms. You can add sand to emulsion to give walls a subtle grain, or layer a base coat onto a piece of furniture, rub over the surface with a candle and then add a topcoat in a slightly lighter shade of the base colour. Sand the whole piece and the paint comes away from the waxed areas giving you the textured appearance of years of wear and tear.*

Q **I've used coir in the room but now I've come to clean, how do I treat the flooring?**

A *If it wasn't supplied with a stain inhibitor then you must get the flooring treated as you need to protect against any liquid spillages. You shouldn't use water or shampoo on these natural floorings as they will absorb the moisture and expand or wrinkle. If something gets knocked over, soak it up instantly. Allow mud or dirt to dry out before tackling it. Simply brush the area to loosen the mud and then give the room a vacuum. Use furniture cups under chair legs or castors, as this type of flooring will mark.*

6

Wet, wet, wet rooms

Take the plunge for a luxury bathroom. The most stimulating experience I have ever had naked was in a hotel in Las Vegas. And if you've never tried out a wet sauna, I can't recommend it highly enough.

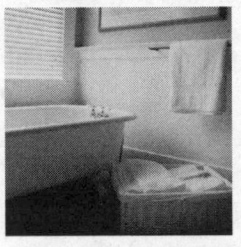

In the middle of The Pink Flamingo spa (even though 'Bugsy' Siegel's original Flamingo is now gone, the hotel that still carries the name is no less glamorous) you can sit until it's hot enough to fry an egg on your leg and then pull a chain and get deluged with freezing water.

Once you can breathe again – roughly 20 seconds later – you do the same thing all over again and again and again. This is the perfect way to wash away the memory of losses at the blackjack table and effective as a hangover cure for the free Jack Daniels at the roulette wheel. (But is not recommended for anyone too highly strung or with any kind of heart condition – but then they probably wouldn't be in Vegas anyway.)

Here's an idea for you...

For the ultimate in luxury include a television in the room: you won't have to miss a moment of a movie or the start of the football. The latest version looks like a tinted mirror until you switch it on (using your credit card sized remote control) and it has a heated screen so that you'll still be able to see the picture however hot and steamy it gets in the room.

A word of caution: *be very careful* when researching wet rooms on the web. Start by going for upmarket bathroom specialists and tile companies to get professional advice. Even on Google, the websites that come up when using 'wet rooms' as a search term include a diverse cross-section of porn available on the net.

When I got home from my trip, I began to research the idea of having some kind of spa at home...and quickly realised that I'd have to go back to the States in order to win enough money to pay for a wet room. But don't let that put you off. You can simplify things and include elements such as a whirlpool bath or a large enough for two walk-in shower cubicle into your bathroom without breaking the bank. You can invest in a specially designed shower cubicle with a gently sloping floor that allows excess water to be contained in a small area. Team that with glass walls for the cubicle and you can kid the pickiest bather that there's a freestanding shower in the room.

If you want to go the whole hog and include a shower without a screen, a 'barrier-free' bathroom where water runs into a well in a gently sloping floor, the most important consideration is to find a builder – or bathroom designer – with experience of wet rooms. The floor may need to be raised to allow for a slope and in older houses the floor may not support the weight of a new stone or fully tiled floor. It isn't just a question of retiling, the surfaces will need to be lined and sealed, which is a specialist job. At this point it is also worth thinking about underfloor heating. I would always recommend installing it as the room will be much more inviting in the winter months. You might also want to consider a sunken tub. Consult with your builder or designer to see if it will fit in with the raising of the floor and can be fitted into a recessed area.

When you are considering sanitary ware and furniture, go for wall-mounted pieces in every situation possible.

LAP OF LUXURY

Super showers now offer such a range of luxury facilities you can easily recreate the spa experience at home. In contrast to the classic over-the-bath dribbling handset, you want a heavy-duty spray.

The importance of a powerful shower cannot be emphasised enough. Showers need sufficient water pressure to maintain a steady flow so the position of your water tank could affect the installation. *Again, this is why you must have an experienced designer or builder on the job.*

If you want to think about the space before you commit to a wet room, turn to IDEA 17, *Bathe in style*.

Try another idea...

'**What would the world be, once bereft Of wet and wildness? Let them be left, O let them be left, wildness and wet, Long live the weeds and the wildness yet.'**
GERARD MANLEY HOPKINS

Defining idea...

Defining idea...

'Some men are like musical glasses; to produce their finest tones you must keep them wet.'
SAMUEL TAYLOR COLERIDGE

When choosing your fixtures look out for a steam version that incorporates an overhead shower, lighting and maybe speakers that can be built into the ceiling. (No point in scrimping on the luxury element if you are doing this properly, and tunes in the steam room are a plus.) Shower designers know that if you are going to steam you need to really relax, so some have thoughtfully added seats to their products. Include a shower design that offers adjustable jets or side sprays so that you can massage whichever bit of cellulite is bothering you that day. After you've steamed you'll want to cool off with a deluge of cold water, so look for an appropriately named flood shower that recreates a waterfall effect overhead. Sound like a lot of fixtures? Well modern technology means that you can find all these features in a single model.

FINISHING TOUCHES

Natural materials suit the style of a wet room. Marble, granite, slate, wood and glass should all be considered in the materials that you choose. Small mosaic tiles on the walls will give the room a Mediterranean feel; duck boarding sets a Scandinavian mood. If you want to add a wall to divide any area of the room – to prevent the basin or loo from getting splashed every time you enjoy a vigorous session in the shower for example – create a panel from glass bricks for a modern look.

The beauty of a spa-type bathroom is that it functions as somewhere to get clean, somewhere to relax and somewhere to indulge yourself. If you are a bit of a water baby, it's the perfect room.

Q   The idea of waterproofing the whole room sounds a bit extreme. I live in an old house and it sounds like a lot of work. Can you tell me more?

How did it go?

A   *Yes it does involve a lot of work, especially if you have a suspended wooden floor which will have to be raised to accommodate the drain. It needs to be waterproofed as this is the only way that you can set up the space so that it doesn't matter where the water flows and which surfaces it hits. Professionals also describe it as 'tanking' the room. More often than not this involves taking up the existing wooden floor. You then angle it to the waste and drain and cover the whole thing with a material such as ply or fibreglass. Finally a rubberised solution can be used to seal the whole surface.*

Q   So if I do have this done is there any point in me putting in a shower screen?

A   *No, that's the whole point. It won't matter where the water from the shower goes. The only reason you might have for using one is if you want to protect the loo or bath from getting a drenching every time you take a shower, but if you position them on the opposite side of the room to the shower head you shouldn't have a problem.*

7

Curtain call

Frame your windows and let the fabric do the work. When you smarten up your sashes or bring colour to your casements, you are complementing a colour scheme or fitting in with a particular look.

Do you want casual drapes running on curtain rings and a pole or are you looking for a more formal treatment where the curtains are teamed up with a pelmet and dressy tiebacks?

Your choice of curtains should reflect the mood of the room. Keep it simple if you are living in a modern environment, a neat pencil pleat heading and plain pole for example, and go OTT if you have a classic look in mind, and I mean indulge your windows with pelmets, tiebacks and tasselled trimmings.

There is a plethora of different looks for your curtains but you should always be generous with the fabric that you use. Whatever the style of the room, the curtains should comfortably cover the window; if the fabric has to be pulled quite flat to meet in the middle they will always look cheap, cheap, cheap. Allow a minimum of two times the width of the window and a maximum of three when you buy it. (You can go for more but it is only necessary for the most opulent of designs.)

Here's an idea for you... If you have a room that isn't overlooked, consider leaving your windows bare of any traditional treatment. With any kind of view outside this creates an amazing impact when people walk into the room. If it seems a bit bare, pick a mixture of vases of different heights. Arrange the same kind of flowers in each receptacle and place in front of one or two panes, keeping the tallest to the side panes of the run of windows. Alternatively use the sills to display pictures or photographs, propped up against the glass and moved around on a regular basis to change the mood.

Those clever designs that seem effortlessly to pool on the floor can look amazing. This look works better with light fabric that flows and drapes easily; anything too heavy will bulk up on the floor into a heavy pile rather than sink down into a light pool.

FABRIC CHOICES

Never buy fabric for curtains based on a tiny swatch. You will have no idea about how a print will look when it is made up into curtains if you have only seen a small square of the design. It would be a bit like buying a still-life when the artist has only sketched a single apple: how are you going to know what the overall finished piece will look like? The best way to get an idea when you are buying fabric for this job is to grab the roll off the shelf in the shop and pull out a metre or two so that you can see the complete repeat of a design. No sales assistant in the soft furnishings department worth his or her salt will frown on you doing this and if they do, just stare them down. After all, if you are dressing two or three windows in the same room you might be investing a large amount of money.

Depending on the place that you are decorating, look to lovely shears, muslins and voiles for rooms where you want the light to flood in. They have a luxurious air when allowed to drape in generous swathes. One trick to add a more formal touch is to hang them behind a pelmet which is covered in a contrasting fabric. Choose damasks, heavy linen and textured silk when you want to make more of a statement with the drapes when they are closed. There is no doubt that you will have already made a decision about your colour scheme when you come to choose the fabric but think about the different effects that patterns can achieve. If you want to create the illusion of extra height, then opt for a design with a vertical stripe. If you want to add width, then pick a material with a horizontal design.

Just a note on poles. If your fabric is opulent, choose a suitably grand pole and make sure that the finials are dressy too. For sheer designs, keep the pole understated – something that ends with a simple curl would be fine.

Take the time to research your fabric choices and match the treatment to the mood of the room and you are on the right road for creating gorgeous windows.

Try another idea...

The dining room is often a place for opulent window treatments. See IDEA 29, *Eating in is the new eating out*, **for ways of designing this room.**

Defining idea...

'*Either those curtains go or I do.*'
OSCAR WILDE

Defining idea...

'*It is god in the house when the curtains lift gently at the windows.*'
ELLEASE SOUTHERLAND,
African-American author

29

How did it go?

Q **I have chosen a patterned fabric for my curtains but it's quite sheer so they will need lining. What type of fabric do you suggest I use?**

A *Have you ever thought about combining different fabrics? A pattern lined with a stripe looks quite special when you can see a little of the stripe when the curtains are pulled back. Use a tieback to make sure you can create this look. You'll need to manipulate the fabric a little so that the stripes show. If you then use some of the same material to make up a couple of cushion covers it ties a scheme together beautifully.*

Q **I have a small window on one wall in the dining room – is there anything I can do to make it seem bigger?**

A *It's easy to alter the proportions of a window by careful positioning of a pelmet and pole. If you fix your pelmet so that the bottom edge just barely covers the top of the window frame, no one will see just exactly where the window finishes. Allow your pole to extend each side to one-third of the width of a small window. When you draw the curtains allow the inside edge to just brush the sides of the frame. No one will be able to guess just how narrow the window really is.*

8

Work that room

Get the best out of your home office. You are saving a ridiculous amount of time by not travelling to and from work each day when you set up an office at home. But if the environment isn't functional and your use of the space less than efficient, you may not reap the benefits.

In creating a work area at home you want it to be able to operate independently from the rest of the house.

Have you thought about converting a garden shed or garage into a work area? Or having a dedicated building installed in the garden that you can then make into an office? I have even read of an office being constructed in a tree house, so think laterally about where you have space that could be used (and just imagine how lovely it would to be stuck up a tree all day!).

If you aren't lucky enough to have a dedicated room, what are your office options? You need to create a space in another place and the dining room is a perfect spot for doubling up. There is already a table and chairs (although you should invest in a dedicated work chair – you are going to be sitting for several hours a day and don't want to end up with backache). You probably already have plenty of lamps and good dedicated lighting in the dining room and adding another piece of storage that won't look out of place shouldn't be too tricky if you pick a unit that matches your existing colour scheme.

Here's an idea for you...

If your office is situated in a dual-purpose room it's more than worth investing in a unit that will house your work area but can be closed off at the end of the day. Faux wardrobes or bookcases are widely available. If you work in the lounge, use leather suitcases or adapt blanket boxes as storage for files. In a guest room you can easily disguise the bed during work hours by positioning it against a wall and covering it with throws and a mix of cushions.

If you need to adopt a corner of the lounge, try and make sure that you position your desk on the same side of the room as the door and preferably behind where it opens into the space. That way, if you don't tidy up at the end of everyday, a cluttered desk isn't the first thing that people see when they walk into the room. I would urge you to invest in a screen. Whether you opt for a Japanese-style paper design, an old-fashioned fabric piece or even a wooden screen, this can be moved into place to disguise the work area and moved out of the way when you have nothing to hide.

Avoid working in the bedroom if you can. You need to get away from the office and if work is on your mind when you go to bed, and within easy reach, it's a recipe for an unsettled night.

I started out with a fairly chaotic approach to the 'office environment' when I started working from home but quickly realised that I needed to address a few specific issues.

■ **Time is money:** Don't start doing all the jobs that you used to fit in at the weekend during your working day.

■ **Good communication is a must:** Have a dedicated phone, fax and internet line for your work.

■ **Organisation is essential:** Make sure that you have storage, then get some storage, and finally bring in some more storage. There is nothing more off-putting when you start the working day than piles of papers on the floor and a desk littered with literature.

■ **Layout is key:** Set up the space so that information you need instant access to is positioned near to the desk. Occasional reference material can go in a cupboard on the other side of the room.

If you are put off by working in chaos, IDEA 15, *Keep it tidy*, may help you clear the decks.

Try another idea...

'The presence of a second building behind the main house made the property all the more attractive to Hemingway, because it was there that he could make his study a refuge, a place where he could create, and was accessible by way of an exterior flight of iron stairs. He lined the walls with shelving, filled them with books, and acquired a plain round table. Here he installed himself, sitting upon a leather-covered stick chair purchased from a cigar factory. The process began every day in the peace of the early morning and generally continued for a good six hours.'
FRANCESCA PREMOLI-DROULERS, *Writers' Houses*

Defining idea...

33

■ **Safety is an issue:** Keep an eye on the number of plugs going into sockets and extension leads and keep cabling organised so that it doesn't get into a spaghetti-like state.

■ **Lighting must be right:** Get dedicated task lighting. Do position a lamp on your desk but don't allow it to reflect on the screen.

■ **You need a good ambience:** I have an 'energising' scented candle to burn and keep flowers on my desk.

■ **Avoid distractions:** Position your office away from the busy or family areas of the home.

■ **Make it a dedicated space:** Try and keep the office area clear of anything that isn't related to your work.

If you try to implement as many of the above as possible, you should find working from home works for you.

Q **I've been getting backache after working for several hours. I'm using an office-style chair that I bought second-hand but I do a lot of keying-in work and my back seems to be getting worse. What can I do?**

How did it go?

A *It sounds to me like you need to chuck out the chair and go to a professional office supplies company. Explain the type (no pun intended) of work that you do, how long you are seated and take along a measurement of the height of your desk or table. You may need a chair with flexible height positioning for the seat so that your feet can sit flat on the ground when you work. Does the back support you when you sit forward to type and sit back to read? You should be looking for a design that supports your spine at all times.*

Q **OK, but I'm still not comfortable for longer than an hour or so.**

A *And why should you be? You must take regular breaks when working at a computer. My optician recommends that I move away from my desk and walk around every 10 or 15 minutes for general well-being as well as to protect my eyes. Get a cup of tea, open the post or grab a snack – but make sure that you are taking regular breaks.*

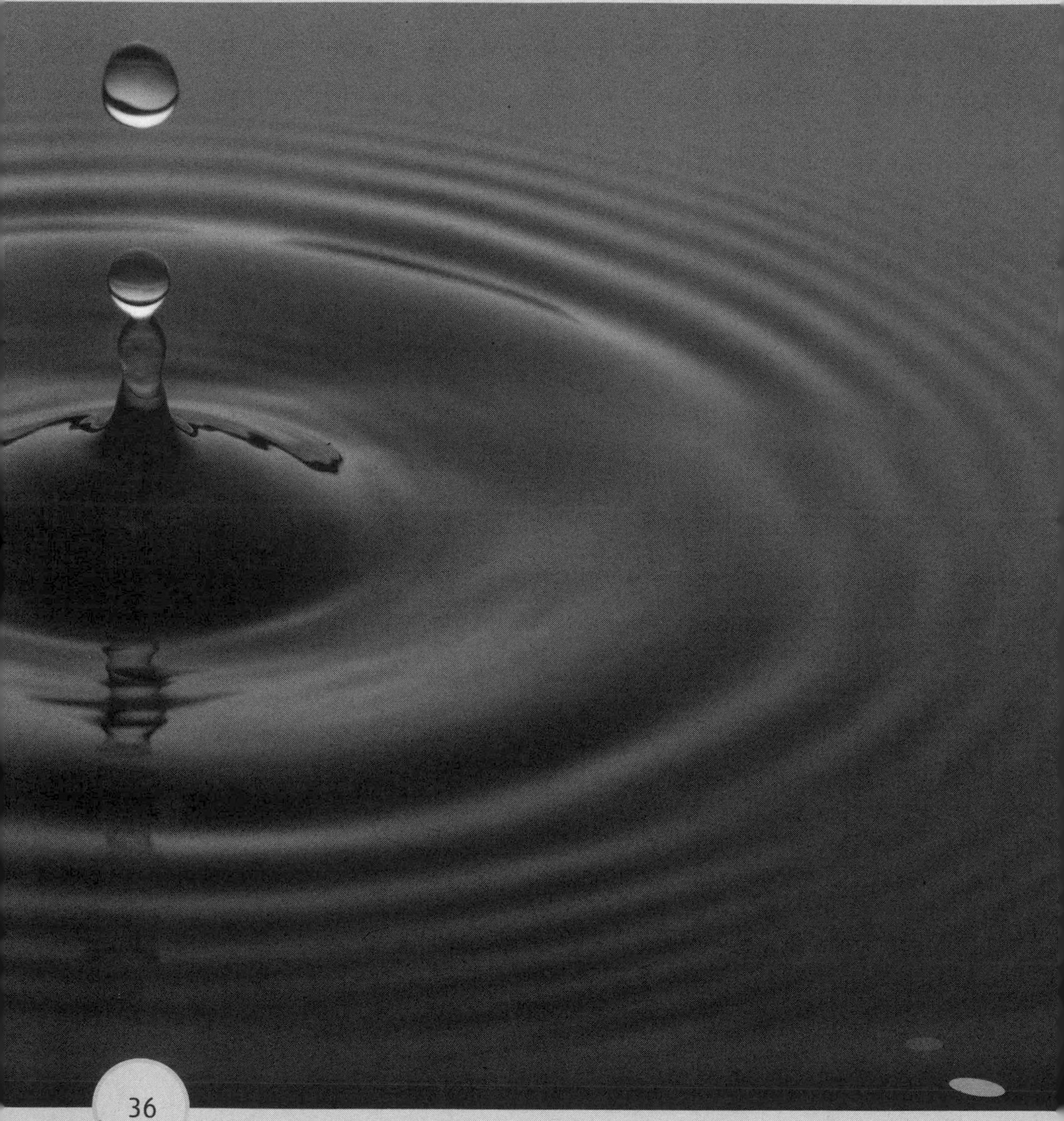

9

Choosing the blues

An ocean colour scene. From tranquil seas and stormy skies to classic tunes and Paul Newman's eyes, the blues can do no wrong.

In choosing blue and including blue, you bring a calming influence to your home. A place or space with a hint of blue is somewhere you'll find that you can relax. I'm not a hippy, but trust me (along with a raft of well-trained and very well-educated colour therapists): colours do affect your mood.

I am that sure whichever colour you are drawn to, blue or red or yellow or black or white, it is tied into memories both good and bad. Holidays, high days, hellos and goodbyes...in the same way that I have a record that reminds me of a certain time, so a colour is evocative. Blue reminds me of years at college beside the sea in Bournemouth. And a once in a lifetime holiday in Barbados, where the sea and sky is always blue and your mood is always good (rum hangovers aside).

Here's an idea for you...

You might find the seaside scheme from the Mediterranean too bright so try out a nautical look that owes more to the yachts and boats of the Isle of Wight. Think about a traditional nautical scene with deep navy heavy-duty cotton fabrics to cover sofas and chairs. Avoid a simple two-tone room and bring in a touch of deckchair stripe with a hint of pink or green for blinds or curtains, and small touches of sandy taupe in rugs or throws. Why not strip back floorboards to introduce a touch of wood or perhaps invest in a classic steamer chair where the combination of canvas upholstery and a wood frame encompass the look of the whole. Think ship's galley. Bring in pebble grey in the form of accessories, whether it's a stone vase or slate bowl, to complete the room.

SO WHY CHOOSE BLUES?

Well, they are calming and serene. They bring peace and tranquillity. They can be austere and they can be welcoming. Cool blues, with a grey or greeny shade, are cold. If you have a north-facing room where natural daylight is reduced to a watery trickle in the winter and a solitary sun-rising hour in the summer, it most certainly isn't an option for the lounge. But it may be perfect for a study or office, where concentration and focus are important. Warm blues that fall towards the purple part of the spectrum are perfect for halls and passageways. Let's think about some schemes.

In the Mediterranean and the Caribbean, bold and vivid blues reflect the colour of a sunny sky and warm sea. Teamed with a liberal use of white this combination is buoyant and bright. If you've had a holiday in such a location, they will bring back great memories and for that reason alone may be perfect for you to use. The bathroom, in particular, with bold blue mosaics as a backdrop for a classic white suite will always look fresh. The blues to choose are bright and vibrant, often shades of turquoise. When you use this palette you can afford to introduce a touch of zingy green. Bring in a lime green cushion cover or throw to add a point of interest in the room. Or pile up limes in a white bowl for a stylish display that complements the colour scheme. Look for chalky whites to work with your blues and find fabrics with their own texture, like linen and muslin.

When all is said and done blues are the ideal basis for well-designed modern and classic schemes.

Defining idea...

'*There is no blue without yellow and without orange.*'
VINCENT VAN GOGH

Try another idea...

If you aren't sure about which fabrics to choose for your window treatments, have a look at IDEA 7, *Curtain call*, and IDEA 22, *Blind ambition*.

Defining idea...

'*A powerful palette to my mind is a palette that's not just a set of interesting or strong colours: it's something that has it's own identity above those colours and which can trigger strong associations, sometimes in our subconscious, of a time, place or emotion. A single colour can of course trigger such associations by itself, like a Miles Davis solo can. The palette, on the other hand, can work like a full orchestra.*'
KEVIN McCLOUD, *Choosing Colours*

39

How did it go?

Q   I like the idea of a blue scheme but I have a home built over a century ago. Any tips for a scheme?

A   *For a more classic look, think about using a period palette. Heritage colours are available in most paint ranges and include shades that are particularly suited to a older homes. These colours are more restrained and can be used across panelled walls and to highlight architectural features. Consider using Wedgwood Blue with its wonderful history. Whites should be flat and matt. Stay away from anything with a shimmer or shine.*

Q   OK, that's the paint. What else should I team with it?

A   *One thing you can do is look to include some decorative prints at the windows in curtains or blinds. Toile de Jouy, which is available in a number of colours but looks particularly stunning in blue, features country scenes, people and plants in historical settings. Team this with a heavy cotton fabric with a slim blue stripe to cover sofas or chairs.*

10

The great outdoors

A well-designed balcony, patio or roof terrace is a joy. This isn't a gardening guide so don't look for planting advice.

However, if part of your property includes one or more of the above, these spaces deserve as much attention as the interior rooms of your home.

And that's how to look at them – as outdoor rooms. They can work year round too – you don't confine your use of the bathroom to two months in the summer and your kitchen works for you twelve months of the year, so why not an outdoor space? If you live in an urban environment you will relish your outdoor space even more, as a peaceful retreat from the city bustle.

LAYING THE GROUNDWORK

Deck the space. Don't mess around with other surfaces unless you already have flagstones, terracotta tiles or cobbles already in place. Timber decking is inexpensive, durable and good looking, and gets better looking with age as long as it is well maintained. (If only we could all lay claim to the above.) There are plenty of designs that you can fit yourself, but if you don't take the DIY approach it's not necessarily expensive to pay someone to fix a deck. Consider getting all the materials yourself rather than asking the fitter to supply them; that way you can shop around. If you

Over time the timber will repeatedly get wet and then dry out and you may see small splits appear in the decking. Any knots in the wood could also exude resin. These are part and parcel of the appeal of timber. Neither will cause any damage, but you can brush away resin with a stiff brush once it has dried, and apply a water-repellent coating or specialist decking treatment once a year that will protect the surface to a large degree.

plan well ahead and buy in winter for laying the following summer you can find real bargains, as garden centres change their stock seasonally.

Brush your deck regularly with a stiff broom and wash the surface down at least a couple of times a year with a specialist cleaner. If you can beg, borrow or be bothered to hire a high-pressure jet cleaner, all the better.

SAFETY FIRST

Unless your space is at ground level make sure that railings around the area are secure. *Really, really* secure. People do like to lean their backsides against a surface when they have a drink in one hand. I went one step further and had walls built on two sides of my roof terrace to give a little more privacy from the neighbours. This means I don't have to worry even when children go out there because it is totally secure. (Then the old school next door that had been empty for years got planning permission to be made into flats. Now I am overlooked whatever corner I choose to sit in, so no more topless sunbathing for me.)

DRESSING UP

Garden canopies – yes or no? To be frank, don't bother with the expense of made-to-measure designs. I think the cost of making and fitting them far outweighs the benefits, although you will find plenty of companies that will totally disagree with that. It's a judgement call. Instead, use parasols on stands (or beach brollies stuck in large terracotta pots filled with dirt or sand), which are far more flexible anyway. You can move them around the area according to the direction of the sun or to protect you from the prevailing winds.

Use solar-powered garden lights. I know intellectually that any qualified electrician can come around and install outdoor lighting with all the appropriate safety features, but emotionally the combination of rain and electricity still alarms me. I inherited outdoor lamps wired into the house. I won't change the bulbs unless I am wearing my rubber-soled trainers and washing-up gloves (yes they're rubber too). Alternatively, rely on candle flares. They're much more fun anyway and also generate a bit of warmth.

Should you cover the outdoor area? See IDEA 18, *People in glass houses...*, if you really want to use the space all year round.

Try another idea...

'*If you have a garden and a library, you have everything you need.*'
MARCUS TULLIUS CICERO

Defining idea...

'*The best place to seek God is in a garden. You can dig for him there.*'
GEORGE BERNARD SHAW

Defining idea...

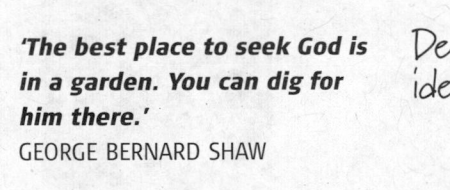

43

Metal or wood furniture? (Don't even think about plastic.) This is a style call. If your outdoor space leads off a modern chrome-filled kitchen, choose a contemporary powder-coated steel or rustproof aluminium set that reflects the mood. Should you have patio doors that lead from a rustic lounge, opt for wood. It's about making the outdoor space an extension of the indoor area and it works much more effectively if the two areas are in tune. Chances are your crockery, tableware, vases, cushions and throws will all coordinate with the outdoor furniture if you operate this way.

Look on your outdoor space as a real part of the home and you'll reap the benefits of having lots of lovely extra space.

Q **I have put railings around my roof terrace but even with the furniture out there I don't feel it looks like a usable space. What am I missing?**

How did it go?

A *Is it that the space looks bare? Why not fix trellis along one or two sides and invest in a couple of potted trailing plants that will grow across the wood. This will give you an air of privacy by creating a natural wall. Is it that the space feels cold? Heaters that run on gas cylinders have come down in price over the last few years and now are within everyone's budget. Alternatively, and only if you are not going to have children around, what about an open air fire? You can buy stainless steel designs that house a central chamber in which you burn wood or coal. Finally, never underestimate the pleasing effect of a group of chunky church candles placed together in a group on the table.*

Q **I have a very long garden that I want to break into different levels. Any suggestions?**

A *You might want to think about terracing, which is the traditional way to create a series of different-level areas up the garden. This isn't a small job so be prepared for a lot of mess. It can be completed in a variety of ways, such as excavating areas completely, bringing in other materials to make up levels or by 'cutting and filling' where you use the waste from one area to build up the space in another. You'll need to approach a garden designer or builder to get a good idea of the costs involved, which will depend on how much digging and waste removal there will be.*

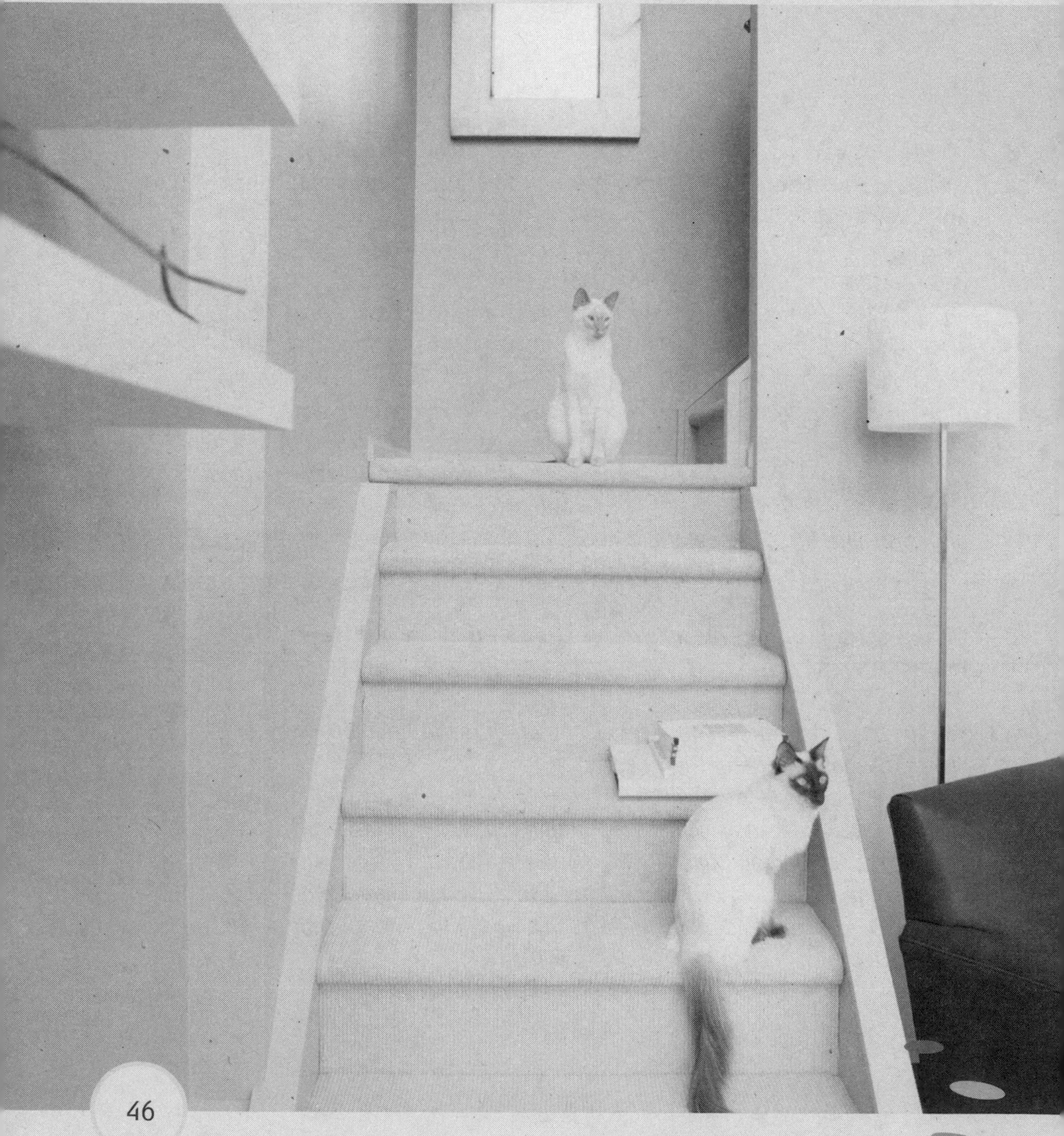

11

When white is right

Create chic interiors that will never go out of style. From pearly glazes to chalky finishes, the sheer variety of paints available means you can have a wide range of finishes when working with white.

It's a brave person that decorates a room with just white. But I would invite you to be bold because the finished look is truly impressive.

To open up small spaces and to create stunning larger rooms, white offers a stylish solution for every shape and size of space in the home. It can also be a good look when you are working to a tight budget. You can strip your old floorboards and wash them with white. You can buy junk furniture and give it a limed or antiqued white paint finish. And if your sofa and chairs are upholstered in a coloured or patterned fabric, you can throw swathes of plain cotton over them to bring them in line with the scheme.

You might think that your choice of colour will be limited. And if it was truly just a solitary colour you'd be right. But look at any paint chart and you'll see the range is vast. There are cool whites with a suggestion of blue, and warm whites that have an undertone of red or yellow. There are antique whites and contemporary whites, creamy whites and lime whites, and as already mentioned there are the different finishes to introduce too.

Here's an idea for you...

When you plan your white room, a good way to bring in lots of different textures is by your choice of fabrics. Consider a waffle cotton throw, white on white embroidered table linen and a muslin blind or curtains in the lounge. Introduce a canvas chair, a mohair blanket or a crewelwork bedspread in the bedroom.

Defining idea...

'White is not a mere absence of colour; it is a shining and affirmative thing, as fierce as red, as definite as black. God paints in many colours; but He never paints so gorgeously, I had almost said so gaudily, as when He paints in white.'
G. K. CHESTERTON

Just pause for a moment and think about a variety of white things that you find in nature: tulips, eggs, shells, stone, milk and fur, to name but a few. Each of these has a different tinge and texture; each one presents a different facet of white, which just shows what tremendous variety this choice presents.

WHERE TO USE IT

All-white schemes have the biggest impact when you are working in a fairly large space. If you have tall windows, high ceilings and a generously proportioned room then you can use white to stunning effect. But the advantage of using it in small spaces like a box room or a tiny bathroom is that it will help to maximise available light.

WHY TO USE IT

It's a scheme that will never go out of fashion. It suits both traditional Victorian interiors where you might want a warmer cosy feeling, and contemporary minimalist homes where you are hoping to achieve a cool mood.

HOW TO USE IT

When combining two or more whites in one room, keep the tone of all the elements the same. For example, if you used a white paint with a hint of pink on the walls, then avoid a greeny white fabric to cover your sofa. Make your choice of warm or cool tones after considering how much natural light there is in the room. South-facing rooms that benefit from plenty of warming natural light are the place to use the cool whites that suggest a hint of grey or blue. North-facing spaces that are darker and cooler for much of the day will benefit if you decorate them with whites that have a hint of pink or yellow.

- Warm whites: cream, buttermilk, limestone and ivory

- Cool whites: alabaster, eggshell, ice white and oyster shell

Be brave and go for an all-white look. You will grow to love it.

You can dress up a one-colour room with the right accessories. See IDEA 39, *The essential extras.*

Try another idea...

'**When the mists roll in and the leaves start to turn russet around the edges, white can still be warming and welcoming. Think of the inviting ivory glow from beeswax candles, a teetering pile of toasted marsh-mallows, a sumptuously thick cream-coloured chenille throw and a vase full of voluptuous white amaryllis scenting the air.'**
STEPHANIE HOPPEN, interior designer, *White on White*

Defining idea...

49

How did it go?

Q **I have used a browny matt white on the walls in the bedroom and then glossed the woodwork with a standard white. Now looking at the room the walls look slightly grubby. Why is this?**

A *It is almost certainly the contrast of the two finishes. Your gloss paint is not only pure white but also shiny so it picks up the light, while your walls are not only off-white but also matt which appears to absorb the light. When painting walls in an off-white colour you ideally need to choose an off-white paint for the woodwork too. Lightly sand your woodwork and repaint it with satinwood or eggshell paint, or try painting over one wall with a pearlised glaze and see if this helps to marry the two together.*

Q **I understand the idea of using different fabrics to introduce texture, but what else should I be looking for to dress the room?**

A *When you are looking for pieces to include in your white room, search out pieces that are made from a mix of materials. I can't overemphasise the appeal of ceramic lampshades. They are a stunning way to dress up your lights. With furniture, search out Perspex tables, leather pouffs and white-painted wood pieces and choose sofas and chairs covered in linen or cotton. Finally, accessorise with frosted glass vases, a collection of white ceramics and groups of candles. I have seen a group of white tea lights placed in glass holders on a dining table with a length of fake pearls trailed around the bases – it made a great centrepiece for a table in a predominantly white dining room.*

12

Decorative effects for a designer home

Walls, furniture, floors and sometimes fabrics can be transformed with a lick of paint.

TV makeover programmes may have given paint effects a bad name, but think again. For every change that you don't like, the screen designers that you watch come up with a good idea that you can use.

You may be weary of the format – horrid room, quick transformation, never want to live with it however will smile for the cameras – but every now and then you see a gem. These designers do have a trick or two up their sleeves.

Not convinced? OK, you are not obliged to watch any more TV. But please don't dismiss paint effects out of hand. They are easy, quick and above all else inexpensive. Also in my experience, if you want to make the best of your home – and why else would you be reading this – you'll explore any channel to achieve your desired look. The beauty of getting 'hands on' with paint is that you can adapt a piece of furniture or change the appearance of a wall to suit your style. After all,

Here's an idea for you...

Go to www.anniesloan.com Now you may have been tempted to skip this chapter because you think you will never want to pick up a paintbrush. I urge you to reconsider. As Annie says, 'With the simple addition of glaze medium to the paint mixture, a door opens onto a whole range of techniques, for it is what you use to make the pattern not the products themselves that create the finished effect. Using brushes, sponges, rags, combs etc. work to combine the base colour with the more transparent glaze colour on top. If you are not satisfied with the result then wipe it off and start again – before it dries!'

How easy could she make it – there's even the get-out clause at the end!

unless you have the funds to commission a one-off piece or pay an artisan, how are you going to get that junk table to fit in with your dining room décor or bring an original touch of the Bloomsbury Group to your living room? Basic rules that you may have heard before but need to be adhered to:

■ **Any surface** – wood, metal, fabric, plaster or fabric – needs preparation.

■ **Buy the right equipment for the job.**

■ **Read the instructions** that come with any product that you are going to use and stick to them – there's no cutting corners if you want the best look.

■ **Don't rush the job.**

■ **Practice on something/somewhere that doesn't matter** – the back of a drawer on furniture or a piece of paper for walls.

START SIMPLE

When I first picked a project, I looked for a piece of furniture that I could transform into an Art Deco drinks trolley. (In fact what I really wanted was a globe of the world that opens up to reveal the drinks – but there's no way that will fit in with my minimalist interiors so I compromised.) I assumed that adding a mirrored top and spraying it silver would work and completed the job in a day. *Hideous*. The point is to plan your work. Buy the piece. Sketch a picture of it – however crap you are at drawing – and then steal your children's crayons or buy a box of coloured pencils and make an attempt to create on paper a rough visualisation of the finished article. Then pin this up somewhere so that you will look at every day. If it's above your bed or on the back of the bathroom door then so be it. The front of the fridge works for me. Give it a couple of days and if you still like the look, then go ahead with your project. If it engenders gales of derision from everyone else in the house and you are not comfortable with it, then think again.

Where can you put your painted piece? IDEA 33, *A piece of the past*, will put it in a period setting and IDEA 2, *You've got the look*, shows how to set a particular style.

Try another idea...

'**Remember that the most valuable antiques are dear old friends.**'
H. JACKSON BROWN, Jr, American author

Defining idea...

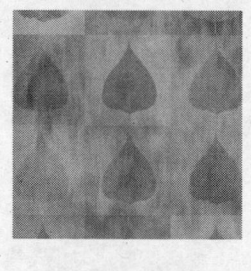 

'**One must act in painting as in life, directly.**'
PABLO PICASSO

Defining idea...

KNOW YOUR LIMITS

It's unlikely that with one or two dribbles around the park you would expect to join
Real Madrid. However if it was your first time with a football you might attempt a
bit of Subuteo given the challenge. So try revamping a chest of drawers or a chair,
but don't attempt to repaint every surface in your house in one go. It will take a
while to get to the Bernabeu.

Pieces may need cleaning, stripping, sanding, filling, priming and smoothing before
they are ready for the finish. And that final touch might be to distress, age, wax,
stencil, lime, varnish, gild or decoupage depending on the effect that you want to
achieve.

Research the type of look you want: an aged, antiqued or really glossy finish and
paint effects offer a stylish solution for decorating your home.

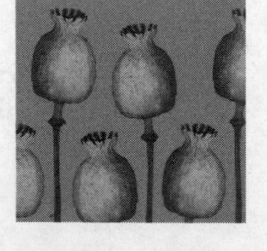 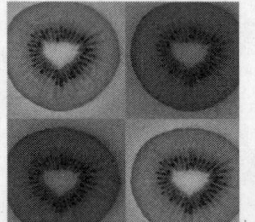 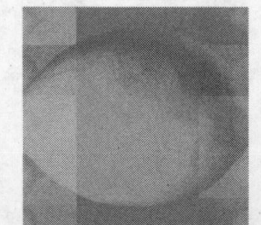

Q **I have picked up an old chest of drawers that I am thinking of painting but I paid a lot of money for it, so should I paint it?**

A *The answer to that is 'don't paint serious antiques'. There is nothing worse than a Lloyd Loom chair that has been bastardised with paint. If you paid good money, chances are that it needs repairing or renovating rather than a complete facelift. When you buy from junk shops check for the following: wonky legs, worm holes or broken hinges and locks that don't work. If you can restore it without changing the overall appearance so much the better. In general, items that are cheap – MDF, some wicker, plastic and pine – might be worth giving a coat of paint.*

Q **I have been thinking of gilding a chest of drawers but am aware that working with metal leaf can be tricky. Any tips?**

A *The preparation is the key as any imperfections on the surface will show. Make sure that you have sanded the area that you are gilding to a smooth finish. Use wood filler on any dents or deep scratches and ensure that the surface is free from dust before you start work. If you are painting the piece first, apply two or three coats and sand with wet and dry paper in between each coat. If this is your first time, you might want to avoid metal leaf and use gilt cream instead which you can simply rub on with your finger.*

How did
it go?

13

Introduce Scandinavian style

Create the perfect setting for your Norwegian Blue. With the combination of countries that make up Scandinavia you can expect an eclectic mix of different styles, but the paired down, clean and fresh, typically termed Swedish look is my choice.

Why? Because it is versatile, simple to achieve and easy to live with — all welcome attributes in anyone's book.

Think rustic wood. Think simple printed cottons. Think fresh blues or muted reds and you are looking along the right lines. More importantly, this style calls for a mix of old and new so it doesn't need to cost a fortune to achieve the look.

FIRST CHOICE FABRICS

One of the most important elements of Swedish style is the use of material. You can happily introduce check, stripe, print and patchwork all in the same room, as long as the colours match of course. A quilt with plaids in navy, red and white is the perfect piece to use as a starting point for your room. Pick out a coral colour from one square and paint a wooden chair to match. Find a blue that you like amidst the checks and use a plain fabric in the same shade to make curtains or a blind. There is

Here's an idea for you... **Take a trip to the southeast of Sweden to Sundborn where you'll find the home of Carl and Karin Larsson. You'll see paintings by Carl, textiles woven by Karin and furniture that she has designed. The interior is a source of inspiration for interior designers across the world. Check out the tourist board website for travel and accommodation information.**

a place for delicate sprigged florals, traditional gingham and even classic ticking in this room.

SOFAS AND SEATS

The finely turned legs and elegantly carved backs that are synonymous with this style owe their genesis to a prince. Back in the eighteenth century when Gustav returned to Sweden (to become King Gustav III) after living it up in the Court of Louis XVI, he brought back the classical form of furniture that he had seen in France.

History lesson aside, that's not to say that you have to invest in stacks of expensive antique furniture. You'll find many furniture companies make designs along Gustavian lines that you can paint yourself. But you can also look out in junk shops or reclamation yards for any sofas or chairs that have simple, clean lines, straight backs and legs that taper to the foot. Give them a coat of clean white paint, reupholster in a pink or blue check or add throw and cushions, and you've got a piece that cheats the look. If your sofa is the wrong colour, you can get away with using a tie-on loose cover in cream or white for this style.

ESSENTIAL ELEMENTS

Wood panelling figures large. Add MDF pieces to dado level or try tongue and groove up to picture rail height. If you are designing a small room, use high-level flat skirting so that you don't shrink the space too much. All mouldings should be simple in style; avoid anything that is curly or looks too ornate.

Stripped or painted wooden boards are the flooring of choice. But you can afford to put down simple runners or rugs to break up a large expanse of floor space.

If you love rooms with a very clear style, this look offers an easy to achieve finish.

> '*Create your own visual style...let it be unique for yourself and yet identifiable for others.*'
> ORSON WELLES

Defining idea...

> **For more advice on choosing and using rugs, see IDEA 43, The best dressed floors are wearing...**

Try another idea...

> '*In a progressive country change is constant; change is inevitable.*'
> BENJAMIN DISRAELI

Defining idea...

Q I have the right fabrics and furniture but the room just looks like it's decorated in blue and white – it doesn't say 'Swedish'.

A *You obviously have all the main elements in place but you need to add some finishing touches. A shelf running around the room at picture rail height will give you the perfect place to display Carl Larsson prints or blue and white china – both key accessories in a Swedish-style room. Simple wood mouldings added to the top of plain cupboards, the front of cabinets, along the edge of shelves and even to table legs all mimic the Gustavian style.*

Think about where you have positioned the furniture. One key part of this look is the symmetry of the room, so place a chair either side of a cabinet with the backs flat against the wall. Or put a footstool either side of a window to frame that part of the room.

Q I'm still not sure it looks Swedish...

A *Carl Larsson was saying 'Chuck out your chintz' years before it became a catchphrase for a Swedish superstore. Embrace the idea that you are going to strip things down to the basics – a clean white wooden floor, a sofa with an upholstered back and neat clean lines to the silhouette. Colours are simple, and so are the rest of the elements in the room. Remember that the finishing touches show an eye for detail rather than a place for clutter. When you put a collection of china or a group of pictures in place, take a step back and just make sure that they work in the room.*

14

Tread softly, because you tread on my dreams

Or where and why to use carpet

These words of Yeats always makes me think of curling my toes into a super-thick pile carpet. It may not have been what he had in mind when he was wishing for the cloths of heaven but it works for me.

The soft solution for flooring underfoot is a fail-safe choice for bedrooms, my recommendation for lounges, and can be used anywhere else in the house as along as you buy the right type for the amount of wear and tear it will receive.

One day, I'm going to have a huge carpeted bathroom. I just love the idea of climbing out of the bath and stepping onto a soft floor for a change. I've walked across enough vinyl to appreciate the difference but I know I'll need to find a design that will withstand the wetness.

Here's an idea for you...

If you have the budget, get the best of both worlds by putting down a wood floor and then adding a large unfitted carpet on top. If you choose a light oak or beech floor and opt for a dark carpet on top, it means you can instantly change the look of the room by keeping the carpet down in cold winter months and then rolling it up and storing it through the summer months.

Familiarise yourself with the jargon of carpets before you buy. The construction, pile, fibre content and texture are all points to consider. Clearly your biggest influence will probably be the colour but these other things need to be factored in. You want a carpet that will last so check a couple of things to give you an idea of how hardwearing it will be. Look at the back of woven carpets and make sure that the tufts are packed closely together. Kneel down or press the pile with the heel of your hand and make sure that it springs back quickly. Good quality woven carpets are sure to last. If you choose a tufted design, go for the most expensive you can afford.

If you are carpeting the whole house and need to cut costs, go for less expensive carpets in the bedroom and spend more money on areas that get constant use such as the hall, lounge and stairs.

THE PROS OF CARPETS

While wood floors have become overwhelmingly fashionable, it's important to remember the benefits that a carpet offers:

- **Keep the noise down:** It dampens down sound between floors and from foot traffic – a real bonus in flats. According to The Carpet Foundation, bare smooth flooring is likely to produce seven to twelve times more noise than a carpeted surface.

- **Cosy up:** It provides insulation for your home – any kind of energy saving is a priority in today's environment.

- **Whoops a daisy:** It offers a cushion for falls, and a non-slip surface to prevent accidents.

The choice of colour of your carpet will have an impact on the mood of the room. See IDEA 3, *Work that colour*, for more on colour scheming. You can add interest to the room by including one or two rugs. If you want to dress up your carpet, see IDEA 43, *The best dressed floors are wearing...*

Try another idea...

'What if everything is an illusion and nothing exists? In that case, I definitely overpaid for my carpet.'
WOODY ALLEN

Defining idea...

63

A DESIGN TOOL

With so many colour choices and such a wide range of textures, carpet is a valuable decorating tool when putting together your scheme. Because of the large amount of space that it covers, plain carpets in light colours will help to make a room seem much bigger. Using the same carpet through two or three small rooms will also create the illusion of a bigger home. Patterned designs have their place if you have kids or pets, helping to disguise wear and tear. If you have opted for plain walls and furnishings in a room, they also function as a tool for bringing in a mix of colours to the area.

Budget for good quality underlay: it prolongs the life of a carpet. It levels out any imperfections in the sub-floor, and is an effective way of preventing heat loss – on average 15 per cent of heat loss from a home is through the floor. The thickest underlay is not necessarily the best, however. Look for one that has been made by a carpet manufacturer from the yarn that is left over from the carpet-making process for a high quality option.

You want to walk over your floors in comfort for years to come so take the time to carefully consider the carpets.

Q   **I have looked at a wide range of carpets and if I buy a wool mix it is going to cost a fortune to carpet my room. Why shouldn't I buy a cheap one and be done with it?**

How did it go?

A   *There is no point in buying cheap carpet. It doesn't wear well and you'll have to replace it so quickly that the cost of buying another new one and having that fitted means you might as well have spent more in the first place. There is also a suggestion that synthetic fibres pose a health risk as a source of volatile organic compounds (VOCs), common indoor air pollutants that can cause allergies. Blow your budget on a high quality stain-resistant wool mix and you'll be able to live with it for years.*

Q   **That's all well and good, but once I have spent a fortune how do I care for it?**

A   *There's a dull job that has to done on a regular basis – vacuuming. If dirt is left to embed itself into the pile it will age the flooring. You can brush floors and sweep floors but really giving it a good going over with a suction pump (that's a vacuum to you and me) is the best solution. Bear in mind that heavy furniture will leave indents in the carpet. The image of little cups under legs may seem old fashioned, but they do do their job.*

65

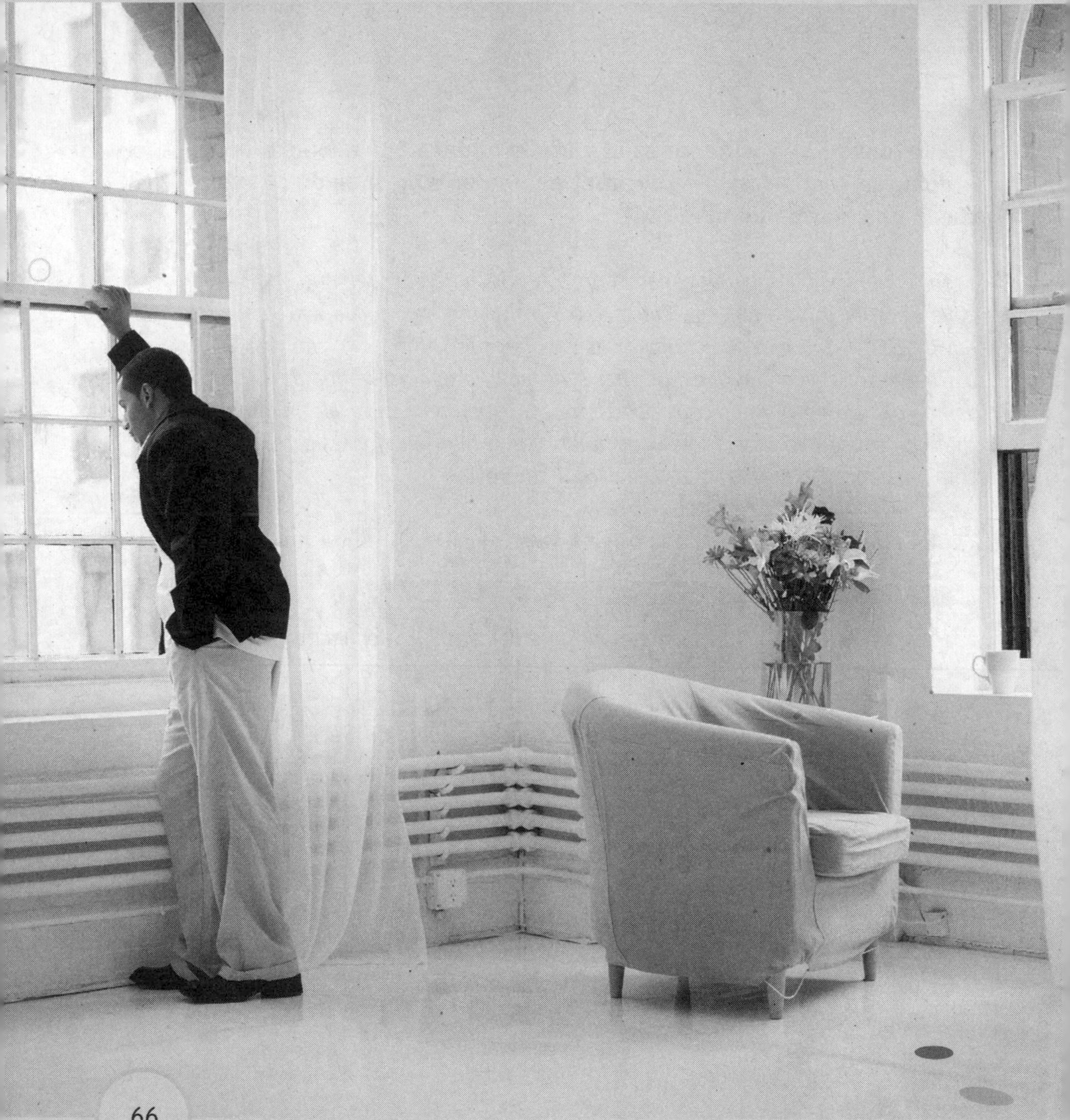

15

Keep it tidy

Decluttering is the new black. Whether you want to make extra space or simply clear up your home, get set for a brutal experience.

There is a way of tackling tidying that lacks commitment. It involves tucking papers in drawers, putting magazines back in the rack and working on the assumption that 'I might use it one day'.

Stop right now, thank you very much, in the words of the immortal Spice Girls. If you are going to declutter you need to approach it with dedication and verve and most importantly, with a lack of sentimentality.

Pick a room – any room – and sit in the middle. What you are about to do is remove roughly one-quarter of the contents in that space. That's your target. (And that's just for starters. Once you have performed your initial declutter, if you are really serious about it I want you to go back a week later and repeat the process.)

In the kitchen: you are chucking out unused spices, old tins, battered bakeware, chipped crockery, fraying table linen, knackered saucepans and unused gadgets

You may want to look at another book in this series, *Detox your finances*, which has a very useful chapter on selling items on the web. 'Car-boots in cyberspace' explains the complexities of the e-bay auction and how you could make money out of your junk.

(bread makers and juicers being chief culprits). In the lounge: you are getting rid of books on the bookshelf (that's where the sentimental bit comes in for me; I hate getting rid of books), China ornaments that were dodgy holiday mementoes or suspect gifts, dried flower arrangements, worn out cushions and old CDs. In the bedroom: you are looking to give many, many items of clothing to the charity shop. If you keep your bed linen in there, how many sets do you realistically need? If you've mislaid one of a matching pair of pillowcases chuck the odd one out – if you take it downstairs to the kitchen to cut up and use as cleaning cloths you are only adding to the clutter down there, so chuck it.

In the bathroom: it's time to dispose of old make-up, old medicines, half-used body lotions and potions and towels that were stained by your last hair-dyeing experiment. It's all very well thinking 'I'll use that at the beach', but when was the last time you remembered to take a spare towel with you?

It's a process that is loosely based on the William Morris principle 'Have nothing in your houses that you do not know to be useful, or believe to be beautiful.' And it makes absolute sense. Most of our clutter is just a home for dust and dirt.
So here's how to approach the job. Start in the corner furthest away from the door. If there's a rug on the floor or a cushion that needs to go, take it out of the room and put it in a pile outside the door. If there's a cupboard in the corner, open the door and, starting from the top, take out everything that's on the shelf. For each item ask yourself when was the last time that you looked at it, read it, used it or

even thought about it. If you can't remember any of the above then take it out of the room and add it to the pile. If the cupboard is not sectioned off, bring in some new storage systems: box files for papers, garments bags for clothes, etc.

I should mention at this point that it might be worth having a bottle chilling in the fridge, because you will need an incentive after and hour of two of doing this. Also, in the same way that people jog to pacey music or work out to funk, make sure that you are listening to something inspirational. I mix up a bit of Barry White, some Stone Roses, very early Michael Jackson and a bit of Bruce Springsteen. It all gets me moving one way or another.

Don't give up when you get bored: the aim is to clear the excess baggage in one sitting. You have to look on it as a job that needs completing before you are allowed that glass of wine, not reach for the bottle when you are halfway through. Take everything that you've removed and recycle it in the appropriate way.

Approach decluttering with the determination of a pitbull and you'll reap the rewards in terms of tidiness, cleanliness and lots of lovely extra space.

The key to decluttering is having good storage. IDEA 49, *An organised mind*, explains the essentials.

Try another idea...

'*Be ruthless with your wardrobe. We wear 20% of our clothing 80% of the time; so make sure the clothes you move are the things you wear. Give away any garments that you haven't worn in the past year.*' 'Life Laundry' presenter DAWNA WALTER, *Your Home*

Defining idea...

'*When we got into office, the thing that surprised me most was to find that things were just as bad as we'd been saying they were.*' JOHN F. KENNEDY

Defining idea...

How did
it go?

Q **I have tried to empty my house of excess bits and pieces, but I'm left with piles of papers that I can't be parted from my work area in the lounge and clothes all over the floor in the bedroom.**

A *You have obviously embraced the principles but please check that you can't get rid of these bits. Go for your second declutter and see if you do really need everything that's left. Failing that, you may need to consider bringing in extra storage. Built-in wardrobes in the bedroom are a brilliant solution for making the most of the space and keeping it free of a clutter. A table with drawers underneath could be just what you need to provide extra storage space in your lounge.*

Q **I understand that, but how am I going to make storage in my study area fit in with the rest of the lounge?**

A *Do you have a dedicated office-style filing cabinet? You don't need to have a piece of furniture that doesn't fit in. Designs are available in wood instead of metal if you are worried about the utilitarian look of metal designs, or you can paint them with a coloured aerosol paint to fit in with your colour scheme.*

16

The sun also rises

Brightening with yellow. When the sunshine pours through a window into your room you can forget your troubles for a while.

There is a reason why Judy followed the yellow brick boad and it's because such a sunshine colour offers a wealth of positive associations.

If colours were people then yellow would be the happy gang. Orange, its close neighbour in the colour spectrum, would be the go-lucky crew. If you need something positive in your life, these are the colours that you should look to use for positive energy and a more invigorated and energy-filled approach to life.

Of course, there's always that occasion when you could happily punch the person who has a permanent smile on their face. That jaunty builder who heckles you with 'Cheer up love, it might never happen' (at which point I always have to resist the temptation to tell them I've just been divorced and the dog has died, but I digress). The point is that sometimes you can have too much of a good thing, and for that reason there are occasions when it's good to avoid using too much yellow or too bright a sunshine shade – in your bedroom for example. It's a full-on colour and

Here's an idea for you...

If you live in a basement flat or have a north-facing room your priority is to make the most of any available light. Choosing yellow for these rooms will boost whatever sunshine reaches the dark recesses of the room. Another point to consider is that often basement or ground floor flats or rooms will have low ceilings. You can create the illusion of height by painting the ceiling a lighter shade than the walls. Try blending colour up the wall. If you have a dado or picture rail then start with a darker yellow beneath the mouldings, choose a lighter shade above, and go for white with a hint of yellow or a creamy white at the top. (If you have the opposite problem try reversing this technique. Move from dark at the top to lightest at the bottom and the ceiling will visually seem lower.) Use mirrors on walls facing the window to reflect light into the space.

one that could set you back hours if you are overstimulated when your body and brain have only just regained consciousness from hours of sleep. It may leave you feeling slightly grumpy and disorientated because you don't exactly know why you are not up to speed. If you do choose yellow for the bedroom, pick a warm primrose colour, which is cheerful enough to kick start your day without being too loud. Clotted cream woodwork will also tone down the effect.

My advice is to choose bright yellow for rooms where you want to be motivated. A sunshine yellow kitchen or dining room will have you cooking up a storm and entertaining guests with inspirational tales. More importantly, it is a warming colour and can be used to counteract the negative effects of being in a north-facing home or a basement flat.

DESIGNS IN COLOUR

For an alternative scheme to lighten spaces, see IDEA 11, *When white is right.*

Try another idea...

Some colours lend themselves to certain patterns, and for yellow it's stripes. A delicate way of introducing yellow to a room is by choosing wallpaper with the slimmest primrose pinstripe. The Laura Ashley wallpaper collection has a wonderful colour called Cowslip. It's a creamy yellow far removed from the brash and bright primary colours in this sunny family. You can also use an orange stripe, although it will have the effect of bringing a retro mood to the room, while the yellow choice will create the mood of a summery country cottage. (If you like the retro look you must see the Ted Baker Wallcoverings collection. Better known for his shirts and swinging Elvis Santa at Christmas, the coverings are set to become classics.)

For brightening up dull rooms and bringing a spring to your step, consider a yellow colour scheme.

'Busy old fool, unruly Sun, Why dost thou thus, Through windows and through curtains call on us? Must to thy motions lovers' seasons run?'
JOHN DONNE

Defining idea...

How did it go?

Q   I've used yellow and white throughout the living room but it seems when I walk into the space the mood is bland, not bright.

A   *It maybe that you were scared to use a bold shade and have gone for a wishy washy colour. One way to liven up the look is to bring a completely contrasting colour into the space. Try raspberry. You could use some blooming floral prints arranged in a group on the wall or a modern 'work of art'. One of the easiest ways to introduce these spots of colour is with flowers so pick up a bouquet of blooming peonies or some lush tulips and position them on a shelf or mantelpiece against the yellow walls. You'll instantly appreciate the difference.*

Q   My room is already very bright as it gets the sun morning noon and night. Can I still use yellow?

A   *You are so lucky. If you have a space that has that much natural light then you can rely on white with a hint or two of yellow to decorate the space. If you think of yellow as an accent, something to bring out the flavour of the room in the same way that a touch of chilli brings out the flavour of certain foods, then you'll realise that you don't want to drench the room with it (it would be too hot) but a pinch here or there is a great way to conjure up a visual feast.*

17

Bathe in style

Washing, crimping, bathing or refreshing – a well-designed bathroom is a versatile space.

Lie in your bath and take a good look around you. The starting point for planning a new bathroom can often be a list of the faults of the existing one.

I inherited a particularly hideous over-the-bath shower with elaborate shower rail system to allow the curtain to be pulled all the way around the bath. It was totally unnecessary, and the poles suspended in a mish-mash from walls and the ceiling made it look like an elaborate industrial mess. By simply taking away the curtain and associated poles and putting in a neat screen I made the room seem instantly bigger, and it's now definitely more pleasurable to lie in the bath and gaze at the ceiling, or my navel.

If you are going to revamp a bathroom, you need to decide whether you want to keep the existing layout and replace fixtures where they are, or move things in, out and around to get better use of what is, more often than not, a spatially challenged room.

Don't panic if you have inherited a coloured suite with co-ordinating tiles. The chances are it's so old that you may want to replace it, but even if it stays you can detract from the hideousness of the tub and walls in various ways. Tile paint is much maligned. Yes, it is a laborious job to recover tiles and no, it won't look as good as replacing all the tiles, but if you prepare the surfaces religiously and follow the instructions as if they were commandments, the finished effect is pretty good. Use in conjunction with tile grout pens and you can refresh the room. Alternatively, you can buy panels with a tile design already imprinted on the surface and these can be fitted over the top of existing tiles.

Clear out anything that isn't white or neutral. Towels, laundry baskets and cupboards should all be replaced with neutral colours (in the case of cabinets, a glass fronted design, maybe frosted, is particularly pleasing on the eye). And consider putting in a new floor. In general the dimensions of the room are so small that it won't cost a fortune to put down new vinyl.

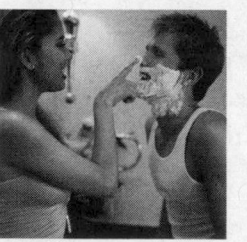
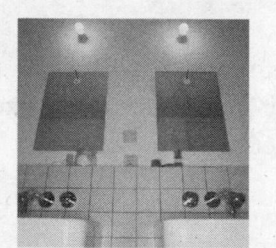

SUITE PIECES

I am a bidet fan and not ashamed to admit it. Let me give you some uses (other than the purpose it was designed for) to explain why, if you have the space, I would recommend that you fit the fourth piece into your suite of bath, basin and WC.

- There's always somewhere to leave the hand-laundry soaking.
- It is the perfect place for washing feet pre-pedicure.
- If you can't use the loo to be sick you have another receptacle.

With both bidets and toilets always opt for wall-hung designs, for one simple reason: cleaning around pedestals is a pain, and they are a place where dirt tends to gather. The joy of being able to mop across a floor unhindered by the usual obstructions has to be experienced to be really understood. (If you are now worried that I am slightly obsessive about fluff on the floor, I'd like to point out that I have a dog whose hair tends to get everywhere.)

It's a frequently overlooked issue that cast-iron baths weigh a ton (give or take a few pounds). If you are looking to recreate the look of a period

If you are going to replace the flooring take a look at IDEA 28, *A tough decision.*

Try another idea...

'*Colour is incredibly important to me, but in the bathroom that means the opposite of what you may think – everything's got to be white. When you're trying out every colour of every item in a make-up range, it's essential to have a neutral background. So the idea of coloured lights and fancy tiles is all well and good, but it's just not for me. And no, I never had an avocado suite.'*
BARBARA DALY, *The Independent Magazine*

Defining idea...

Here's an idea for you...

bathroom, check that your floor will take the weight. Also remember that with a freestanding bath the amount of water that splashes over the edge will increase considerably (more sides for the bath water to slop over) so you do need flooring that will withstand regular soakings. While the idea of picking up an old fashioned piece from reclamation yards may have a romantic appeal, don't bother. Brand new is easily affordable and reproduction designs are so good that I would buy new every time.

SINKING IN

If you live with a partner or have kids, fit in a double sink wherever possible. There is great pleasure in having your own sink. I once stayed in a glorious hotel in Edinburgh for New Year where the bathroom had 'his and hers' sinks. My contact lens solution, make-up, body lotion, electric toothbrush and cotton wool pads all had a space, and didn't get shoved aside when 'him indoors' wanted to shave. Now translate that into your own home. Kids' stuff on one sink and adults' on the other for example – it's a cleansing experience.

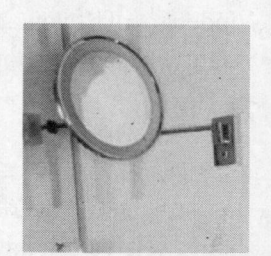

Q **I have roughly planned the layout of the bathroom but there isn't enough space along one wall to fit in a sink and a bidet. Also, with a towel rail on one wall and the tiles above the bath on the other, the window on the third and door on the fourth, what can I do about storage?**

How did it go?

A *Take another look at your plan and see if it's possible to put a corner basin at either end of the window wall. It may need to be slightly smaller than the sink you have chosen, but it has the benefits that if it is fitted into the top of a cabinet you will gain extra storage as well as free up wall space for your bidet.*

Q **I've opted for an all-white room but in winter it feels desperately cold. The walls are completely tiled so I can't introduce a warmer colour with paint. Any ideas?**

A *Instant changes can be wrought. Invest in some towels in warm colours – ruby red would be perfect. Try bringing in some natural wood and wicker in the form of a cabinet, towel rail or linen basket. Put a rug on the floor; use something with a rubber backing so that it won't slide around. And invest in toiletries or accessories in pink, orange and red: soaps, oils or candles, whatever you fancy.*

18

People in glass houses...

Forget that image of a tacky white plastic extension on the back of a house in the suburbs: conservatories can be gorgeous.

This is particularly true if you are lucky enough to have a south- or southwest-facing garden that will allow the maximum amount of sun into the room.

If you are in this position I really recommend that you start saving or go and get a loan straightaway to pay for the job. You will have the luxury of an extra room in your home all year round and one that, if planned and decorated with care, will become the most popular room for reading, drinking and chilling out (or getting a bit of privacy if you're lucky).

THE PLANNING GAME

Ignore anyone who says that you need to decide on the use of your conservatory before it is built. This is nonsense. After all you don't just cook in the kitchen, you also eat, entertain, argue and do laundry. In the lounge you may have supper on your lap, watch the television, read or fool around (you can do that last one in the kitchen too). The point of putting in an extra room is to give your home some extra

Here's an idea for you...

Find furniture that you like, rather than feel the need for dedicated conservatory pieces. You might see a better selection of tables and chairs in the garden section of your local DIY superstore than on a specialist conservatory furniture website, for example. Fading is obviously an issue in a room that is exposed to the sun so don't spend a fortune on fine fabrics for cushion covers. Lightweight pieces are clearly a priority so that you can move them around the room to maximise hours sitting in the sun. I have seen the prettiest wirework tables and chairs used in a conservatory – reclamation yards might be a good place to check out – and you can dress these up or down according to the season with cushions and throws plundered from other rooms in the house.

interior space – what you choose to do in there will certainly change through the seasons and very probably through the years. You can decorate it, accessorise it, and furnish it in such a way that it can fulfil multiple roles.

First consider the following:

Budget. Spend the max to get the best. Bear in mind that blinds can eat up a large chunk of money if you are fitting them across the whole extension.

Which way will it face? North – will need attention paid to heating and lighting for the winter months. Ask your installer about specialist types of glass that will offer extra insulation. South – good quality blinds or shutters are essential for the summer. Good ventilation is vital too, so plenty of roof vents and some opening windows. Consider tinted glass for the roof. East – it will catch the morning sun so use materials that retain heat, like thermal glass. If you are thinking about an extension to the kitchen this will give you the perfect breakfast room. West – make sure ventilation is good to prevent condensation from hot evenings and cold nights.

Shape. How much of the garden and which area are you willing to give up? If you have a small side passageway that leads to the garden but serves no other function why not start to extend there and use that wasted space? If you are seriously spending, consider a two-storey affair.

Material. Make it blend in with the rest of your house. Here are the options. PVC – durable and virtually maintenance free. This is often installed in white but you can find wood-look options. This is the C-list celebrity of the conservatory world. Aluminium – strong, so can support large predominantly glass structures but may be prone to condensation – the B-list candidate. Timber – what it loses in terms of ease of maintenance it gains in versatility and style. A-list (Oscars, all the best parties, Gstaad in the winter, St Tropez in the summer).

Just like outdoor spaces, you want to get maximum use out of your conservatory. IDEA 10, *The great outdoors*, will give you some useful hints for co-ordinating it with the rest of the house.

Try another idea...

'The butler opened a door for me and stood aside. It opened into a vestibule that was about as warm as a slow oven. He came in after me, shut the outer door, opened an inner door, and we went through that. Then it was really hot. The air was thick, wet, steamy and larded with the cloying smell of tropical orchids in bloom. The glass walls and roof were heavily misted and big drops of moisture splashed down on the plants.'
RAYMOND CHANDLER, *The Big Sleep*

Defining idea...

'If slaughterhouses had glass walls, everyone would be a vegetarian.'
PAUL McCARTNEY

Defining idea...

Heating. Underfloor heating is the best. You don't see it but you know it's there and in winter you'll be glad you have it. Choose this option if you are going to lay ceramic tiles or stone flooring. Radiators are another option. You may be able to simply add them on to your existing central heating system if your boiler has the capacity for the extra work. Or invest in one or two oil-filled radiators, which are quite an efficient way of heating if you can't extend your existing system.

A conservatory can mean a substantial financial investment and you want to use it all year round, so get the basics right from the start.

Q   We have just started using our newly built conservatory but the condensation in the room seems excessive even after I have opened windows and left a heater on. What can I do about it?

A   For the first few months after the building has been completed it is drying out so levels of condensation will be particularly high. These will reduce after 6–12 months; during that time you should keep the windows open as much as possible. Keep the heating on low for a few nights, especially through the winter months (warm air holds more moisture than cold air). You could invest in or hire a dehumidifier for a week or two and accelerate the drying out process.

Q   Can I just build on to my house or do I need permission to extend the property?

A   This all depends on where you live, and size also matters. If you live in a conservation area you will almost certainly need planning permission. You may also need Building Regulation approval on certain designs, for example, if it is a kitchen conservatory. Your builder or conservatory designer should be able to advise you, so get this query out of the way before you start planning your extension.

How did it go?

85

19

An illuminating experience

Get the lighting right and it can be the making of a room; skimp on this essential design detail and you may end up in gloom.

There's a good, a bad and a downright ugly way of lighting any space. Look at it this way: if lighting is an ingredient in the recipe of putting together a room, then it's the icing on the cake or the exquisite sauce on the steak. If it's good then it's Michelin starred.

If it's bad you may have perfected the main part of the dish but the overall meal will be just average. And if it's downright ugly then you have ruined the meal. You waste all the effort of putting together a lovely interior if you fail to pay attention to how the space is lit. Lighting ties quite neatly in to how the area will be used. Every room in your home serves a variety of purposes, so allow for an assortment of lighting options to fulfil each and every need. Lighting also has a role in drawing attention to specific features in a room, and the reverse of that is that it can be used as a means of disguise by leaving certain areas in darkness.

Do you have a collection of objects on a shelf or an amazing print on the wall that could be highlighted with a specific source of light? Firstly move a lamp near to the piece and send the beam so that it casts light straight on to the group. That may be too strong. Point the beam down and see what effect that creates, and then position the light source so that it shines up towards the group. Each position of the light will create different shadows so play around until you have the most pleasing combination of light and shade.

SORTING THE STYLES

You can reduce lighting to three basic types, and to create a successful scheme you need to layer all three: ambient, task and accent lighting. Ambient light is designed to offer an all-over well-lit room. This is the starting point to any scheme and the most basic type of lighting. Task lighting, as the name suggests, works to illuminate specific tasks. These might be working at your computer, applying your make-up or cooking. Its purpose is to provide enough light for the activity concerned – enough to prevent eyestrain. Accent lighting is the type that can often be neglected but brings out the best in a room. It will highlight the best features such as works of art, pieces of furniture or a particular area – a dining table in a kitchen/diner is a classic example.

ROOM BY ROOM

The first space that you come to in a home is the hall. Do something different on the stairs. Position a recessed spot light or low-level wall washer beside every second or third step, making sure you have an on/off switch at the bottom and top. Moving into the lounge, why not avoid an overhead light altogether and have an electrician put two or three lamps on a circuit that is operated by a single switch? If you have shelving in alcoves either side of a chimneybreast, then use down-lighters to highlight the items that are displayed. Through to the kitchen, make sure that you include lights that run underneath wall-mounted cabinets as well as your overhead strip or spots. Have the different lights on separate circuits so you can use as much or as little light as you

There is an art to lighting and displaying objects. See IDEA 30, *The art of living*, for some ideas on grouping pieces and positioning pictures.

Try another idea...

need. This will also mean you can transform a practical and functional working area into somewhere appropriately lit for an intimate dinner party. Jump up the stairs to the bedroom, and you must have lights at either side of the bed. Move to the bathroom and make sure that you can see to cleanse your face. An illuminated mirror is a must.

When dressing up your home, lighting is an essential tool in creating the right look and style for every room.

'Sometimes our light goes out but is blown into flame by another human being. Each of us owes deepest thanks to those who have rekindled this light.'
ALBERT SCHWEITZER

Defining idea...

 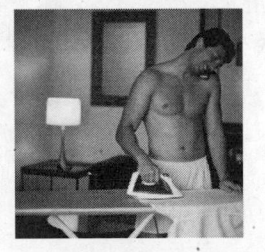

'It is not economical to go to bed early to save the candles if the result is twins.'
Chinese proverb

Defining idea...

How did it go?

Q **I know that I need to mix up different kinds of light in a room but where do I start?**

A *Let's take the lounge. If the only source of light is a central pendant fitting then you need to do some light work. The first step is to fit a dimmer switch. It's a basic step but it does mean you can lower the lights to create a subtle glow. Next, while there are no fixed rules, if you can introduce downlighters, uplighters, wall washers and lamps you are well on the way to improving the look of your room. (You'll be familiar with all of the above except possibly wall washers. These are lights that cast an even glow across and down a wall.)*

Q **I have mirrored tiles on one wall in the bathroom and I am getting a real glare rather than a pleasing glow when I switch on the overhead light. Even putting in a low wattage bulb hasn't really cured the problem. Any suggestions?**

A *I presume that you operate the light with a pull switch at the moment. If you have the space, try putting in a wall cabinet with integral light on the wall opposite to the tiles and use this rather than the overhead light when you are in the room. Another option would be to get an electrician to come in and move the control to the outside of the room. Then you can use a dimmer switch (safety regulations mean this type of fitting should be outside the room).*

20

Bold reds make for instant impact

Or...la vie en rose. From the hottest scarlet to the subtlest pink, this palette can create instant impact or a subtle glow.

The woman with the red Chanel lipstick makes a striking statement in a crowd; the girl with the English rose complexion takes more time to spot and longer to appreciate; but both have their inherent appeal. So it is with rooms where you choose to use red.

Are you decorating your den? Work with claret and create a cosy space – somewhere you'll retreat to when you feel cold or even lonely.

The mere act of enveloping yourself in a room of ruby shades suffuses the body with warmth. I'm not becoming an advocate for any therapy that takes you back to the womb, but you'll get that safe and warm feeling in a lounge decorated in Tudor red. When I plan a room with red, I embrace these historical associations. I think of it as somewhere that will look well worn, like a dusty old library or one of those

Here's an idea for you...

When was the last time you ate Neapolitan ice-cream? If you really want to work with pink, then think of vanilla-, biscuit- and rose-coloured ice-cream melting together into scrumptious fluffy shades. This is your modern look for pink. The very nature of these pastel colours will dictate a feminine feel to the room but you can counteract that with clever use of fabrics. If your walls are painted in pink, choose a biscotti brown suede sofa in the lounge or a cappuccino-coloured fabric for your bed head. Then add a creamy sheepskin rug to go in front of the fireplace or a heavy cream eiderdown to throw over the bed. Allow just enough pink pieces to peak through, be they crisp cotton bed linen or taffeta and silk-style cushions to pull the look together.

wonderful country house hotel bars where you have a Kir before going into dinner.

I would advise you to avoid department stores when looking to furnish such a room. Try auction rooms or second-hand shops where you can pick up old and worn leather pieces and wooden tables, chests and bookcases that might show the odd knock or scratch. A battered Chesterfield is the perfect piece to place amidst deep red panelling, an oak side table the ideal spot to stand your crystal decanter filled with the finest port. Look for cushions and throws in chocolate brown and consider an old tapestry or hand-embroidered pieces to add to the comfortable air. A pair of rich velvet curtains will complete the look – hang them from a chunky wooden pole.

SUBTLE COLOURS

The delicate shades of pink, synonymous with a perfect English rose, are as much in contrast with the above colour scheme as chalk and cheese. While deep reds suggest passion and power, pink has lighter associations: the Pink Panther, tickled pink, in the pink – a sign of good health. There was a trend a few years ago for shabby chic: the look that relies on pretty chintzes, antiqued white furniture, rag rugs, a sort of tatty Laura Ashley catalogue from years gone by. This is the perfect style for using pink. A feminine look – no, not girlie, more a room that is comfortable with its age and knows it still looks good. If I say to you it's Katherine Hepburn, while the bolder reds would be Sophia Loren, does that give you a clearer idea?

This is about a subtle use of the colour, more simple touches than whole swathes of a certain shade, because I firmly believe no one (with the exception of girls under eight) would want to – or probably should be allowed to – decorate an entire room in pink.

So, in the kitchen it could be a pink gingham blind at the window above a cream butler's sink, or a collection of rose-patterned china in a farmhouse glazed top or open rack dresser. In the hallway it should be a scalloped edge lampshade atop a simple white candlestick base on the consul table, or a flower in the print of a heavy chintz curtain that covers the front door when it's closed. In the bathroom it could be the soaps, lotions and potions that adorn an open shelf, maybe the ribbon edging on fluffy white towels.

Working with red gives you the opportunity of creating real impact with a colour scheme – don't blush at the thought but go for it.

'When in doubt wear red.'
BILL BLASS, American fashion designer

Defining idea...

If you want another way to use pinks and purples, see IDEA 26, *Welcome to my boudoir.*

Try another idea...

'The true colour of life is the colour of the body, the colour of the covered red, the implicit and not explicit red of the living heart and the pulses. It is the modest colour of the unpublished blood.'
ALICE MEYNELL, poet

Defining idea...

93

How did it go?

Q   I've painted all the walls in red but the room now seems to have shrunk to about half its original size. What can I do to reverse the effect?

A   *If the room was small to begin with it may be that you will need to rethink your colour choice because such a strong shade will visually shrink the room. Get two people to hold up a white sheet against the wall at the far end of the room (or use a staple gun to temporarily hold it in place). You'll see by lightening the colour there that it immediately changes the perspective of the space. So the first thing to do is paint the wall that is opposite the door (the first wall you face as you walk into the room) in a lighter colour. Choose any neutral – a soft grey, off-white or beige are all options. Alternatively, do you have a dado or picture rail? Experiment with changing the colour in one of these areas, again to a neutral colour.*

Q   So I know I want to use some red, but any tips for introducing just a touch?

A   *There's no reason why you can't introduce any style or colour in small doses. If an all-red room seems a bit too much, then use it on a small scale. Red can be added to alcoves or the occasional architectural detail: skirting boards, picture rails and cornices spring to mind. Just take a step outside. What would your house look like with a bright red front door? Now there's a bright idea.*

21

Something's cooking

Take the fitted approach to streamline your kitchen. The beauty of investing in a fitted kitchen is that it can be tailor-made to suit all the quirky corners or awkward shapes that exist in most homes.

It's also a way of maximising space and can provide some brilliant storage solutions, designed to make your life that much easier.

With the luxury of starting from scratch you can make sure that the light is right, that the power points are in the correct places for all your gadgets, and that your day-to-day use of the space is a joy. After inheriting a kitchen that had clearly been built by the previous owner's DIY-mad husband, I rejoiced when my kitchen had to be ripped apart. Oh the joy of a new beginning!

I have to say at this point that when you move into a new home, budget often precludes you from investing in a whole new kitchen however much you might hate the previous owner's colour scheme or layout. By using paints, replacements doors and perhaps a new floor, it's possible to give the room a facelift that might make it more bearable. You'll just have to live with the layout, but buying a freestanding kitchen trolley is one way of getting an accessible work surface if that is what you lack. However, we are dealing here with the extravagance of a whole

Here's an idea for you...

The list of requirements is complete, but have you overlooked some aspects of the room?

Could you lose a pan cupboard and make it the space for storing equipment by having a rack suspended from the ceiling for hanging up saucepans? Have you had to reduce the number of cabinets in a run because there is a radiator on the wall? You could take it off and have plinth heaters instead. Have you had to devote a chunk of work surface to house a large microwave? Choose a built-in combi-oven that includes a microwave facility.

Defining idea...

'Some of our most exquisite murders have been domestic, performed with tenderness in simple, homey places like the kitchen table.'
ALFRED HITCHCOCK

new design so be clear about your budget before you start. Costs can easily run away with you and a cheaper option is always available for most things.

THE TRIANGLE PRINCIPLE

This is an age-old device that kitchen planners have been promoting for years when they start to lay out the room.

It goes like something like this: the cooking area, preparation area and storage should each be at the point of a triangle so that you can move efficiently between the three work areas. I choose to ignore it because everybody cooks in a different way. While the sink may be one of your three important areas if you don't own a dishwasher, if you do it means your priorities will be different. And with microwaves replacing ovens for a lot of people who reheat ready-made meals, that lovely high-tec fan/gas/electric combi-cooker may only be used at the weekends. You want a layout that suits you for more than two days a week. I like space in my kitchen so have fitted everything along one wall to leave the rest of the room free of cabinets. It's a simple 'line' design with the cooker, sink and fridge positioned along the same side of the kitchen in a run. That way I can move easily and 'crablike' along the work surface and between the three – take potatoes out of the fridge, wash them in the sink and put them on the hob to boil. I predict I will save myself (over several years) hours and hours of running backwards and forwards across the kitchen. Well, quite frankly, if I needed that much exercise I wouldn't be cooking with real cream and butter.

MAKING PLANS

If the number of people hanging around the Ikea kitchen department on a Saturday morning is any indication, you'd think putting together a kitchen required a degree in design. It doesn't, but the sheer volume of options for cupboard doors, work surfaces, appliances, etc., can be intimidating. It does help when you are planning a kitchen, probably more than any other room in the house, if you can make a decision. If you are the kind of person who takes half an hour to choose which toppings you want on your pizza, give yourself a year to put your room together.

Considering that cooking, eating and even watching TV all take place in the kitchen, it's worth spending time to put together your perfect room.

Does your kitchen double up as the dining area? Turn to IDEA 29, *Eating in is the new eating out*, for some hints and tips on combining the two functions.

Try another idea…

'The doorway led into a short hallway, lined with closets, and then into the butler's pantry, lined with glass-front cabinets containing sparkling battalions of crystal, and stainless steel sinks. The cabinets, with their beadings, muntins, mullions, cornices – he couldn't remember all the terms – had cost thousands… thousands… And now they were in the kitchen. More cabinets, cornices, stainless steel, tiles, spotlights, the Sub-Zero, the Vulcan – all of it the best Judy's endless research could find, all of it endlessly expensive, hemorrhaging and hemorrhaging…'
TOM WOLFE, *The Bonfire of the Vanities*

Defining idea…

97

How did it go?

Q   **It all sounds too much – there are so many things to consider. Where do I start?**

A   *Let me make it more approachable. Break it down into the following areas: cooking, storage, preparation, washing up and eating. Compile a list of all your requirements in these areas and you're well on your way to designing your kitchen.*

Q   **I have designed the kitchen with some interior-lit cabinets, but how do I know if I have adequate lighting in the room?**

A   *One way to guarantee that you have enough light in the room is to include a track system on the ceiling, fitted with swivel spot lights. This means you can always point a beam in the right direction.*

 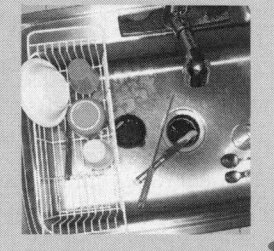

22

Blind ambition

Simple lines and a structured design make for the perfect window dressing. A lovely window treatment doesn't have to rely on swathes of fabric.

The beauty of blinds for me is that they sit neatly in their designated space. You know where you are with them; there's no tweaking of tiebacks or messing with a pole and rings.

Once a blind has been installed it's a straightforward up and down, or down and up routine, and if you think they are too plain, then think again. A patterned fabric made into a blind can have just as much impact as a dressy curtain.

I have an intense dislike of wooden Venetian blinds. I think it's because they can be used at virtually any window so people use them far too much. I always feel that no thought has gone into the window treatment when I see it dressed up like this – it's as if someone has taken the easy option and hasn't even considered that a softer blind might be better suited to the room.

So please think about how you dress your windows. They may be at the very edge of any room but they can take up a large proportion of the wall space and need the same consideration that you give to your paint colour or choice of wallpaper. Which

Here's an idea for you...

Vertical blinds make brilliant room dividers. If you have an open-plan living/dining room and want to break up the space to create added privacy or more clearly define the two uses of the areas, they can fit neatly across an alcove or can be suspended from a fitting in the ceiling. This is a more contemporary approach then putting in folding doors. Choose a colour that is close to the paint or paper on the walls.

Consider your choice of material when buying blinds for the kitchen and bathroom. Look to use wipeable PVC blinds in the bathroom where they may get splashed on a regular basis. In the kitchen, and for safety reasons, make sure the blind is made in fire-retardant fabric.

brings me neatly to a point that you will want to consider. If your walls are painted in a single colour, you can use your choice of blind to introduce an interesting contrast to the space. If you have chosen to hang a patterned paper, then a plain blind may be just what you need.

CHOOSE A STYLE

I'm not sure it is even worth discussing festoon blinds. Does anybody still choose this frou-frou style? Perhaps I'll just say that if you were unfortunate enough to inherit one when you moved into your home, then you should take it down this instant. Pin up a sheet instead. Roller blinds bring simplicity to a window – just a flat piece of fabric that neatly rolls away. Dress up a plain roller with a contrasting panel at the bottom, or if you are a fan of stencilling they provide a perfect canvas for your work. If you are thinking about a treatment for your bedroom and need to preserve your privacy, choose a bottom-up design. With a box fitted to the window sill (preferably), or outside the bottom of the frame (this can look bulky), you raise them up rather than drop them down. This means the bottom half the window can remain covered while the top is clear to allow light into the room. You also have the option of combining an opaque panel with another material, perfect for a lounge that is overlooked.

One of the greatest new innovations for rollers is the huge variety of pulls from which you can now choose; wooden blocks, jute balls, leather laces and ceramic beads can all be added to the bottom of your blind if you feel the need to dress it up a bit.

Have a look at IDEA 36, *Softly, softly*, for ideas on using different types of fabrics.

Try another idea...

All of my windows have Roman blinds. How boringly unimaginative of me. It's because I love their clean lines: the way that the pleats sit neatly when they are open and the way that the fabric lies flat when they are closed. I like to be able to choose any fabric I want so rather than buying from a catalogue I always buy my own material and then have them made up by a professional curtain maker. It's an approach I would recommend because it doesn't cost a fortune. You can buy an inexpensive fabric to compensate for the making-up costs and once it is up no one will know that's where you cut costs.

Reefed blinds make a more quirky statement but can end up being a pain to operate and keep looking neat. These are pulled up and down by cords, which run through eyelets at the top of the blind and loop down and around the fabric. This means you can pull them up very tight, but you often have to fiddle with the fabric to allow it to roll up neatly. It's the sort of blind to use at a window where it may stay half down for any number of days.

If you pick the right design of blind your windows will always look good.

'Relying on the government to protect your privacy is like asking a peeping tom to install your window blinds.'
JOHN PERRY BARLOW, retired rancher and cyber rights activist

Defining idea...

How did
it go?

Q My kitchen window is in a recess. How do I know what size I need?

A *You can measure up inside or outside of your recess. If the window you are dressing is flat, then measure across the frame; if it is recessed, then you need to measure between the walls at either side or in which case you can make the blind as big as you want.*

Q How do I know which style to choose for my kitchen?

A *Well, as we have discussed, I would ignore anything very flouncy. Roman blinds are a great option in a kitchen because there is very little material to trap dirt and dust and they can be made in almost any fabric. This means you can match them to the colour of your cabinets, your floor or anything else you choose. The design means that they are simple to operate so you can get them out of the way of wall-mounted units or the cooking area.*

23

To sleep, perchance to dream

Design your bedroom with comfort in mind. While buying a house may be the biggest financial investment we make, buying the right bed is one of the most important.

Really. Sleep deprivation caused by a crying baby, pressure of work or a snoring partner may not be easy to resolve, but if it is a direct result of an uncomfortable bed, then the solution is in your own hands.

But more of beds later. Let's consider just how you want your bedroom to look and how to achieve that before we get into the specifics of furniture. Start with the style, which will dictate colour choices, fabric types and furniture design, and bear in mind that there are endless variations on these themes.

RUSTIC LIVING

Bring the comfort of the country into your bedroom. Yellows and greens or rosy pinks can form the basis for the scheme. Keep a light touch when decorating. Opt

Some notes about buying beds...

- **Buy the largest bed you can fit into your bedroom. That way you and your partner will have your own space to sleep in.**

- **If you and your partner have different requirements, then consider investing in two different mattresses that will zip together.**

- **A hard mattress is not necessarily a good mattress. What you are looking for is the right amount of support. Lie on your choice for a good few minutes before you buy.**

- **Turn your new mattress every time you change your bed linen.**

- **Forget fashion – is the height of the bed you are buying right for you?**

for wallpaper with a delicate print, and if you can't face papering every wall, then just use it in alcoves or on the wall facing the door. Choose carpet for the floor and reflect that cosy mood with wool blankets on the bed or a patchwork quilt that matches your colour scheme. Indulge yourself with a curvy wrought iron bedstead and plump for painted or pine wooden furniture for storage. Lamps with pleated fabric shades would be apposite for the bedside table, as would a blanket box positioned at the end of the bed.

CONTEMPORARY ROOMS

The art of Feng Shui and the influence of the Orient have had tremendous impact on interiors, and nowhere more so than in the bedroom. Work with a colour scheme including white, shades of grey, cream and brown. The mood is minimalist so hide or disguise clutter in the room. Opt for a laminate or real wood floor that you can dress up with rugs for extra comfort. Select natural linens to deck out the bed, calico or cotton pillowslips, for example, and put wooden Venetian blinds or shutters at the window. A low-level wooden bed would suit this style, and fitted wardrobes would contribute to the clean lines of the space.

CLASSIC LIVING

Consider a muted yellow or duck egg blue as the starting point for your scheme. It may be appropriate to pick a patterned carpet so you will need to choose your bed linen to co-ordinate accordingly. Curtains are a must. If you want to add a dressy pelmet at the window then echo this look with a canopied bed and be lavish in your use of fabric. Feel free to introduce a gilded mirror or arrange classic prints across one wall. It suits the mood to display a collection of perfume bottles or perhaps have an antique set of brushes and hand held mirror on display. A slipper chair, fabric-covered ottoman or chaise longue will add the finishing touch.

Next consider how you will layout the room. Can you create a focal point with the bed or will you rely on architectural features such as a fireplace to draw the eye? Maybe you have invested in a magnificent old armoire that you are going to use for storing clothes and linen, or have a dressing table that will sit in the bay of a window.

Where are you going to put the mirror? Don't leave it out but don't just stick it on the wall. Consider a freestanding design or a large framed mirror left on the floor to lean against the wall.

If you want some inspiration in your choice of accessories, see IDEA 39, *The essential extras*, for ideas to dress up your bedroom.

Try another idea...

'The bed is a bundle of paradoxes: we go to it with reluctance, yet we quit it with regret; we make up our minds every night to leave it early, but we make up our bodies every morning to keep it late.
OGDEN NASH

Defining idea...

105

Where are the lamps? A reading light mounted at either side of the bed or lamps positioned on bedside tables will add symmetry to the space.

Given that we spend up to a third of our lives in the bedroom, it is worth getting a style that works morning and night, summer and winter to fulfil every requirement.

How did it go?

Q **We have bought a new low-level bed but now our old bedside cabinets are too high for us to use. The budget's virtually all spent, so what can we do?**

A *Can you scrape together enough to buy two cheap occasional tables? Simply cut down the legs to the height that you require. Alternatively find two tablemats (leather or glass would be ideal). Take them along to your local wood merchants and get two blocks of wood, as near to the height of your bed as possible, cut to their dimensions. Paint the wood to match your colour scheme and place the mats on top.*

Q **What do I do if I can't budget for a new bed?**

A *This is tricky because there is nothing worse for your body than a second-hand bed. I am going to suggest a compromise – a new mattress on top of an old frame, although no one who is worth their salt in bed design or sales would agree. You could look for a frame in a junk shop – hospital and old school dormitory beds might suit the guest room because they are sturdy but will not be used that often. Remember that ideally a bed has only a 10-year life, so while you may need to save money, don't expect someone else to sleep on a bed that would give you nightmares.*

24

The green room

Create a cool, calm and collected mood. In colour therapy green is the colour of healing and growth. It's calming and restful and brings balance to the soul.

Now that I know this, I understand why I feel so much better when I have a piece of lime tucked into the top of my beer bottle, and why when I don't I can get very, very angry.

It's also a lucky colour, so invest in some green underwear for when you go to buy your next lottery ticket or go to watch your team. But how does this affect where we use it in the home?

If you consider the choices in the green group, many of the colours are inspired by nature. There's the previously mentioned lime, plus evergreen, moss, grass, avocado, apple, clover and fern. The list goes on and on.

Choose paler shades of green when you want to make a room seem larger. Introduce it into spaces that face west or southwest and need cooling down to counteract the heat from the sun. Introduce it on the wall where patio doors lead into the garden and you'll find it has the pleasing effect of picking up on the colour

If there is a particular area in the home which you would like to make more relaxing, paint one or two walls with a light green wash. Bring in some houseplants, not spider plants, but a bamboo or glossy ficus tree. Get two or three green throw cushions and chuck them on chairs or the sofa. The soothing effects of this quick makeover should be felt straight away.

'**Green Eggs and Ham** *was the story of my life. I wouldn't eat a thing when I was a kid, but Dr Suess inspired me to try cauliflower.*'
JIM CARREY

of the foliage outside, thereby unifying the two spaces. It is that reflection of nature that contributes so much to the restful effects that the colour can achieve. It is also why it works so well with other natural materials like bare wood, stone, wicker and cotton.

Use your imagination for a minute. Picture a well-scrubbed pine wooden kitchen table. The backdrop is a combination of cupboards dragged in a light green wash of paint and the floor is a pale limestone flag. Copper-coloured pans hang from a ceiling rack and a light gingham check dresses the window. Doesn't that sound appealing?

Now go into a lounge where the walls are papered with a slim green stripe. The two sofas that face each other across a low-level maple coffee table are covered with loose cream cotton covers and the floor has a sisal-look carpet. A mirror is framed in faded grey driftwood and the wooden shutters at the window are painted white. Doesn't that sound relaxing? These are the reasons to use green.

Give green it's due: decorate at least one room using this scheme for a well-balanced and relaxing home.

If you are thinking about painting wood furniture to match your green scheme, see IDEA 12, *Decorative effects for a designer home*, on the rules of using paint effects.

Try another idea...

'*Green is the colour associated with the fourth chakra, located in the heart area, and so is connected to matters of the heart. On the physical level, this includes the functioning of the organs close to the heart region, such as the lungs, the chest and the whole circulatory system. It can be helpful for someone suffering from asthma or bronchitis. Green also helps to balance the flow of blood, and it is interesting that doctors and nurses often wear green gowns in the operating theatre.*'
CATHERINE CUMMING, *The Colour Healing Home*

Defining idea...

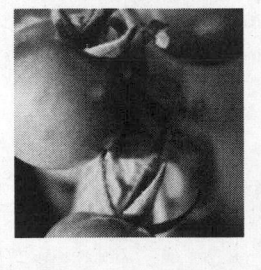

How did it go?

Q   **Right, I understand that I need to calm down, but where are the best places for green?**

A   *Green is a good choice for the bedroom, where you want to be calm. If you have a hyperactive child, try decorating their room in green and you might be surprised at how positively it can affect their moods. It's also ideal for kitchens where you can sometimes get stressed out over the cooking. Because it's a cool colour it can also counteract the effects of all that heat and steam.*

Q   **I have decorated a couple of rooms in green but while they are relaxing to spend time in, I also sometimes long for a little more stimulation.**

A   *It sounds like while you might never want to leave your sanctuaries of calm, you're finding the overall effect a little too laid back. If you have found these ideas just a bit too mellow, you may want to introduce a contrasting accent colour to add a bit of zing to the room. Opposite green on the colour wheel you'll find red, orange and purple in varying degrees. If you think about the impact that a vase full of purple and green irises can have, then you're working along the right lines. Introduce a vase of purple flowers into a green lounge. Alternatively group together a collection of purple candles on a table in front of a green painted wall. Leave a bowl of red apples in the middle of the green kitchen's table and pile up a platter with red cherries – it certainly adds a vibrant touch.*

25

A professional opinion

There are some occasions in life when you have to call in the experts. Whether you need an architect, builder or estate agent, they all need managing.

Looking to improve your home, create extra space or merely flog it? It is certainly wise to rely on trained professionals to help you in your quest, but how do you know you are going to get the best service and not run into one of the following scary scenarios?

'I paid the 10% deposit in cash and never saw them again', or 'the architect says the building time is running two weeks over', or 'its been on the market now for three months and we haven't had an offer anywhere near the asking price'.

HOW DO YOU AVOID THIS?

Don't be scared of them! The technical terminology may be confusing but pin them down until you understand exactly what is going to take place, when, how and for how long.

Here's an idea for you...

Draw up a shortlist of possible architects and then request a portfolio from each one. You will get a much clearer idea if you can compare and contrast work at the same time. Use this opportunity to get a list of their qualifications and any references from previous commissions. That way you have all the information you need before you make your final choice.

It's all in the planning and channels of communication. Get these right from the start and the experience should be bearable – let's be realistic: it's never ever going to be a joy letting someone else get involved with your space, but the least you can do is try to set up the situation so that it doesn't end in tears. In practical terms that means a time-line for builders and architects and a clear understanding of how the estate agent is going to market your home.

BRICKIN' IT

If builders were obliged to carry ID cards and register with a professional body, it might solve some of the problems associated with the trade. Here's my advice. Keep a logbook of the job. It needs to be dated – add times if it seems appropriate – and you need to keep a comprehensive list of who does what on the job. This is in addition to any contract that you sign. You can use this log to compare against the progress of the agreed timetable. (In addition to the costs and outline of the work involved, look for a start and completion date, a start and finish time each day, any safety and security provisions and an assurance about the disposal of any waste materials.) This advice comes from harsh experience. One team not completing a job properly and another team then also failing to finish it left me with a leaking roof. If you can pinpoint exactly who is responsible you will stand a much better

Defining idea...

'When one has finished building one's house, one suddenly realises that in the process one has learned something that one really needed to know in the worst way – before one began.'
FRIEDRICH NIETZSCHE

chance of getting things finished satisfactorily. You also stand a much better chance of success if you name the individuals concerned rather than referring to them generically.

You'll need a builder if you choose to put in a conservatory, see IDEA 18, *People in glass houses...*, for some more information.

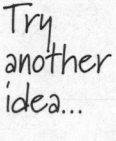

Try another idea...

BUILDING IT

In the best scenario an architect can manage the job, dealing with the subcontractors who are working on your home. First and foremost, when you want to use an architect look at as much of the finished work of the firm as you can. Their style will influence your style. You might meet a 'glass and steel' man who you get along with famously but will the finished design work on the extension to your country cottage? It's all about building up a relationship so that you have a mutual understanding and respect. Architects can be relied on to cope with any legal requirements that you may have to fulfil, knowing who to speak to in order to get planning permission for example.

Be strict with them about your budget. Costs can easily creep up when you are choosing materials, for example. A granite worktop will elevate the costs of a kitchen extension dramatically and there are thousands of alternatives.

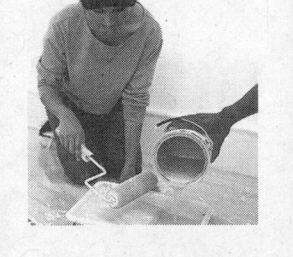

Defining idea...

'Got home, late and
exhausted, to find Gary the
Builder still there and house
completely taken over with
burnt toast under the grill,
washing up and copies of the
Angler's Mail and Coarse
Fisherman all over the shop.
'What do you think?' said
Gary, proudly nodding at his
handiwork.
'They're great! They're great!'
I gushed, feeling mouth going
into funny tight shape.
'There's just one little thing.
Do you think you could make
it so the supports are all in
line with each other?'
HELEN FIELDING, *Bridget Jones:
The Edge of Reason*

SELLING IT

Do estate agents always have your best
interests at heart? It would be in a perfect
world (no wars, no plagues, no famine) where
they did. No of course they don't. The
commission cheque looms large over any
negotiation. There's your starting point. Haggle
over how much you are going to pay them. If
it's a large chain which offers advertising in its
own brochures or local press, a web presence
and window display you're going to pay a little
extra, but if you don't actually like being
passed from one agent to another you might
be better off going with a one-man band – at
least you always know with whom you are
dealing. The highest value isn't necessarily the
best. An agent can inflate a price to get your
signature on the contract (and get your hopes
up of trading up) but then the price will have
to be dropped to get a sale and you may be left
short for your next purchase.

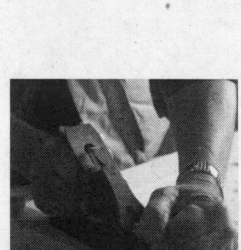

Q **I have seen several architects and narrowed my choice down to two companies having seen their portfolios. I need to provide them with a brief for the job so that I can get a more definite idea of costs. How do I approach this?**

How did it go?

A *You should by now have a clear idea of the work required so grab some magazines and compile a selection of tear sheets that show the style, materials, colours and rough size of the job. With this include a list of your expectations, how the space is going to be used and how soon you want the job started/finished. Copy this to both companies and you should by their respective responses be in a position to make your final selection.*

Q **Contract aside, how do I know that they are going to do the job well for me?**

A *A good builder should be able to supply you with references from satisfied customers. You may even want to go and look at some work before you employ them. Check the finish on any job. If they are running late they may not give the finishing touches the same care and attention as the rest of the job.*

26

Welcome to my boudoir

Think glamorous, think gorgeous, think about a sexy and sensuous space. If you hate design rules and like to mix things up then boudoir style is for you.

It conjures up for me a mix of rich fabrics, curvaceous furniture and a room filled with all sorts of unusual accessories. It is laid-back and bohemian and it embraces a wide variety of materials in its style.

In boudoir style, you won't find many straight lines or a structured layout to a room. What you may see is a pile of cushions spilling from an old chaise longue onto the floor where they double up as footstool or seating when required. A bed will be dressed with a silk bedspread and a mixture of pillows in different shapes and sizes. Detailing on furniture in the room is curly and ornate, and positioning of these pieces takes a fairly random approach: they don't have to be flat against the wall but can sit at an angle in the middle of the floor. If you have a chest of drawers or desk that you think might fit in terms of shape, then you can replace plain wooden knobs with glass ones to fit with the look. In the same mode swap wooden shelving for glass and change plain supports to a filigree design. If boudoir style is

Here's an idea for you... **Try using pearlised paints on one wall in the room. This finish comes into its own if you position a lamp so that the light catches the reflective surface.**

applied to the bedroom you might find an antique wrought iron washstand alongside a battered armoire. If it's in the lounge there could be a velvet-covered slipper chair sitting beneath a wall-mounted candle sconce.

With the flamboyant nature of this style of room you can afford to go a little over the top when dressing up the space. If you like the idea of a fabulously fluffy sheepskin rug, then position it beside the bed or in front of your hearth. Faux fur throws and cushions can find their place across the bed or draped over sofas and chairs. Include baubles, trinkets, embroidered cushions and old lace. Go to antique arcades and rummage to find interesting pieces, or raid the old family home for an heirloom or two.

Look out for:

- Mother of pearl accessories
- Antique gold frames
- Coloured glass and pearl-glazed lustre ceramics
- Anything with a beaded trim

COLOURS AND FINISHES

Work with a palette of purples and pinks. Look for richly coloured beaded silk cushions or trim plain ones with lengths of organza ribbon. There's no doubt this is about indulging your feminine side so make the most of really pretty pastel shades. You might also want to consider a course in gilding if you are serious about working with this look. A touch of gold here and there in the room creates just the right sense of decadence for this style, and you can add it with gold leaf, wax or paint to a variety of surfaces once you know the tricks of the trade. Take an old wrought iron garden chair, for example, and add patches of gold to the frame. Have a little round cushion made up to fit the seat so that it feels like it belongs inside the house. You can also use a length of silky fabric to wrap around the back and legs of a plain wooden chair transforming it into a lavish and stylish piece.

There is a place for reflective surfaces in this room. Can you track down one of those wonderful Venetian-style mirrored console tables where the drawers are etched or painted with a floral design? If not get a suitably decorative mirror. You are trying to find something with a rippled edge or a design that has an elaborate motif at the top and bottom of the frame.

If you want to live with a relaxed atmosphere and missed out on the tidy gene, boudoir chic could be just your thing.

Boudoir chic is perfect for the living room, but if you want some more suggestions for this room, see IDEA 38, *Lounging around.*

Try another idea...

'As she sallied forth from her boudoir, you would never have guessed how quickly she could strip for action.'
WILLIAM MANCHESTER,
American historian

Defining idea...

'Poetry is a mirror which makes beautiful that which is distorted.'
PERCY BYSSHE SHELLEY

Defining idea...

How did
it go?

Q **My whole house is fairly bohemian and I've pulled together this look in the lounge by combining lots of different bits and pieces from the rest of my house. The one thing I am lacking is some boudoir lighting. What should I be looking for?**

A   *What you want is something really flamboyant. Your choice of light fittings is crucial with this look. A chandelier is essential for the sumptuous mood of the room. Try and find a design that has been dressed with murano glass drops or add your own crystal drops. You can drape a length of fake pearl beads between two fixtures for a decorative touch. Candle style fittings for the bulbs are something to look out for, or get decorative bulbs not plain designs.*

Q **I've got the basics but it needs a few frills.**

A   *Remember that it's the quirky details that contribute to the overall appeal of this look. It's OK to drape a fringed shawl over the end of the sofa or leave a silky nightdress hanging from a pretty padded hanger suspended from the front of your armoire. Be relaxed and laid back and you'll get the look that you want to achieve.*

27

Young at heart

When you design a child's bedroom you want a space that can adapt as they grow.

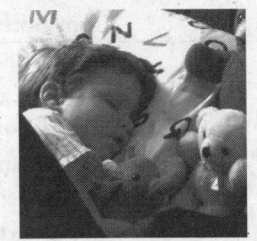

And boy do they grow. From the toddler who has no say in how you decorate their space to the independent child who wants it all her own way, you need to create a flexible scheme.

Not having kids of my own I don't have first-hand experience, but with nine nephews and nieces I can lay claim to some knowledge of the subject. If you need to give the room a single priority it has to be storage. A couple of drawers under the bed and a set of crates for toys makes a good starting point but however much storage you start with, multiply it three- or fourfold and you'll be getting close to the real demands that will be made on the space over the years from baby to toddler to youth. You can stop worrying there because after that it's pretty much up to them what goes on. A teenager's space is a sacred retreat – enter at your peril.

A WORK IN PROGRESS

Start with some basics in the room that will stay in place for several years. It has to be said that a good quality carpet is worth the investment as it will be crawled over, played on and might even have to survive the odd drenching from a drink thrown

Here's an idea for you...

Fabric drawstring bags provide practical storage for everything from clothes to toys. They make a versatile option and bought in different colours and designs are one way of adding colour and fun to the room. The quickest and easiest way to add lots of extra storage space is to put up a peg rail around the room from which you hang any number of bags. Make sure that when you put it up, you drill good deep holes and use rawl plugs for extra strength. You have to figure that at some point children will pull on bags and put the rail under considerable pressure.

mid-tantrum. Any cheap flooring just won't withstand that much wear and tear.

Next think about your choice of bed. You can buy cots that convert into a child size bed. They may be pricey but make a good long-term investment. If you choose to buy a cot and then replace it when the child has grown out of it, you are looking for a bed that will last for ten years. That's about the maximum life span for any bed anyway, but if you spend wisely at the beginning you won't have to worry about it again for sometime. A bed that has another mattress which slides out from underneath, with legs that pop up to make another bed, is a sensible choice given that you are bound to have to provide more sleeping space at some point for pyjama parties.

Don't bother to wallpaper the whole room. If your child requests a paper with a favourite football team, cartoon character or doll, then buy a roll and use it on just one or two walls so that when they get bored with a design you aren't stuck with repapering the whole room. Paint the remaining walls in a neutral colour that will work with other changes in the place. Hardwearing finishes are essential so why not add tongue and groove around the bottom half of the room? (Also that way you would only have to wallpaper the top half anyway.) If you paint it in a hardwearing oil-based paint it will also be stain resistant and easy to wipe clean. Alternatively opt for a wipe-clean vinyl wallpaper which cleans with the sweep of a wet cloth or sponge.

Be realistic about how many times you want to refurbish the room through the years. Baby-sized furniture is very cute, and all well and good if money is no object, but I suggest you invest in 'grown-up' pieces from the start. If you want to change the handles on a wardrobe or the knobs on a set of drawers with suitably cutsie designs, it's a considerably cheaper way of making the furniture match the room. Look for pieces with lasting style and ones that could, should you wish, be repainted to update them – pine wardrobes and MDF shelving spring to mind. Bookcases, chests of drawers and blanket boxes are all valuable sources of storage in a child's room. They will be there for several years.

If you are thinking that it all sounds a bit boring for children, then the list of goodies that are comparatively cheap to buy and easy to change runs something like this:

- Lampshades
- Bedlinen
- Blinds
- Bean bags / floor cushions
- Rugs
- Fabric wash bags
- Door / drawer knobs

You can happily let your children choose these according to their current passions, which at certain ages can change as quickly as their shoe size.

Choose practical and durable furniture and furnishings and your child's room will last through the ages.

For more ideas on choosing carpet, see IDEA 14, Tread softly, because you tread on my dreams.

Try another idea...

'**What might be taken for a precocious genius is the genius of childhood**'
PABLO PICASSO

Defining idea...

'**All the time a person is a child he is both a child and learning to be a parent. After he becomes a parent he becomes predominantly a parent reliving childhood.**'
Dr BENJAMIN SPOCK

Defining idea...

123

How did
it go? **Q** **I have finished the room but my daughter is a light sleeper and even if I draw the curtains they let in too much light during her afternoon sleep. They co-ordinate with the rest of the fabrics in the room so I don't want to replace them. What other option do I have?**

A *You have a couple of choices depending on how you have hung the curtains and what type of window you have. If there's a recess, then have a roller blind made in black-out fabric and fit this to the frame. Alternatively, pick out a dark colour from the pattern and buy another pair of curtains to match this and hang them from a supplementary pole.*

Q **I indulged my son's choice for Super Heroes wallpaper but he's now into football and wants a change. Any ideas?**

A *Buy some of those little football stickers and position them randomly among the heroes. Then explain that even Super Heroes need play time and tell him he can change the room when he's ready to redecorate it himself.*

28

A tough decision

Choose stone floors for their looks and durability. In my fantasy world where money is no object, marble floors are available to everyone and limestone and slate find a place in the appropriate space.

I'm talking about lovely great big slabs of the stuff. Not neatly cut, squared off tiles (they are the subject of another chapter in the book), but substantial, large and lengthy pieces that take a mountain of a man, or more probably several, to move.

Have you seen the recent version of *The Thomas Crown Affair*? (One of the only remakes, incidentally, that comes anywhere close to being as good as the original.) Piers Brosnan and Rene Russo have a passionate session on the stone staircase in Thomas Crown's immaculate apartment. Now that's not the everyday sort of punishment that you subject your stairs to, but it is an example of how floors can be put through some pretty vigorous workouts. The great news is that you can rely on most hard floors to offer the ultimate in durability and this contributes much to their appeal. (That, and you don't get carpet burns.) If you are subjecting a hall to

Here's an idea for you... There is a world of difference between the supplier and fitter of a floor. Someone sourcing stone may well have a life-long love affair with the product and an intimate knowledge of its quirks and qualities. They'll know how to coax out the best features and disguise any failings. A fitter is there to lay the floor whether it's marble, slate or limestone. If one company is providing the complete service, all the better. If you are sourcing the stone from an importer and getting someone else to fit it, then make sure your supplier gives you some back-up. You'll need the proper sealant and a specification sheet with details on how to treat the stone which can be passed on to your fitters.

constant traffic or a kitchen/diner to regular entertaining, then a hard floor can take the punishment when a softer option might show signs of wear and tear.

There is something about stone that says timeless luxury. Is it because we know that these materials have formed over millions of years and so deserve to be treated with the respect and deference that their age commands? (There is a small quarry in central France, for example, where limestone is extracted from beds which were laid down in the early Jurassic period some 140 million years ago.) Or is just that we are familiar with seeing them used in grand houses and historic buildings which make them an object of desire?

WALK ON BY

Marble is to floors what diamonds are to jewellery: an expensive choice but one that rewards you with its sheer beauty and dramatic impact on the eye. In sheet form it is always going to break the bank (sort of like a four-carat emerald-cut stone), but there is the less pricey alternative of tiles, although these are more likely to be a backing material with a veneer of marble laid on top. Marble is one of those materials that makes a real statement. It needs to be used in big spaces and grand locations. That's why you find it used in luxury hotel foyers.

Granite is in the luxury goods department too. The choice of colours, from pink-hued and speckled white to blue-grey and black, means it can fit in with most colour schemes. Can I say it's rock solid? Well it really is incredibly hard and will be in place for longer than you or I will be able to enjoy it. Just be careful if you choose a polished finish as this will make it slippery. (Again, it's available in tile form, which would make a really good choice for a hallway or vestibule.)

If you are wondering about terracotta or mosaics, **IDEA 48, A night on the tiles,** addresses these materials.

Try another idea...

'*Joseph Ettedgui, innovative retailer and fashion entrepreneur, believes that lighting and flooring are the two most important elements in the home and if these work, "everything else will look wonderful". Whenever he is creating a home, he always spends as much money as possible on good quality flooring, whether stone, wooden parquet or the softest carpet. "The floor is one of the very first things you feel when you enter a place", he says. "Your feet actually feel quite a lot."'*
SIR TERENCE CONRAN, *Easy Living*

Defining idea...

'*Nothing is built on stone; all is built on sand, but we must build as if the sand were stone.'*
JORGE LUIS BORGES

Defining idea...

Slate has a much more rustic appeal, and if you want an immaculately smooth finish to your floors look elsewhere. It can be slightly rough with worn edges, but its waterproof qualities makes it a good choice in the bathroom, for example.

For those of you who are looking for a lighter option, you should be asking about sandstone and limestone. In creamy whites, buttery yellows and pale grey, these would be suited to areas where you need a floor in keeping with a light colour scheme. (Some of these are named after the area in which they are quarried just to confuse you: Cotswold stone, for example is a limestone.) Now if these floors are laid properly, sealed and maintained they will look great. However, because they are porous they will easily stain so make sure that you get them treated. For that same reason you must also be careful about the type of cleaning solution that you use. A black mark in the middle of a large expanse of light stone will ruin the luxury look, and you can't just scrub it off with bleach.

Here's an idea for you...

Q You say that stone must be sealed properly, but with what?

A *It can be any product that penetrates the upper surface of the stone and and protects it from dirt and scratches. Your supplier or installer should be able to supply a special stone floor sealer. Once that is done you can always apply something extra – on slate, for example, a water-based, self-polishing wax can be applied over a sealed floor for extra protection.*

Q Right, but how do I then clean the slate?

A *The best way to keep it clean is with regular vacuuming to get rid of any grit and a weekly mop over with a damp (not sodden) mop. If you need to apply detergent make it a really weak solution and rinse it well.*

29

Eating in is the new eating out

Relax at home with a dedicated dining space. Why the rush to run out with your credit card and pay for a meal that might or might not be worth the monthly interest?

A friend of mine recently went to the new and highly lauded restaurant set up by a young chef to train teenagers with no skills (social or work that is) for a career in the catering industry.

Now the food wasn't great but they drank enough wine to dull the edges of their disappointment and made it from start to finish without sending back a single dish. When the bill arrived my friend's husband grabbed it as the couple they were out with had just recently decided to get married. 'Look on it as our engagement present', he said. The words were hanging in the air, like one of those cartoon bubbles, as he opened up the bill. It was astronomical, I mean more than enough to feed a small nation. His response was to burst out laughing. Sometimes when you feel you've been taken for a sucker that's the best response. When I heard about it all I could think was 'imagine how many takeaways I can eat at home with that amount'. (Also, how much good wine I could buy, because we all know that the mark-up on a restaurant wine list is enormous.)

Here's an
idea for
you...

If investing in a matching set of chairs is beyond your budget, go for an alternative. Buy four or six wooden chairs from junk shops. They can be all sorts of shapes and sizes but *must have* removable fabric-covered seats. Take out the seat and remove the fabric. Lay it on a piece of paper and cut round to give yourself a paper pattern. Then simply position this on a new fabric, cut out your squares and centre the seat cover on top. Fold over one fabric edge and staple to the underneath of the seat. Then do the same with the opposite edge. Make sure that you keep the fabric taught. Repeat with the other two sides and put back in the chair. Repeat for all your seats – and now you have a matching set.

Now I'm not saying that there aren't many, many occasions when we want to go out and eat. I crave the social atmosphere and general *bonhomie* that being in a restaurant generates as much as the next person. But what I am suggesting is that if you set up a dedicated dining space at home which has all the attributes of a good restaurant and none of the bad (leave the food aside at the moment), then you might find just as much pleasure in staying in and getting the friends to come to you.

Whether you cook for the family or entertain on a regular basis, a well-designed dining space should be on everyone's wish list. It might be a dedicated room or it could be part of the kitchen or lounge, but it is somewhere that you will want to sit, eat, chat, drink and relax. If you have a separate dining room you can indulge any design choices, however, if it is part of another room you need to be clever with the area and you may just resort to dressing the table to create the mood for the meal. It's a tall order for just one space, so how do you tackle it?

STUCK FOR SPACE?

It is frequently the case that you will need to eat in a corner of the kitchen or at one end of the lounge. You will need to choose furniture that fits in the space. This means looking for adaptable tables that can expand to accommodate a group of people and that fold up when they aren't in use so that they don't take up too much space. Whatever style of dining chair that you fancy, make sure that it's one that can stack. Six chairs take up a lot of space if they have to stand alone and will clutter up a room, but if they can be put in a pile you can store them more easily when they aren't needed. They will fit into the space under your stairs or can be tucked into a corner out of the way.

'Few things tend more to alienate friendship than a want of punctuality in our engagements. I have known the breach of a promise to dine or sup to break up more than one intimacy.'
WILLIAM HAZLITT

If you are looking for ways dress up the space, see IDEA 39, *The essential extras*, on essential accessories

Defining idea...

Try another idea...

A DEDICATED ROOM

You can indulge your desire for a very specific look if you have a separate dining room. Whatever the style of the rest of your home, should you wish for ruby red walls, rich velvet-covered seats, a dramatic chandelier and floor-standing candelabras, then here's the space where you can create that look. And boy-oh-boy will you have some parties in there. Without wanting to dampen your enthusiasm for a room that stands alone in the overall scheme of your home, I would suggest that you think about how you are going to prepare the table and present the food. Here's what I am thinking. The room described above will call for gold or silver chargers set beneath the finest china with exquisite glasses for red wine, white wine and water, teamed with fine cutlery and the finest starched table linen. Now if you usually eat from plain white plates, eat with plastic-handled knives and forks and use a handy chunky tumbler for a glass of red wine, these items will not translate into your designer dining room. My point is that you will need to invest in a complete set of glasses, platters, cutlery and serving spoons, mats and all the associated tableware to make such an extravagant scheme work. Do you have the budget to do that or should you work to design a room which will work with items that you already own?

You can treat the preparation of your dining room as putting together a puzzle. The design of the room is the main part of the image and you need all the other pieces in place for it to look complete. Whether you are having a formal dinner to impress the guests or a casual meal for good friends, the same principles apply.

How did it go?

Q I know all the elements that need to go in, but how do I decide on my scheme?

A Well, let's go back to the restaurant theme. Start out by thinking about your favourite one. Is it minimalist and modern with lots of chrome and glass, industrial lighting and chic white china, or is it cosy and dark with rough plaster walls and candles stuffed into Chianti bottles to illuminate the meal? Whatever the elements that make you return time after time, you want to achieve the same effect in your home.

Q I have a dining table at the end of my lounge but people always seem to go and sit on the sofa as soon as the meal is over and it breaks up the party. Any solutions?

A The real beauty of restaurants is often in the intimacy of the space. It feels right to linger over your coffee and a cigarette. However, at home when you eat at a table positioned at the end of an open-plan lounge, people drift off towards the sofa too quickly once the pudding has been demolished. There is a simple solution. Use a screen to divide the two areas quite clearly into spaces with different functions.

30

The art of living

From a photograph to a print or a collection of glass to a single much-loved piece of sculpture, you can find a way to display your treasured work of art.

If I ever win the lottery, I will buy an original Elizabeth Frink. I don't want something on the scale of 'Risen Christ' outside Liverpool's Anglican cathedral, but a Goggle Head would be amazing. I'd love to own a Degas bronze — not the ballerinas but a racehorse in motion.

Buying a piece of art is quite an emotive moment. Your choice is such a personal one. And once you get it home and can sit and enjoy your purchase in private it is a thrill that defies any simple explanation. If you think I am getting a bit carried away, just bear with me. I have a limited edition photograph of James Dean that I bought with a whole month's salary in 1987. It would be the first thing that I rescued in a fire. A cast-concrete silver-leafed bowl from a designer whose work I coveted for years, and was finally given as a leaving gift, is a constant inspiration to me. The point of these biographical details is that once I had these pieces, I took some time to decide where and how they would be displayed.

Here's an idea for you...

You may have items in your home that you haven't considered as art but that you can use to make displays. Take glass flower arranging beads for example. Fill two or three plain, straight-sided vases with a variety of different coloured beads and group them together along a windowsill – when the light catches them they look amazing.

What about fairy lights? Wrapped around an empty picture frame and hung on the wall, or curled up inside a big glass bowl and placed in the middle of a shelf they make stylish pieces of 'art'.

Now what we consider as art is a very personal preference, and how we choose to display it comes down to much the same thing. However, there are certain ways to focus attention on a picture or to draw the eye to a much-loved collection that could help when you choose to put these things on display. And the way they are displayed should be sympathetic to the style of the pieces – for example, you can use open-plan shelving for modern collections and lit glass-fronted cabinets for more classical art.

You should take into consideration the following when displaying pieces:

- Wall colour
- Situation
- Lighting

Starting with colour, while most art galleries choose white as the colour against which to hang or display pieces, the walls in your home are likely to be painted or papered in any number of colours. Now you can hang a Mondrian on a wall papered with a stripe but you wouldn't be very happy with the resulting effect it creates. If you have a spectacular picture is it worth considering repainting a recess or chimneybreast in a colour that complements rather than crowds the image? Does the situation show the piece off to its best? A large modern vase calls for space around it so that it can be appreciated without other objects distracting the eye, so maybe you need to consider moving a table into an uncluttered area of the room to allow the art to breathe.

Is there a corner of the room that gets flooded with daylight but then spends the rest of the time in shadow? Your object might look great by day but get lost at night. In which case you should think about getting a light to illuminate the object. If you don't want to start rewiring the room, a lamp moved so that its beam can be directed on the right spot when required is a quick and easy solution to the problem.

Look around your home for a blank wall or empty corner and be open to the idea that a picture destined for the lounge wall might be perfectly placed when hung in the bedroom. Think about moving pieces around and you'll surely end up with the perfect display.

See IDEA 49, *Keep it tidy*, for more information on storage.

Try another idea...

'Without art, the crudeness of reality would make the world unbearable.'
GEORGE BERNARD SHAW

Defining idea...

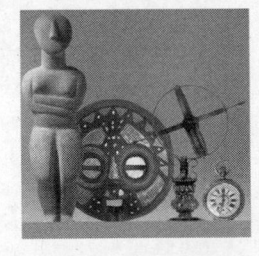

'The object of art is to give life a shape.'
JEAN ANOUILH, French playwright

Defining idea...

Q **Well, I understand how to position a piece, but what sort of prints should I be looking for?**

A   *Pick pictures that suit your space. If you live in a loft you'll have large expanses of wall where you can afford to hang huge dramatic canvases. Think about a big Warhol print mounted on a canvas and left unframed. Or go for a dramatic black and white photograph – views from the sky of urban or rural landscapes can look stunning when reproduced on a large scale. For homes decorated in contemporary style, look at graphic prints or hand-printed silkscreen prints. Mount in beech or light wood frames.*

Q **I have looked around and these all seem pretty pricey – any other alternatives?**

A   *You'll be amazed at what you can put together without much of a budget. It tends to work out a lot cheaper if you buy a picture and then a frame separately; that way you can shop around for less expensive designs. Take sepia photographs for example. You'll usually find a box full of them at street markets and in the back of antique shops for which you'll pay a few pence. A single picture might have no impact but a line of them across a wall, or a group put together, looks great.*

If you haven't bought a digital camera yet, go out and get one. I know you haven't got much of budget but it could save you a fortune in posters and prints and the possibilities are endless once you can print images from your own computer.

31

Social graces

Get your house dressed up and ready to impress. Have you got one of those friends who you love to visit on a Saturday night? Somehow the house is always welcoming, the lounge looks lovely, the dinner table inviting and if you end up sleeping over, the guest bedroom is a delight.

Your cooking may not always be perfect, but it's more about the ambience that you create when you ask people round to dinner.

And your guest room might double up as a study and have computer equipment and filing cabinets juggling for space with the bed, but it's about making the room welcoming – working around what you have got in place.

Part of getting it right is in the planning. Allow yourself time to prepare the food, tidy the house and get yourself ready. There is nothing worse than the guests arriving in their finery when you haven't had time to get dressed up, never mind that you don't have anywhere to go. It may sound very dull, but a list of jobs and a rough estimate of the time they will take should set you on the right track. Only you know how long you spend on folding eight napkins, laying out eight table settings, getting eight matching glasses together and arranging your flowers. Now that's out of the way, how do your dress up your home?

Here's an idea for you...

Choose a seaside theme for your dinner party and use shells as tealight holders. Make a piece of driftwood into the centrepiece for your table. Go for a Japanese mood and use your coffee table instead of your dining table to eat from. Bring in big floor cushions instead of dining chairs for seats. When you want something rustic, search out those tiny terracotta plant pots, plug the hole in the bottom and use them to hold the pepper and salt.

The finest china, the most elegant linen and some sparkling crystal makes a wonderful setting, but I have found that a few inexpensive 'home-grown' ideas will have guests passing the complements along with the condiments far more effusively. You can make a lovely display even if you are designing on a shoestring. The easiest way is to work within a theme.

TABLE STYLES

If you want to choose a floral theme try some of the following ideas:

- Float a single flower head in a bowl beside each place setting.

- Use brightly coloured tins that held fruit for example and put a posy beside each setting.

- Scatter petals along the length of the table (red roses look amazing against a white cloth).

- Tie a long ribbon around the back of each chair and thread a single stem though each bow.

- Freeze edible flowers in ice cubes so that the drinks match the theme.

There are hundreds of other possibilities but do you get the idea? Think about the theme then write down as many items that are associated with it as possible and see how many of these you can use or adapt to work in the room.

If you are stuck for space to store things in the guest bedroom, see IDEA 42, *It works like a dream*, for some useful hints.

Try another idea...

OVERNIGHT STAY

Scent has a powerful effect on people. If your guests walk into their bedroom and there is a wonderful perfume in the air, it immediately says 'welcome'. The subtext is that you have made an effort for them and it makes the room all the more attractive because of that alone. Leave scented candles on the windowsill. With good quality ones, you don't even have to light them because with the heat of the sun, they will give off a scent anyway. Use a fragranced air freshener in the room roughly half an hour before it is going to be used. That way the scent will not be overpowering but will still linger in the air.

'Without friends, no one would want to live, even if he had all other goods.'
ARISTOTLE

Defining idea...

If you do have to disguise a work area I would recommend that you buy a folding screen. It may seem like an extravagance for just one night, but this is a versatile piece of furniture that you are investing in. It can go into other rooms and be put to use on other occasions. For hiding clutter there is nothing better.

Entertaining at home should be about both you and your guests being relaxed, so make sure you plan the occasion.

'Most women put off entertaining until the kids are grown.'
ERMA BOMBECK, American humorist

Defining idea...

How did it go?

Q   **I'm having a dinner party but while it would be nice to fold up the napkins, I can never seem to get that professional look, all neat and starched. Any tips?**

A   *I know this can be a challenge because it took me a year to perfect the 'table lily'. However, you can just roll up the napkins and use a variety of lovely items as napkin rings to dress them up. Matching up colours can be useful, so if your room is green, tie bear grass around them. If you have a very pretty floral room, use lengths of organza ribbon. For a rustic scene try a length of brown raffia, and if you want to add a bit of glamour, then you can't beat jewel-coloured beads threaded onto fine wire and looped into a ring.*

Q   **OK, I've done that, now what about candlelight. Is it essential?**

A   *Well I would always say 'yes'. It creates an intimacy that overhead lights just can't match. Did you know that if you store your candles in the fridge for a while before lighting them, they will burn for longer? If you don't have enough candlesticks you can use shot glasses to hold them. Also tealights or floating candles placed in a bowl of water tinted with food dye can look amazing.*

32

Things are hotting up

Combine functionality with style when heating your home. Why not have a new hearth custom-made to the exact specifications of your existing design?

You won't have to worry about any gaps between your wood floor and the surround and there will be no need to replace the carpet.

The reason that I bring this up is because quite often we think we are stuck with a fireplace. It seems like an immovable object, but if you want to change your wood surround for marble or your dark hearth for a light stone there's nothing stopping you. The fireplace should be the dramatic focal point of your room, so it needs to be in keeping with your chosen colour scheme and style.

Here's what I suggest. Think of your various heat sources as pieces of furniture. You wouldn't just stick any old sofa in your lounge or any old cabinet in the kitchen – they need to match the mood and the same applies to radiators, fireplaces or stoves. Because there is such a vast array of designs you can match any colour scheme and every style of home.

If your radiator is positioned on the main wall in a room, think about having it moved. That's usually the place where you want to put the bed in the bedroom or the sofa in the lounge, and with furniture in front of the radiator you will be wasting most of the heat.

If you are going to choose a heated towel rail for the bathroom, make sure that you opt for a dual fuel design. These can run off the central heating in the winter, working in tandem with your radiators. They are also wired into the electricity so that in the warmer months you can operate them independently when the heating in the rest of the house is switched off.

FIRESIDE STORIES

If you have inherited a fireplace with a dark slate surround and you want to use a white colour scheme in the room, then switch it for a design in limestone or one of the modern materials that fire manufacturers have developed that allow an amazing amount of detail to be moulded to the design. Ceralite™, for example, developed and copyrighted by Elgin & Hall in the UK, derives its base from limestone rock but is modified in a process that results in it being much sturdier than normal gypsum-based plaster fire surrounds. At the end of the handcrafted manufacturing process, the material has the qualities of a ceramic, and will 'ring' when tapped. (Which will give the party guests something to do as they lean against it with their glass of wine.) I'm not saying that the process of changing a fire is without grief. There will be a lot of mess and dust will get into nooks and crannies that you may not have thought possible to reach. However, the dramatic difference a change of fireplace can make to the room means it has to be considered.

While you are considering this, call in a chimney sweep. Once a year you should have the flue swept to remove soot deposits, to clear old coal and to make sure that it isn't blocked by anything. Birds and their nests can be a problem. If your fire doesn't seem to be burning properly, get the sweep to burn a smoke pellet. This will show whether it is drawing properly and identify cracks in the flue that can be repaired.

There are ways to dress up a plain fireplace and surround. If you are looking for some inspiration, see IDEA 39, *The essential extras.*

Try another idea...

STOVE STYLE

The Swedish know how to do stoves. Their homes often feature grand ceramic designs, tiled or left plain, which can reach from floor to ceiling and make a magnificent feature in a room. If I had a big enough living room and the money to spend, it would be something I would consider choosing.

Stoves can offer the ideal solution if you don't have a fireplace but want some kind of focal point to heat the room. They don't have to be huge or old fashioned and there are designs to run on any type of fuel. Plus you can pick a design with a built-in boiler that will run your radiators and hot water. They are certainly more stylish than the classic white box on the wall type of boiler.

- **Electric**: Plug it in wherever you need a boost – perfect for the conservatory.

- **Gas**: Practical if you can't bear the thought of clearing out a solid fuel design – would suit the bedroom

'Love can bottle the heat in July to warm the chill of December.'
MARGARET GREGSON, author

Defining idea...

145

Defining idea...

'Don't you stay at home of evenings? Don't you love a cushioned seat in a corner, by the fireside, with your slippers on your feet?'
OLIVER WENDELL HOLMES

- **Wood:** Make sure you have a plentiful and reliable source of wood (and only wood can be used) – fit for the kitchen.

- **Multifuel:** Burns smokeless fuel but also wood or even peat – a rustic touch for the lounge.

WALL STORIES

If the most complementary thing you can say about your radiators is that they make somewhere useful to hang the washing, then you really need to get them changed. There is no excuse for living with the classic ugly white designs that you probably inherited with your home. In a modern setting change them for long spring-shaped designs than can run around the room just above skirting board height. Or choose one of the many contemporary shapes available: you can buy a cactus-shaped radiator these days, or if you are looking for something to go in the children's room a design shaped like a big bear. So there's really no excuse for being boring with your choice.

Radiators can also be used as features in a room. Find a design that can also function as a room divider and you combine two elements, heating and design. (That's a good principle to apply to a lot of things in your home – can something fulfil more than one purpose? For example, a screen can be decorative and hide a workstation too. A radiator cabinet can cover an ugly radiator and provide a handy shelf for keys and post in the hall.)

Given the choices in colour and design, there really is no reason why your source of heating can't be as stylish as your curtains, your furniture or your flooring.

Q **According to you the fireplace should be the focal point in the room, but I have a plum sofa and fairly opulent curtains so it doesn't seem to draw the eye.**

How did it go?

A *The simplest solution is to paint the breast above your surround in a colour that contrasts with the surrounding walls. Pick paint that's a slightly darker red than your sofa cover. Also, invest in three tall vases in complementary colours – they should be slightly different heights but make them large. Place one at one end of the mantel and two at the other side. This will help frame the area and draw the eye to the fireplace.*

Q **I've tried that, but the empty fireplace still looks very dull.**

A *I would always recommend putting something in a fireplace when it's not lit. If there isn't a flaming fire to draws the gaze, then make sure there's a pile of logs, a lovely floral display or a decorative fire screen.*

33

A piece of the past

Bring classic style to your home with traditional furniture and furnishings. The year in which somewhere was built, the architectural details included in each room and the overall ambience of the place will lead you towards a particular look.

Pick up your house keys and purse and head to Blockbusters or your local multiplex. If your home has a history you'll want to reflect that in your design, and one of the best ways to research a look is to watch a classic movie.

Think about the interiors in Scorsese's *The Age of Innocence* or Merchant Ivory's *The Remains of the Day*. Consider the backdrops in *Dangerous Liaisons* and the sets in *Guess Who's Coming to Dinner*. They all place you right in a particular period from which you can pick out ideas. Clearly museums offer a visual resource too. And there are magazines dedicated to period homes and the way to dress them that offer endless listings of useful stockists and suppliers.

By researching the period you'll be guided towards particular colours, patterns and designs. And while you may want the authenticity that antiques provide, you can use your research to include reproduction pieces that reflect a particular age. Don't

Here's an idea for you...

If you are trying to recreate a period look, remember that designs and styles will have developed over a number of years. The Victorian age, for example, spanned several decades, so allow yourself some flexibility when putting together your room.

be too rigid in your interpretation unless you want to live in a museum – it could leave you with a 'repressed' room. Stay in sympathy with your chosen style but feel free to allow one or two quirky elements to creep in to create a more relaxed environment.

MAIN FEATURES

You have really lucked out if your house already has particular features that reflect its age. An original fireplace or architectural mouldings like dado or picture rails, wood panelling, cornicing or even a tiled floor could all be the starting point for your design. Can I just say that if you have an original parquet floor then you must lavish it with affection and show it a great deal of love. Treat all of your original gems with respect. Too often people rip them out without due regard for how this will change the face of the place.

But don't despair if you lack these kinds of details, they are easily introduced. Original and reproduction antique fires and mantelpieces can be sourced from manufacturers and reclamation yards. Wood mouldings are simple to fix in place by anyone with even a smidgen of DIY ability and are available in a mix of shapes and styles to suit.

DESIGNER DETAILS

Fabrics have an important role in the period home. Depending on the theme you'll want to look out for sumptuous silk, delicate lace, floral patterned chintzes, heavy damasks or richly coloured velvets. Consider how they were used in the past and you can introduce them today. You could pleat silk and use it as a wall covering for example, a lace panel may make a perfect table runner and a length of velvet might make an ideal throw. The shape of furniture can also influence a mood. Introduce a heavy. imposing mahogany piece for a Victorian-style bedroom or a streamlined sofa in an art deco lounge.

Adding a single choice piece like those above can also create the focus for your room. My advice would be to look out for one purchase that is indicative of the period that you wish to work with and then dress the rest of the room around that. Invest in a chandelier for the lounge, a cheval mirror in the bedroom, an antique washstand in the bathroom or a vintage bedspread in the bedroom.

CHOICES FOR WALLS

From Shaker style to art nouveau and from the eighteenth century to the present day, certain colours are associated with certain styles. If you are looking for a guide you'll find period collections available wherever you shop for paint. It's important to get your walls the right shade because they provide the backdrop to the furniture and furnishings that will dress your room. Also don't forget that wallpaper is an option. If the historians who trace its use back to the 1400s are to be believed, then it has most certainly earned a place in the history of home décor.

If you are looking to create a period setting, treasure your original features, supplement them with some reproduction designs, and history shows that you are on the right track.

You might want to create a period look by changing the fireplace in your lounge or bedroom. IDEA 32, *Things are hotting up*, might help you make the decision.

Try another idea...

'*Just build a classic horseshoe of wood and plaster, and fill it with statuary and curtains, then sit back and savor the beautifully blended results.'*
MICHAEL WALSH, author

Defining idea...

151

How did
it go?

Q **I've been collecting antique and reproduction pieces for the dining room and have put together my scheme. It has become a bit of an obsession, and I'm wondering if I should continue the look into another room.**

A *You can have one space dressed in period style but, as with any look, if it's not in keeping with the adjacent rooms it can create disharmony in your home. Home design works best when the look is reasonably consistent throughout. If you are going to commit to a period look, you want to consider introducing one or two pieces into other areas but make them background dressing rather than the focal point in the rooms. Make sure that they are complementary to the scheme rather than allowing them to dominate the space – that way they become signposts towards the room that is dedicated to a particular look.*

Q **So you think it's OK to put an antique desk in a contemporary setting?**

A *Every house should have some flexibility to mix and match old and new. Sometimes it is just a matter of making sure that the colours work together and at other times you need to be more blatant about mixing the two styles. If you have a piece of Chinese lacquered furniture, for example, it will sit happily against plain white walls when the floors in the room are made of wood. If your wooden sideboard dates from the nineteenth century perhaps all it needs to make it work in your modern home is for you to dress it up with two or three contemporary vases and some elegant flowers.*

34

That hits the spot

Don't rush the layout of your room. Wouldn't it be perfect if there was a place for everything and everything had its place?

The goal of this exercise is harmony in your home. If you have a feeling that Feng Shui might be the answer, then read a book dedicated to that principle.

I am not in possession of the knowledge to direct you to identify your wealth corner and won't be able to guide you to clear out your relationship area, but I do believe that if you believe in those methods, then they will be beneficial to you. This is a more mundane but still valuable guide to setting up spaces.

THE PERFECT POSITION

Placing furniture can affect the mood of the room and how it is used. The lounge is a good room to use for this exercise.

If you want to create a formal look, keep pieces of furniture square on to each other, chair backs should be flat against walls and tables put at right angles to chairs. Keep coffee table books in carefully stacked piles of two or three diminishing in size from bottom to top.

Here's an idea for you...

Think about the balance of the room. Are all of the larger pieces of furniture on one side of the room and smaller items grouped together on the other? Doesn't just reading that make you feel a little unbalanced? If you can draw an imaginary line across your room from the door to the far wall and position equal sized pieces on either side of the divide it will help to add symmetry to the space.

In contrast, chairs placed at an angle in the corners of rooms, sofas placed to create an L-shape or things displayed at random will seem much more relaxed.

Two large sofas positioned face to face on opposite sides of a large coffee table make it difficult for people to conduct a conversation. A sofa with two armchairs placed at right angles at either end mean a person in each seat will be able to contribute and be heard.

Try this. Draw a floor plan of your room. Try and be accurate with the scaled-down measurements so that you have a realistic idea of how much the chimneybreast sticks out into the space or how much extra floor area there is in the bay window. Remember to put any 'permanent' fixtures like radiators onto the plan and also indicate which way the doors open into the room. Light switches and power points need to be noted so that you don't obstruct them with furniture. Take the plan away with you and sitting somewhere else list all of the furniture that is currently in the room. Beside each piece put down its function (seating for chairs, lighting for lamps, storage for bookcases, etc.)

Now think about how you use the room and assess whether you need every piece that is in there or whether there is something missing that would make the room work more efficiently. Think about whether the coffee table is actually in the wrong place for people to reach it with ease when they are sitting on the sofa. Or is a lamp positioned so far away from a reading chair that it can't possible function as a task light? These are just some of the things that you can easily change.

I am a fan of open, airy spaces. So I would also recommend that you decide if you really need every piece of furniture in the room. Could one of the three bookshelves be moved to the hallway? Would it be possible to take out the second armchair and still have enough seating for everyday use? There is nothing better than imagining a room with nothing in it and then mentally placing the pieces on your list in one by one according to the importance of their function in the room. (A sofa is the most important piece in the lounge, a bed the most vital item in the bedroom.) As you work down your list you may realise that a writing desk would function just as easily in the dining room as the lounge and by removing it you would be uncluttering a crowded corner.

Look at IDEA 49, *Keep it tidy*, if you are worried about your storage solutions

Try another idea...

'I have been black and blue in some spot, somewhere, almost all my life from too intimate contacts with my own furniture.'
FRANK LLOYD WRIGHT

Defining idea...

Here are some things to consider when you are planning other rooms...

■ **Hallway:** Does the table you have put beside the front door make it difficult to negotiate the space and would a wall-mounted narrow shelf provide an alternative solution?

■ **Bedroom:** Is all the storage that you have in there essential or could a dressy cupboard be positioned on the landing in a recess at the top of the stairs? (Remember that you have to allow space for the sweep of the opening doors.)

■ **Dining room:** Would you be better to get rid of two half-height cabinets and replace them with a taller unit that will house the contents of both but free up floor space, somewhere that you can stack chairs when you take the leaves out of the extending table, for example?

Plan the layout of your room with care and you'll find it both pleasurable and practical to use.

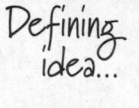
Defining idea...

'*Plans are nothing; planning is everything.*'
DWIGHT D. EISENHOWER

Q **Well, I have drawn the plan but I can't see how I can remove any of the pieces in the room as they all serve a purpose.**

How did it go?

A *OK, but can they be put to that purpose in another space? We are back with the wardrobe on the landing which can house clothes that don't need to be accessible every day – formal dresses, coats, winter shoes in the summer months for example. You might also want to go through a decluttering exercise (see IDEA 15, Keep it tidy) as it could be that you can get rid of things and so reduce the amount of storage that you really need.*

Q **But what if I am still left with the same amount of furniture?**

A *Planning a space should also include thinking about alternatives to the items that you already have in place. So while you may currently need a cabinet for the television, is it possible that you could be investing in a wall-mounted flat screen design at some point? And while the freestanding bookshelves seem essential in your study, would it be better in the long term to get some custom-built shelves put into the alcoves at either side of the door where currently the space is wasted?*

35

Left on the shelf

Choosing and using the simplest of storage solutions. How many? How deep? How high? It is impossible to live without a shelf somewhere in your house.

There, I have laid down the challenge for someone to prove me wrong, but I say the more shelves the merrier.

When you consider that everyone has something that needs a home, and everyone has the desire to store certain items where they can not only see them but also easily reach them, then shelving is a logical solution.

This is the shelving chapter – you might think it crosses over with storage, and you'd be right. I'm not talking about cabinets – just simple shelves. If this seems a bit polarized look at the following issues which you need to consider when planning your shelves:

- Built-in or freestanding?
- Glass or wood?
- Suspended in space or with obvious supports?
- Deep enough for books or slim enough to suit CDs and DVDs?
- Long enough to stretch across an entire wall?
- Short so that they make a feature on their own?

Do you have a room that is chock-a-block with furniture? Work out how much floor space is taken up by cabinets and cupboards. Then assess the contents of these pieces of furniture and consider whether they would fit on wall-mounted shelves. (Do a quick decluttering exercise while you consider this.) The amount of wasted wall space in any home is immense. The number of rooms that would benefit in terms of looks and ease of use if some floor space was freed up is just as great. So put the two together and the solution is to put up some shelves.

Defining idea...

'Life has a way of setting things in order and leaving them be. Very tidy, is life.'
JEAN ANOUILH, French playwright

Whether you opt for built-in or freestanding is as much to do with the layout and design of your home as your personal preferences. If you live in an older property with architectural features, the natural place for built-in shelves is the alcove either side of a chimneybreast. But in a more modern home, there are still areas that can be used. Think about the area above doors and the space underneath a staircase. These can be fitted with shelves or provide somewhere to introduce a freestanding unit. Now a thought about materials. One of the finest makeshift shelving systems I have seen was in a student flat. Financially challenged but needing some storage, they had used breezeblocks and glass to create a set of shelves. The pleasing contrast of stone and glass gave them a designer air, and because the glass wasn't too long and the breezeblocks were very sturdy, they were an example of the safest form of shelving – where the shelves aren't too long to support their load and the supports are strong enough to withstand a few knocks. Wood shelves are all well and good – practical and easy to buy 'off the shelf', as it were. However, it's important to think about alternatives and that is where glass comes in. If you wish to display a particular piece, then glass has the advantage that you can shine light on the object of your affections from below.

If you are wondering if you missed a storage opportunity, take a look at IDEA 47, *Have you wasted that loft space?*

Try another idea...

In the kitchen it may fit in with your style to put up a slatted metal shelf, something that will fit in with an industrial look. The advantage to this kind of shelf is that you can also hang butcher's hooks from the underside, which increases the number of storage solutions that they offer.

Other issues that relate to shelving can be easily resolved. Measure the depth of your biggest books for the shelves in the library. Work out how much space your kitchen equipment – with all necessary attachments and accessories – will take up. Consider whether you have enough floor area in the bathroom for a freestanding set of shelves or whether you are going to have to settle for a space-saving solution.

Above all, it takes an honest assessment of the objects that are going to live there so be realistic about how much room they will need when you plan for your shelves.

'As the biggest library if it is in disorder is not as useful as a small but well-arranged one, so you may accumulate a vast amount of knowledge but it will be of far less value than a much smaller amount if you have not thought it over for yourself.'
ARTHUR SCHOPENHAUER

Defining idea...

161

How did it go?

Q   Are you saying that I should get rid of all my cabinets? Surely there are certain things that are better hidden behind closed doors.

A   *Not at all. I agree that if you are a clutter queen then you need to be able to hide lots of rubbish where it won't become an eyesore. But you would be amazed at how good even the most basic of things can look if you make the effort to put them on display; a set of white china can be appealing in a dining room; a collection of jugs in all shapes, sizes and colours will look wonderful in the kitchen, and on a practical note, information stored in stylish box files is more easily accessible when all you have to do is reach up to a shelf and not go rummaging in a cupboard.*

Q   But shelves are all basically the same shape, which is pretty dull.

A   *Again, not at all. There is a classic design to look out for which is a piece of curling wood that makes a shelf. I have seen a luggage rack from a train used as a place for pots and pans to live. You can use wire or wicker baskets in a run as a kind of shelving system, and don't forget that corbels make neat shelves for positioning a candle or a small vase.*

36

Softly, softly

Weave a mix of materials into the fabric of your home. Whether you are a fan of patterns or like to keep things plain, the fabrics that you choose to use play a huge part in developing the style of your home.

The soft side of any home encompasses a great range of items: upholstery, curtains, throws, blinds and bed linen to cover just a few. Now there are certain fabrics that will be ideal for certain jobs and others that are so versatile that you can put them just about anywhere.

Light linens will make super curtains but are not good for upholstering chairs that will get a lot of wear and tear; velvets are ideal for upholstering pieces but don't make up into good loose covers.

The most important role of fabric is to bring colour and comfort into a room. If you imagine a space decorated in plain neutral shades, then the inclusion of a blind in a contrasting colour adds interest to the room. If you think about a bedroom that is predominantly dressed in cool colours, then a fluffy chenille throw on the bed introduces a cosy touch.

Here's an idea for you...

When you come to dress your windows, don't just think curtains or blinds – you can use all sorts of different lengths of fabrics there. In a room decorated along exotic lines, a sari might be the perfect window covering. If you are creating a cosy country cottage mood, how about using a blanket? Little clip hooks that run along curtain poles to which you attach the fabric mean you can dress your windows even if you have no sewing skills at all.

Let's approach this by looking at some rooms. There may be places where you can use fabric that you hadn't considered, for example in the bedroom. Is your headboard hard wood or iron? Would a padded or fabric-covered headboard be a better option if you love to sit in bed and watch TV or read? I don't mean that you necessarily have to have a fitted, frilled and pleated design – very country house hotel – you can have a reasonably plain one. A large oblong of fabric that you simply fold over the headboard and tie in place has the advantage that you can take it off to wash it. Still looking at the bed, if you have invested in underbed storage, would the addition of a valance make the set-up look more attractive? Once again, you don't need to have frills. A neat kick-pleat valance sits flat all the way around the bed – it looks smart rather than flamboyant and if made to match the headboard brings a scheme neatly together.

Dressing the bed offers a perfect opportunity for introducing stacks of lovely fabrics. Although most of us use duvets, there is something wonderful about getting into a bed that has been made up with sheets, blankets and an eiderdown or bedspread. Of course you can layer these on top of a duvet too but for the sake of neatness make sure that the various layers are large enough to completely cover the edges of the duvet beneath. Layering with fabric like this means you can have some fun with colours and patterns. Combine plain fabrics with chintz and checks. Use stripes with ginghams and simple florals – make sure that the colours match and you can introduce all sorts of different designs to the bed. And never forget to pile it up with lots of lovely cushions in addition to your pillows.

If you are thinking about underbed bedroom storage, see IDEA 42, It works like a dream.

Try another idea…

The lounge is home to all sorts of items that will need to be dressed with fabric: chairs and sofas, pouffes and footstools and of course the windows. When you are thinking about the fabrics for this room, remember that one of the functions of fabrics can be to bring different textures into a space. Imagine that you are having loose cotton covers on your sofa – you might choose a damask to upholster an armchair that will sit beside the sofa and a heavy velvet or suede for the footstool. You could then pick heavy linen for your curtains or blinds. It's quite astonishing how much of an impact this can create. On a simpler scale, just draping a woollen throw over the back of a chair adds interest to the space.

'We live in a web of ideas, a fabric of our own making.'
JOSEPH CHILTON PEARCE, scholar and scientist

Defining idea…

Another room where fabrics can be used for visual impact is the dining room. If you think about the combination of a tablecloth, napkins, upholstered seats, table runners and again the window treatments, there are plenty of places to play with different patterns within your chosen colour scheme.

If you have a designer wood or glass tabletop that you wish to show off, then use a table runner in place of a tablecloth. The contrast of, say, a washed white wood table and a green checked runner bordered with a floral fabric is pleasing to the eye.

'Man never made any material as resilient as the human spirit.'
BERN WILLIAMS, author

Defining idea…

Remember that the comfort of your guests is important when they sit down to eat, so if your chairs have hard seats think about having some padded tie-on cushions made to match your runner – it's a neat way to pull a scheme together.

How did it go?

Q I am thinking about combining a blind and curtain at a window. Should I go for contrasting colours or is it more important to make sure that the texture of the fabrics is different?

A *I would opt for colour contrast first. For example, a taupe linen blind can sit happily behind cream linen curtains but if you were to mix cotton and velvet it might look a little strange. There are certain combinations that can work, voiles teamed with cotton for example, but first get as large a piece of fabric as you can for the two different jobs and lay them together to see if the textures work.*

Q Are there any recommendations for which tiebacks to team with particular fabrics?

A *Unless you are going to have them made up in the same fabric as the curtains, then use your tiebacks to add a touch of contrast. I would put traditional coloured cord tiebacks with fringed tassels in classic settings where the curtains are made in heavy chintz and opt for something more casual like rope if you have used cotton or linen for your drapes.*

37

An informal affair

Why should you choose an unfitted, freestanding kitchen? If you have a large enough room, then the freedom of a freestanding design is very hard to beat.

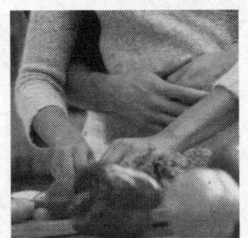

That I might one day be able to include an old or antique piece of furniture like a big French armoire alongside an Aga or island unit is one of my dreams.

This is part of the appeal of such rooms – that everything in the space doesn't have to match perfectly. There might be modern items alongside more traditional pieces, and you might have pine mixed with oak or chrome mixed with wood. Another advantage to this type of kitchen is that if you are vertically challenged you can buy pieces which are at the perfect practical height for you. Now of course it is possible with a hand-built fitted kitchen to get your work surface put in at any height, however designs bought off the peg are usually standard heights – not designed for those of us with shorter legs.

I would say at this point that you must have a room of generous proportions to be able to get away with a freestanding kitchen. All the elements will take up much more floor space than a fitted design. But if you do have such a luxury, then you can really enjoy putting together a room over a period of time. Put the basics in – your

Here's an idea for you...

In a freestanding kitchen you must be aware that your work surfaces could be more fragmented than in a fitted room. On the one hand this means you need to carefully consider just how much surface room you need, and on the other it gives you the perfect opportunity to pick more expensive materials for the smaller spaces. Corian is a wonderfully practical material but pricey, and granite is wonderful in a kitchen but again at a much higher price than laminate designs. In general, stone and solid surfaces make the most expensive choices while wood is just ahead of laminate.

cooker, fridge, sink, etc. – but then rummage around for junk buys to complement your room and allow the scheme to grow over months or years.

If you are already falling in love with this idea, it may be worth getting in a builder or kitchen designer at this point. This is because with freestanding kitchens you may need to reroute plumbing, gas or electricity supplies depending on where you are going to position your sink, dishwasher and cooker – it is possible to have a lovely contemporary cooker hood hanging from the ceiling in the middle of the room, but you would be advised to get an idea of the costs involved before getting too carried away with your ideas for an island hob with griddle on one side.

There are certain things to bear in mind when putting together your floor plan for the room: foremost is that you need space around each item in the room. Try to visualise the different areas that you are going to need – the preparation area, the cooking space, the storage area and, if the room is large enough, the eating and seating area too. There is something very appealing about a kitchen with a lovely worn sofa stuck in one corner – somewhere usually for the dogs to sleep! Now while all of the above may require specific spaces, in certain cases they can be moved around. I am talking about introducing a portable island that will offer you more flexibility than a built-in design. A butcher's block on wheels can be moved to the sink when you are chopping vegetables so

Read **IDEA 25, *A professional opinion*, before you bring in your builder.**

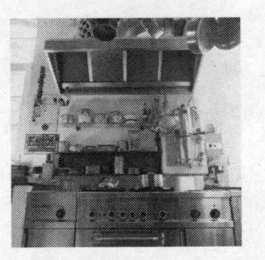

Try another idea...

that you can rinse and chop in the same area, and then it can be wheeled over to the cooker when you want to start making the meal. There is another advantage, which is that it makes it much easier to clean the floor when you can move a trolley out of the way while you mop.

In a kitchen where the walls will not be covered with cupboards, you need to consider what type of splashback you require on the walls. It's clearly vital around the cooking and

'If you can organize your kitchen, you can organize your life.'
LOUIS PARRISH, author

Defining idea...

food preparation areas, so what are your choices? Stainless steel will fit with a modern kitchen and you can buy ready-made panels to fit behind the cooker, while glass allows you to see through to the surface behind so would be perfect if there is a paint effect on your walls. Tiles are the norm and within everyone's budget, but if you have the cash splash out on granite for a stunning effect when combined with a work surface in the same material. Laminate designs will offer you a wide range of colour options if you are looking to stick with one particular colour in your room.

So you can see the appeal of putting together a freestanding kitchen. Now start searching out lots of lovely furniture for your room.

How did it go?

Q   Without fitted cabinets, under which or inside of which I can put lights, how do I tackle the lighting scheme in a freestanding kitchen?

A   *I would always favour recessed spotlights, but make sure you don't put them all on the same circuit. For example, have one set specifically positioned to illuminate the preparation and cooking areas in the room. Have another set that illuminates the dining area or if you are lucky enough to room for a sofa, then the seating area. Make sure that both sets are on dimmer switches.*

Q   No pendant lights then?

A   *Are you thinking about having a hob with extractor fan positioned in the middle of the room? Is one of the ways you are going to increase storage by having a hanging rack for saucepans suspended from the ceiling? If so you can see why it would be better to avoid pendant lights as the fittings may well jostle for space. It's much better to keep the ceiling clear of any other clutter.*

38

Lounging around

**Design your living room for each and every situation.
Disagree with me if you wish, but I would maintain that
your lounge is the hardest working room in the house.**

Morning, noon and night it has to be available for watching TV, reading, snoozing, entertaining and eating. When somewhere is on call for all of these activities there is a long list of requirements, but combining comfort with practicality is a must.

If you put together the 'near as perfect as you can' living room, you have achieved a level of success in interior design for which you can be truly proud. It means that you have understood the principles of laying out a room, embraced the idea that a space works on many levels, and made no mistake in choosing furniture to fulfil a whole range of requirements.

Let's start with seating. Supplement your sofa with one or two armchairs so that should you wish to sprawl out, then everyone else can relax too. If you bring in a pouffe and some floor cushions other people can put their feet up or relax on the

Be prepared to rearrange the furniture to make better use of the space. You may be wedded to the idea that the sofa should be the place that you sit when you want to watch TV, but is it possible that if you shift it to a different part of the room it will serve more than that one purpose? Could it be repositioned so that when every seat is occupied it makes it easier to chat? Would it make sense to move it from in front of the radiator so that you are heating the room more efficiently?

floor. Look through any contemporary mail order catalogue and you'll find wool-, felt- and suede-covered stools that are a far cry from the designs available to our parents' generation. While you are flipping through the pages keep an eye out for beanbags. Of course now that they are made in leather they are no longer called 'beanbags' but have been tagged with the far more sophisticated label of 'floor seats'. Whatever. They can still be chucked at the person who complains that there is nowhere to sit.

Now, what about reading and watching the television? You might be thinking that they require nothing special, but have you got your lights positioned so that there is no glare on the screen and so that you aren't going to strain your eyes. A lamp that can be moved around to accommodate your activities is an essential piece of kit in the lounge. Without it you have to rely on overhead or wall lights and these can seldom be positioned perfectly to suit every activity.

Next, have you got a table close to hand? Whether it's a coffee table that stays in one place or part of a nest of three that you pull out and use according to your needs, you want somewhere that you can set down the remote control or pile up the numerous sections of the weekend papers, not to forget an easy-to-reach surface for a cup of tea (daytime) or a glass of wine (after 5 o'clock).

By the way, a nest of tables sounds horribly old fashioned but designs in maple, glass with alloy and acrylic make them suitable for modern homes.

Any space that accommodates all of these activities also has a responsibility to cope with the associated flotsam and jetsam. There will be books that need a home and videos or DVDs that you have got to store somewhere. If you have a stereo in the room, then you can't just leave CDs littering any available flat surface. This is the ideal opportunity to make use of any area that has been created by the construction of your home. If you have a space either side of a chimneybreast, for example, then put it to use as the perfect place for housing custom-built shelving. A recess created by the positioning of a dividing wall can serve the same purpose. Alternatively, buy a freestanding unit but make sure that you can adjust the height of the shelves. There is nothing more frustrating than a bookcase where every single shelf is positioned at a uniform height. It means a lot of wasted space when you are using it to house a range of books, magazines and videos all of which have different dimensions.

Designing a practical lounge takes some amount of planning, but once the pieces are in place you'll be glad that you spent the time getting it right.

If you want to dress up the space, see IDEA 39, *The essential extras.*

Try another idea...

'Television is like the invention of indoor plumbing. It didn't change people's habits. It just kept them inside the house.'
ALFRED HITCHCOCK

Defining idea...

'The time to relax is when you don't have time for it.'
SYDNEY J. HARRIS, American journalist

Defining idea...

How did it go?

Q **I have brought in storage and moved the furniture around but every activity seems to call for a different layout. It's not practical to constantly move the furniture around so what do I do?**

A *Prioritise. Do you mostly entertain, watch TV or relax and read a book? Is this space the kid's playroom as well as your lounge? Set up the room to fit with its primary function and then create other spaces in your home. Put a sofa in the bedroom so that you can stretch out and read in there. Make the kitchen somewhere that you sit around a table to entertain. Clear out the box room and make it into a den for the children so that they have a space that they can call their own.*

Q **Right I've done that and decided that my priority is entertaining. Which piece of furniture belongs where?**

A *Create areas in the room that are conducive to different uses. Put two sofas or a sofa and chair at right angles to each other so that people can sit down and chat within hearing distance of each other. Make sure that you position a side table between two armchairs so that the people who don't wish to settle into a long conversation can sit for a minute but leave their glasses behind when they wish to move on. Also if there is one perfect place to stand with a glass and observe what is going on around you, it's against the mantel around a fire, so don't clutter up that area with a table or chair. Leave the floor clear for people to lean.*

39

The essential extras

Add the finishing touch to any space with a few fundamental pieces.

After the decoration is done and all of the furniture has been positioned in the perfect place, your room will need titivating. This is the technical term for those final touches that give a scheme life and interest.

They are the bits and pieces that can be collected over time, added to with holiday mementoes, wedding gifts and an occasional collector's piece. They might be a chance buy or a carefully chosen and saved-up-for design classic, but whatever their provenance their job is to dress up a space. Let me explain it like this – think of these items like fashion accessories. You've got your your basic outfit; then you add jewellery, shoes, a belt or a scarf to complete the look. In terms of your home these translate into mirrors, vases, cushions, throws, bowls, pictures, frames and clocks.

Sometimes you need to add a focal point to a room. These 'essentials' can perform this role and a larger-than-life accessory may do the job. If you have ever walked into a restaurant and seen a huge clock on an otherwise bare wall, you'll appreciate how it can grab the attention. My kitchen is a plain oblong shape with no

You can never have too many vases. Vases are one of those items that when put in a collection can become like still-life works of art. Imagine gathering together different shaped designs but all in shades of cream. Group them on a side table in the corner of a room and they draw the eye and give that area of the room a purpose, where previously it was just an unexciting space for the table. Start collecting glass designs in various different shades – in this case it is the material that unifies the collection rather than the colour. Whether you favour huge floral displays or prefer the minimalist approach of one or two stems in a run of two or three matching vases, they offer an easy way to add an injection of colour to a room, dressing it up before your very eyes.

architectural details or decorative effects to draw the eye. I have positioned a large clock on the bare wall that faces you as you walk into the room. It adds a touch of drama to the space.

There isn't a room in the house that won't be improved by the introduction of a mirror, and the bigger the better as far as I am concerned. If you are choosing one for the bedroom make sure that it is tall enough to give a full head-to-toe reflection. This might mean investing in a cheval-style design which comes complete with legs and is more like a piece of furniture than an accessory. Or it might mean that you simply stand the design on the floor rather than mount it on the wall. (Don't worry that this might appear to the untrained eye like you haven't bothered to get out your drill and screws, this look is very much in vogue.) Just make sure that the mirror is also wide enough to lean without falling over. Mirrors can be used to bounce light into dark corners and create an illusion of space in a small rooms – they are a must-have accessory.

There are lots of pieces that taken one by one perform different jobs in a room. Let's take cushions as another essential accessory and one that can be used to bring comfort and colour to a room. Now everyone is familiar with a standard square design and these are all well and good. However, I would urge you to try and mix in some different shapes and sizes. Place a large continental cushion behind a couple of the classic size when you are dressing your sofa. Include one or two bolster cushions with the pillows on your bed. Look for oblong designs and tiny squares and mix them all together. Also choose designs with different trimmings and edgings – look for some with tasselled edges, some with fabric-covered fastening buttons and one or two with mother of pearl or wooden toggles. By mixing up these different elements you are adding lots of interest to the space in which they are placed.

Remember that every room will benefit from a little dressing up and enjoy working on this, the last stage, in putting together your scheme.

See IDEA 30, *The art of living*, for more ideas on displaying items.

Try another idea...

'A flowerless room is a soulless room, to my way of thinking; but even one solitary little vase of a living flower may redeem it.'
VITA SACKVILLE-WEST

Defining idea...

'It is the unseen, unforgettable, ultimate accessory of fashion that heralds your arrival and prolongs your departure.'
COCO CHANEL

Defining idea...

How did
it go?

Q **This all sounds lovely, but if I go out and buy lots of accessories it's going to cost a fortune!**

A *OK, if everything was supposed to be brought into the room at the same time it might. However part of the fun of accessorising a room is to introduce pieces over time. A rummage in an antique shop might produce a lovely old clock. A trip to your local junk shop might result in you finding a slightly worn (but all the more attractive for that) mirror. The idea is to accumulate your collection over time.*

Q **But I need some accessories *now* to dress up the room.**

A *Please try to think a bit laterally. In the case of vases, for example, have a look around your home for other items that can be used in a floral display. Jugs are the obvious one but do you have an old metal kettle or an unused china teapot? Have you got any designer water bottles or wine carafes that can be brought into service for this job? Remember that the item itself doesn't have to be inherently waterproof. You can place a plastic bag full of water inside an object so that the flowers can drink. How about using an upturned straw hat or a handbag to create an unusual display?*

40

Small but perfectly formed

Simple solutions for pocket-sized spaces. With clever use of colour and careful planning, even the smallest space works as a fully functioning home.

If it's true that our possessions expand to fill the available space, then give me a studio flat every time. Not an expansive loft-style studio but a well-designed and compact home.

It has to be said that if you are hopelessly untidy then you are going to have to work harder at this than if you were born with that elusive neat and tidy gene.

However, there is something very appealing about a space that works as a kitchen to cook in, a dining room to eat in and a bedroom to sleep in. It presents a challenge whether you are a slob or impeccably neat. How do you divide the different areas to define the disparate uses? How do you maximise the look of the space while creating different zones?

That's studio living. But what about a house conversion where each floor of the building was originally designed as one-third of a functioning home and is now divided into three separate units where the rooms seem very small?

Here's an idea for you...

You can use light, both natural and from fixtures and fittings, to manipulate space. In a small room, make sure that your window treatment doesn't obscure any of the window – you need to let as much sunshine in as possible. If part of your home is in the roof, keep the skylights clean and clear. One useful tip in small spaces is to use lights at floor level to lead the eye. Spotlights installed just above the skirting and running away from a kitchen area and towards the lounge will draw the eye away from the kitchen if you have extinguished all the lights in that area.

For both situations, let's start with an illusion. In any situation where your floor space is limited you need to decorate and design it so that the area seems larger than it is. In the first place, choose a light colour to paint your walls. In the second place choose a light colour to decorate your ceiling. In the third place choose a light-coloured flooring. (You will bring in other details later so that this isn't as bland as it sounds.)

Now let's be realistic. You can't have a massive sofa, you can't have a king-sized bed. Apart from the style issues that need to be considered, they probably won't go up the stairs or get through the door. In the same way that a doll's house has pieces that are miniaturised versions of the real thing, you are going to have to sit on a diminutive sofa and sleep in a moderately sized bed. (If you can't bear the thought of that, a wall bed might be the answer; a design that folds away can be huge because it won't take up floor space when shut away.)

Just as a jug can also function as a vase and a mug might be the place where you keep your pens and pencils, so when you buy furniture for small spaces work on the principle that, where possible, you want to get two uses out of one item. A coffee table doubles up as a dining table if you have floor cushions to sit on while you eat, a storage chest functions as extra seating when covered with lovely blankets or throws, and a set of shelves can also become a room divider. Once you start to work on this principle you'll find your own ways to adapt things in your home.

If you are struggling as to how to lay out your rooms, see IDEA 34, *That hits the spot*, for some guidance.

Try another idea...

Colour is a useful tool in defining spaces. Variations on the walls and in the floor can be a great way to signpost a change of use. While I have said, and stick to the idea, that everything should be kept light, you can still use a slightly darker paint in two different spaces. If your kitchen is pure white, then decorate the adjacent designated dining area in a shade of stone. And you can change the flooring – if the lounge area in a studio is covered in wood laminate, then choose seagrass to cover the space that you use as a study.

I would also urge you to consider investing in vertical blinds or sliding panels to screen off spaces. These can be fitted to run from floor to ceiling and are easily pulled out of the way when you want to be open plan, and drawn back into place when you wish to separate off your sleeping area for example.

(Just another quick note about decorating – your use of patterns should ideally be kept to a minimum in small spaces. I'm afraid you would be unwise to use a boldly patterned wallpaper even if you have fallen in love with the current trend for retro-style bold designs that seem to be used in every designer home in the magazines.) Much as I hate to state the obvious, storage will be a priority in your compact home. You need to take an uncluttered approach to living in any small space so have a good look around your home and pinpoint any areas that are completely clear. You can look at the floor for starters but then include the walls all the way up to the ceiling too. There is an area above every doorway that can be used to house a set of shelves. You'll find space beneath each set

'Room service? Send up a larger room.'
GROUCHO MARX

Defining idea...

181

of stairs that might be ideal for hanging hooks. Invest in clothes bags that fit under the bed in the bedroom, inset a basin into a cabinet in the bathroom and use the plinth space in your kitchen for extra drawers, and you'll be well on the way to making the most of any dead space.

How did it go?

Q   I don't want to start messing about with the existing lights in my studio. What are my options?

A   *I would recommend investing in two or three lamps in a range of heights. If you have the ability to direct beams into different areas of the room you can create different focal points depending on which space you are using. Remember to turn off ceiling or wall lights in any area that you are not using and use the lamps to illuminate the space that you are currently occupying. Point one up towards the top of the wall to wash it in light and focus another on a particular item in the space, be it a picture, a table or a chair.*

Q   But doesn't that mean I'm going to have to keep moving the lamps around?

A   *Well yes, but that's why they are lamps – the idea is that they are portable, not fixed lights. You have to be flexible in small spaces. If you can't bear the idea that you will have to unplug them and trail flexes around, then it is possible to buy little lights that are battery powered and can be easily stuck in place. Of course you will need to position them so that you can easily replace the battery but it might be one solution. Also never forget the power of candlelight. A group of candles lit at one end of a darkened space will immediately draw the eye into that area.*

182

41

The soft side

Floors that feel supple underfoot. Kick off your shoes and take a walk. Cushion each step with a covering that keeps your feet warm and that cuts down on noise.

Take a walk on the natural side or vote with your feet for vinyl. If you are into that kind of thing, run your feet over rubber just for the thrill of it. There's no reason to not mix your choice of flooring throughout your home and the soft options are vast and very versatile.

If you are tempted to dismiss all natural floorings as just grass, then you need to take a closer look. Each type has different qualities that you will come to appreciate over time, and surprisingly, paper is in this category too. While it may not be the first type of material that you consider for your floors, it's now very much part of this popular group. It's woven into a durable flooring material and the addition of resin to the mix increases its resistance to moisture.

Coir is the tough face of this family and makes a great choice for hardworking areas such as the hall. It may be a little rougher underfoot than the rest but practically it

Here's an idea for you...

Make sure that you clean all these floors in the proper way. For example, water and coir *do not mix*. You need to make sure with many soft types of flooring that they have been treated with a stain resistor, then you just need to vacuum regularly. Laminate, cork and vinyl can all be treated in much the same way. First vacuum, then go over the surface with a damp (not sopping) mop.

makes a lot of sense. If you are looking for a more sensitive option here's a tip: jute makes the ideal choice for bedrooms because it is much softer underfoot, though of course much less durable to traffic. Somewhere in between these two in terms of comfort sits sisal, so that may suit your dining room or lounge. Seagrass works happily in most spaces because it is smooth in texture but tough on the ground.

(Just a quick note for those who love to research, in depth, items for their home. Natural flooring comes from places as diverse as Brazil and Africa, Bangladesh, India and China, and it makes fascinating reading when you look into the various sources and manufacturing of these types of flooring.)

Vinyl may have an image problem but do give it a second thought. It's durable, it's washable and it offers comfort underfoot. Another plus is that there is such a wide range of colours and designs available that if you have inherited a room where you are quite happy with the décor but need to change the flooring, you are bound to find a colour match for the existing scheme. Top quality vinyl reproduces the look of stone and tiles, and there are some wood finishes that would defy the most rigorous comparison with the real thing (albeit from a distance of about 10 metres).

Linoleum is very different from vinyl although the two are often grouped together. The former is a natural product while the latter comes from synthetic materials. As with many natural materials lino improves, if cared for properly, with age. And it is a good choice if you are asthmatic as it won't attract dust and dust mites.

Rubber and **cork** are both soft options. Rubber is resilient, water resistant and it's available in some amazing colours too. If you want it, patterns can be part of the make-up with grooves, squares, circles and studs all available. If you want a scarlet floor in the bathroom, this is the material to look at. If you are planning a modern kitchen and are unsure of which flooring to choose, this would be perfect for the job.

Cork can be dyed, so you would have the option of a coloured floor, but the reason to settle on this is for its softness and soundproofing qualities.

You may want to consider a different type of floor. See **IDEA 28, *A tough decision*, and IDEA 48, *A night on the tiles*, for other floor options.**

Try another idea...

'*My kitchen linoleum is so black and shiny that I waltz while I wait for the kettle to boil. This pleasure is for the old who live alone.*'
FLORIDA SCOTT-MAXWELL, American writer

Defining idea...

How did it go?

Q So which natural flooring would be best for an older home?

A *Because of the range of textures and colours available, you can find a design for both modern and traditional interiors. If you look at historical buildings you'll often see grass mats used to cover floors, but because we live in modern times I think you should consider the use of the room over and above the material. Remember that all flooring should be able to withstand the wear and tear it will receive. Having said that, the roughest type of coir will suit a rustic setting, while the finest sisal would be better for a more formal room.*

Q If I want to use vinyl flooring should I opt for tiles or buy it on a roll?

A *This is a consideration for many types of flooring. One simple way of making your choice is to consider the size of the room that you are working with. Any flooring sold in sheet form gives you a lovely seamless finish which is ideal for a large area. Where there is little floor space and you have to fit the flooring around lots of recesses or cabinets that project into the room, tiles might be a better choice as they can be cut to fit perfectly.*

42

It works like a dream

Sensible storage solutions for the bedroom are a must. You know those mini-mail order catalogues that drop out of the middle of your magazine?

They are filled with miracle cleaning products, mug trees, scented drawer liners and an assortment of gadgets that you never knew you needed, or even thought existed. You flick through them wondering who buys a miniature cabinet for keys or a mitt for removing fluff from clothes. But every now and then you spot a gem of an idea.

Next time you get such a catalogue don't just bin it but see if you can spot plastic bags that you fill with clothes or bed linen then attach to the nozzle of your vacuum cleaner to suck all the excess air out of the bag. They don't rate in the looks department, but what a great way to reduce the amount of space you need for storage. When summer comes and you are putting away your winter wardrobe you could store it in a fraction of the space it would normally take up. Now that we've

Here's an idea for you...

Before you buy furniture for the bedroom decide on the position of your bed. Does positioning it against one wall mean you have a wasted area behind the door? If you want it under the window are you going to lose the use of a recess that could be made into a seat with a space for storage beneath? Work with the architectural features of the room so that no area becomes a dead space.

shared that neat idea we can address other storage issues in the bedroom.

It must be every woman's idea of heaven to have a walk-in closet or room dedicated to the storage of clothes. Imagine how easy it would be to organise your jackets, jumpers, suits and shoes if there was a room set aside with stacks of racks and rails all dedicated to that one purpose. No bed to climb over, no dressing table to walk around, just a clear run of outfits. Joy. It's a fact of life that very few of us have enough space in our homes to accommodate such luxury (but if you do, lucky you).

So what are the alternatives? Put aside any prejudices you have against built-in wardrobes. The image of awful white or cream plastic-looking fronts is outdated, and chic modern designs offer mirrored units that don't look like they belong in a 70s porn movie. They are not everyone's cup of tea and don't suit every style of room, but because they can be built to accommodate sloping ceilings, awkward recesses and changes in the floor level they make efficient use of the space that they take up.

What's the first thing you do when you get home after a shoe-shopping spree? Pull open the boxes, chuck them aside and try on your new footwear? That's fine, but if your next course of action is to bin the boxes you need to retrain yourself to put your shoes back in the box. I would guess that the amount of money spent on shoes racks and those awful hanging canvas or plastic shoe stores is astronomical. Why waste your cash when all you need to do is retain shoeboxes that can be so easily stacked? And there's usually a picture of the shoe on the box so you'll know which is which. I once saw a magazine feature recommending that you take a Polaroid of your shoes and stick it on the end of a shop-bought box so that you could identify the contents. What a waste of time when if you keep the original the job has been done for you!

If you are running out of storage space consider decluttering the room. IDEA 15, *Keep it tidy*, will guide you through the process.

Try another idea...

Tailor-made storage in the bedroom comes in many guises. Wardrobes, chests of drawers and blanket boxes all have a dedicated purpose, but each takes up an area of the floor and there is the wasted space between each item to consider (it would look ridiculous if they were rammed together side by side). Rather than buy lots of smaller pieces that are not too expensive, have you thought about investing in a larger bit of furniture, something that combines hanging and drawer space for example? The cost might be higher but in the long term it could make more efficient use of the area that it takes up.

Efficient use of space is what it boils down to, and if there is one obvious space-saving solution it is underbed storage. You don't have to buy a bed with drawers built in; why not invest in a set of drawers on castors that you can wheel in and out as required?

Side tables provide a place to put your tea in the morning but if they don't also have drawers you are again wasting a space that could provide a storage solution.

'If you can't get rid of the skeleton in your closet, you'd best teach it to dance.'
GEORGE BERNARD SHAW

Defining idea...

The primary function of the bedroom is to provide a restful and relaxing environment conducive to a restful night's sleep, so keep your bedroom clutter-free. Well-planned storage is the solution.

Q **My bedroom is pretty tiny and while I appreciate the benefits of a built-in wardrobe, I just feel that dedicating a whole wall to this would make it feel much smaller. Is there an alternative?**

A   *Think back to the key issue, which is efficient use of space. By moving your bed around would it give you access to any alcoves or recesses in your bedroom? Are they deep enough to take the width of a hanger? It's quite simple to fix a pole across the space but if you think about it why have just one? If you consider the length of shirts and jackets you could easily fit in two poles, thus doubling your storage. A blind is a much more contemporary way to cover up these areas, though curtains could be better suited to the style of your room. Could you have cupboards built around the door? The space above the door is often left bare but it could provide storage for items that you don't need on a regular basis.*

Q **If I do decide to have built-in cupboards, what will I gain?**

A   *The benefits of floor-to-ceiling wardrobes built to accommodate any recesses or angles in your room is that you can design the space to provide storage for all your clothes and shoes and bed linen. If you include some wire trays or baskets on runners, you will also have somewhere for underwear and even toiletries.*

43

The best-dressed floors are wearing...

Rugs come in a range of classic and contemporary designs. Are you familiar with the feeling that comes when you arrive somewhere and wish you'd made a bit more effort with your outfit? If you leave all of your floors without rugs you are condemning them to a similar fate.

Even the finest carpet or most expensive stone floor will look a million dollars when it's dressed up with a rug.

What do they bring to a room? Sometimes colour, sometimes a change of texture, sometimes they are there to define a particular space. But the beauty of rugs is their versatility.

Imagine a room in summer with a lovely stripped wooden floor. The sun is pouring through the windows and the light colour of the room is perfect for the season. Go on and picture the scene in winter when the floor seems to be draughty and the cool colours send a chill through your heart. Now introduce a lovely, thick rug into the room, something with lots of texture which will contrast beautifully with the smooth wood, in a warm colour that draws you in to the space. It's a quick and easy way of adapting a room through the seasons.

Here's an idea for you...

If you've already designed and decorated your home, you can commission a rug to work with a particular colour scheme or style of interior. There are skilled crafts people who will endeavour to work to a brief. You can contact them through local art galleries or by searching on the web. Have a clear idea of how much you wish to spend, but more importantly a definite picture in your mind of the colours and patterns that you would like to include. Make sure that whoever you work with has seen the room.

They may be just a finishing touch, but what a finish they deliver.

Aside from the comfort issue what else do they bring? They can be used to delineate different areas of the room. If you have a dining area at the end of the lounge, putting a rug down in that space creates the visual illusion of a different area. If you have an enormous lounge or live in a studio-style space with no dividing walls, use a rug to mark out different territories. Place one in the middle of a group of chairs and a sofa and it draws everyone into that space. Put one down in between the kitchen and the seating area and it breaks up that part of the room and emphasises the fact that there are two distinct zones in use.

The successful positioning of rugs relies on drawing the eye to a particular space. This might suggest that the rug needs to be brightly coloured or boldly patterned, but that isn't the case. The mere fact that it sits proud of the floor beneath is enough to work its magic. You can use a pale-coloured rug on top of a natural wood floor and still achieve your aim, but if it has a border in a contrasting colour that may help.

Anyone who is well travelled will have tales of bargaining with a rug dealer somewhere in the world. It almost seems to be a right of passage. Whether you buy an authentic oriental rug, a kelim or a dhurrie, one of the best things about purchasing these pieces is that you have something with a memory attached, but also something that is actually useful. Amazingly, these ethnic items will suit a wide range of interiors. Somehow the woven patterns, stylized motifs and knotted construction of these different rugs blend and complement everywhere from traditional cluttered country cottage to a modern, minimalist, loft-style interior.

I seem to have dwelt on one particular style and should now say that many modern designs are considered works of art. They are so gorgeous that you will consider hanging them from your walls (which is easily done with good strong carpet grippers by the way). Companies commission designers to produce rugs that reflect their personal style and it is not just interior specialists that they choose. The cross-over between fashion and furnishings is nowhere more evident than in rugs. Paul Smith may have designed the perfect suit and diversified into glasses, bags and shoes but you can now also walk all over one of his striped rugs.

Try another idea...

See **IDEA 39**, *The essential extras*, **for other ideas on how to accessorise a space.**

Defining idea...

'*To me a lush carpet of pine needles or spongy grass is more welcome than the most luxurious Persian rug.*'
HELEN KELLER

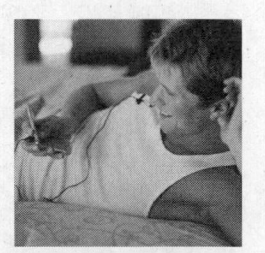

If you have any lingering doubts about rugs, then consider the following scenarios:

- You have a wood floor in the lounge, all the seats are taken but you would like some people to be able to sit on the floor: a thick rug provides some cushioning for their bottoms.

- The colour scheme in your bedroom is fairly neutral but you are aware that a subtle touch of colour would add the finishing touch: a striped cotton rug, laid beside the bed, will introduce a bit of pattern to the room.

- The stone floor in the hall is very practical but it is also extremely cold: a rug placed away from the entrance but running down the rest of the room is much more inviting to new arrivals.

If you want a subtle way of adding warmth, comfort and a touch of colour or pattern to a room, you can look to rugs to provide a solution.

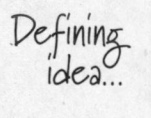
Defining idea...

'A woman telling her true age is like a buyer confiding his final price to an Armenian rug dealer.'
MIGNON McLAUGHLIN, American author and editor

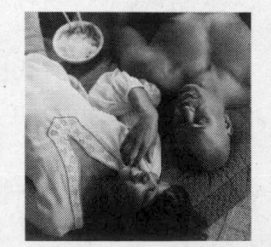

Q **I'm convinced that I need a rug but won't it slip all over the place on a stone floor?**

How did it go?

A *This is a joy to answer because I am addicted to stupid gadgets and the ridiculous bits and pieces that every house should have – even if you don't know it. There are many products that will fit under rugs to keep them in place. Look for something that you can cut to fit to exactly the right size. Search for names like 'stay put' and 'non-slip' on the web and you'll find what you need.*

Q **If I use one of these products, will it damage the rug?**

A *It's highly unlikely. In most cases it could be really good for your rug because it will provide a barrier between the rug and the floor so protecting it from a certain amount of dirt. You'll also appreciate the fact that your rug will not be constantly moving about which makes it much easier to vacuum – essential for removing residual dust and dirt from any kind of flooring.*

44

Take a seat

Comfort and style are essential requirements for your sofas and chairs.

Do your feet swing half-way to the floor? Does your head loll about without support when you sit down to watch the television? It probably means that you didn't put your sofa or armchair through all its paces when you went to choose it from the showroom.

The first rule of buying any piece of furniture is to sit, lie, snuggle and be a drama queen – act out all of your usual positions before you hand over the cheque. If you like to curl up in comfort, make sure your design comes with lots of throw-on cushions. The second rule is to measure it and make sure that it will get into your home.

Imagine the disappointment after waiting weeks for your custom-made sofa when it won't make it through the front door. Winch hire is an expensive business unless you are friendly with the owner of a large construction firm. You'll also have to deal with really grumpy delivery men, not a nice prospect at any time but particularly stressful when you've been camped out on the floor for weeks and are desperate to sit down in comfort.

Stick with the following guidelines when buying a chair or sofa and you can't go wrong:

- **Have some idea of the shape and style that you like.**
- **Work out your budget before you hit the shops.**
- **Be sure of the space that you have allocated for your furniture.**
- **Test every seat and then test them again.**
- **Consider going direct to the manufacturer. This is a good way of saving money because you cut out the middleman, but as with buying from catalogues which could also seem a cheaper option, you have to remember that you won't get to try them out.**

The idea of the three-piece suite has a place for some people. I tend to associate it with the design of a bygone age. It is much better visually to have different pieces of furniture in a room that are tied in by colour or style but not necessarily because they are a perfect match. That way you can put a cotton-covered sofa next to a leather armchair in the lounge or a couple of armchairs in the same room as a chaise longue. I do think you are limiting yourself if you buy every seat in a matching design. Avoiding the three-piece also frees you up to spend more on a spectacular sofa, one with wonderfully luxurious feather-filled cushions and a frame which has been dowelled, screwed and glued and is constructed in hardwood. Yes it will cost a lot, but you can be sure it will last for years. You can then choose chairs that cost a little less but if upholstered in a complementary fabric and dressed up with cushions will look quite OK beside your designer sofa.

When you are investing in these pieces of furniture you should also bear in mind that you may well decide to redecorate and change the colour scheme in your room long before they are worn out. Now it is possible that if you have a small armchair upholstered in blue, which was one of the colours of the scheme that you were working with when you brought it, you could afford to have it reupholstered when you decide to opt for an all-white room. However, with a red sofa that no longer works with the room, you are looking at a much larger investment to replace the covers. I'm not saying that you should always choose neutral colours for sofas and chairs, because that would be very boring indeed. But what I am suggesting is that you have in mind future options. Loose covers might be worth considering, for example. Sometimes you can get two sets for the price of one in summer sales and that opens up your options considerably. For this same reason, unless you are wealthy enough to change sofas and chairs every few years, it's a good idea to avoid high-fashion or gimmicky designs that will look dated quickly.

Antiques and collectable pieces really sit outside of this framework. The sheer diversity in chair design can be quite bewildering, and these are pieces of furniture that become collectable items much more quickly than sofas.

Of course there are the historical designs. A classic Charles Rennie Mackintosh curved wooden armchair or an upholstered Bauhaus design by Walter Groupius, for example, would both be happy additions to any expert's chair collection. But if you aren't looking for investments and just want somewhere comfortable to sit, then one or two different armchairs from a high-street department store are just what you need.

Whatever style of furniture you choose, make sure it fulfils the most important criteria of all: comfort.

Defining idea…

'*A chair is a very difficult object. A skyscraper is almost easier. That is why Chippendale is famous.*'
LUDWIG MIES VAN DER ROHE

Try another idea…

Take a look at IDEA 50, *The pattern rules*, for some thoughts on choice of fabrics.

Defining idea…

'*The discontented man finds no easy chair.*'
BENJAMIN FRANKLIN

How did
it go?

Q **I am thinking about buying a second-hand sofa to save money. Is this a good idea?**

A *Sadly, what you save on the initial purchase you may have to spend on restoration. Restoring an old sofa is a skilled task. The piece may have to be stripped back all the way to the frame. Then it's possible any rotten elements will need to be replaced and, of course, it will need restuffing. Also you have to figure in the cost of new fabric which, depending on the size of the piece, could prove very costly indeed.*

Q **What if I wanted to invest in an antique?**

A *Make sure that you examine any piece carefully. If the legs, for example, look a different colour to the wood on the back of a sofa or chair, it could mean that they are replacements rather than originals. Look at all the different parts of the piece – there will be fabric, wood and metal components and if each one needs repairing it will add to the cost. You might want to consider restoration, where a craftsperson will try to return it as close as possible to its original state. Or you could consider conservation, where repairs will be made but the priority is to preserve the integrity of the furniture, so that work is kept to a minimum.*

45

A taste for tiles

Dress up your walls with pattern and colour – oh, and tiles are practical too. If you are considering how to treat the walls in your bathroom, kitchen or hallway, you could do a lot worse than to tile them.

The hardwearing quality of tiles is enough to recommend them for any hardworking area. Resistant to dirt and easy to clean, they make a logical choice for rooms that receive a lot of wear and tear.

If you think about the volume of water that gets splashed around in the bathroom, the amount of steam in the kitchen, and the rain and dirt that flies around in a hallway, it becomes obvious why tiles are a good choice for the walls.

So how do you choose your tiles? Some of the things you need to consider are common to all of the areas above; others may be more specific to a particular room. You are going to be influenced by the colour, pattern and texture of a tile. If you have already decided on the scheme for your room, then are you going to match the colour of the paint on your walls with a slightly lighter or darker shade or do you want to pick a completely contrasting colour? Are you interested in creating a

Don't just place tiles on your walls – you can use them to dress up window sills too. If you have a deep enough sill, then cover it with colourful designs to add interest to what is frequently a bare and undecorated part of the home. They can be used to add a quirky touch where the window treatment that has been used is quite plain. And they are hardwearing too. You won't need to change them as often as you would need to repaint the surface.

If you have lots of tiles left over from tiling the kitchen, think about using them to cover the top of a table – it's a neat way of dressing up a junk shop buy.

pattern or introducing a picture or mural in the room, or do you want to define two spaces with a tiled dado?

If you think about your kitchen, here are some elements that might influence your choice:

- How much wall space are you looking to cover with the tiles? If you have wall-mounted cabinets, then you may only have a small area to tile and can afford to choose more expensive hand-made tiles over mass-produced ceramic designs.

- Is there a space that you want to fill with a panel or mural of tiles? You could commission something from an artist but quite frankly there are a huge variety of designs that can be bought off the shelf. You'll find trees, fruit, plants, flowers and animals to name a few. These can be set on the wall in the middle of plain tiles or surrounded with a contrasting colour to frame the view.

- Do you want to combine mostly plain tiles with just a scattering of patterned ones? A few hand-painted delft tiles might look perfect introduced at random in a rustic country kitchen, while metallic abstract designs could be a way to add an intriguing detail in a modern room. In the bathroom you are likely to be covering large areas so cost is much more of a consideration. I would recommend that you budget to cover the largest area possible. It makes cleaning and maintaining the bathroom so much more easy if virtually all the walls are tiled.

For other ideas on covering walls, see IDEA 46, *It's in the papers*.

Try another idea...

- Do you have a separate shower area that needs completely tiling? If that cuts into your budget, then limit yourself elsewhere, for example to a tiled splashback above the sink. Stand up in your bath and tile to the height of your shoulders around that area. That should be sufficient to protect the wall from even the most vigorous of splashing bathers.

- Where you don't cover an entire wall, you may want to finish the top of these tiles with a smaller border design for the sake of neatness.

- Have you considered mosaic tiles in the bathroom? These look absolutely stunning whether they are in bright colours or natural shades. Bright Mediterranean blue mosaics have a visual impact that is unrivalled in the tile world.

Tiling the walls in your hallway may sound distinctly old-fashioned and of course this is a feature of many Victorian homes. But there is no rule that says you shouldn't use modern, cool-coloured tiles in place of the dark greens and blues that were traditionally used. Oblong-shaped designs are most definitely an option for this area.

'Decorate your home. It gives the illusion that your life is more interesting than it really is.'
CHARLES SCHULZ, cartoonist, creator of *Peanuts*

Defining idea...

How did it go?

Q **Once I've got my tiles up, how do I maintain them?**

A With a great deal of ease. A simple wipe will usually do the job, but if you are trying to remove a build-up of limescale from water splashes, use a proprietory cleaner. You will need to leave some solutions on for a few minutes but do make sure that you rinse the surface well with lots of clean water. Leaving any traces will contribute to the build-up of dirt on the surface.

Q **If I can't be bothered to take down some old tiles, can I just retile over the top?**

A This isn't ideal because of problems with sealing them at the top and bottom of any run. However, it's easy enough to tile over existing tiles as long as they are still very firmly attached to the walls. There should be no loose or cracked ones in the area. Then all you need to be concerned with is cleaning them thoroughly and removing any grease from the surface before applying the new ones over the top. Do tell your supplier that this is what you are planning so that you get the right type of adhesive for the job.

46

It's in the papers

Back in fashion and burgeoning with design potential, wallpaper has a place in everyone's home.

I know what you are thinking. The paste pot, the collapsible table, the lining up of seams, the cutting and measuring, this is a real fag. I agree.

Save up and pay someone else to do the job. Or embrace the concept of the many new developments in wallpaper technology – it's true – and pick an easy-to-hang design. For example, wallpapers where you paste the wall and not the cut strip make the job much more approachable. You won't need masses of equipment but there are two essential tools: the paper-hanging brush, which you use to smooth over the surface and squeeze out air bubbles and excess paste, and the seam roller that ensures a flat join between two drops of paper.

Remember that you don't have to tackle an entire room. You can choose to paper just the alcoves either side of a chimneybreast, or make a feature of a single wall with the rest of the room decorated with paint. Wallpaper can hide a multitude of sins. If you use lining paper first on an uneven wall or surface with hairline cracks (check that they are not caused by any structural problems before you cover them, and that they won't get any worse) and then add the decorative paper on top, you'll

Here's an idea for you...

If you are going to use a border to create panels and frame pictures you need to make sure that the two work in harmony and don't clash. First, make sure the design of your paper complements the colour of the picture frame. Second, allow a reasonable amount of space between the edge of the frame and the border both at the sides and the top and bottom – ideally your picture should sit in the middle of your panel.

get a superb finish that paint just can't deliver. You mustn't think of wallpaper design in terms of woodchip, bubbles or garish patterns. A muted print with a sprigged flower can add a hint of pattern to a room that is so subtle as to be almost subliminal in its effect. Or a large pattern applied to just one wall will create an instant impact in the room. Retro designs can be used as the backdrop to a fifties-themed interior, while classic prints are the perfect way to complement a traditional home. Don't just limit your imagination to rolls that cover the complete wall. There are decorative friezes, borders and dados that can be used to define different areas in a room and to break up vast expanses of plain wall. For example, you can use a border design to create panels on the wall; a run of two or three across a large space gives a lovely effect and each one can frame a painting, a mirror or a print. If you have a very high ceiling, a wide border run around the room at picture rail height will help visually draw the eye down into the room. You can also use them to highlight architectural features like sloping ceilings, recesses and chimneybreasts, or run them around window and doorframes where again they will draw attention towards each particular feature of the space.

PERFECT PATTERNS

Using decorative wallpaper throughout one room will have a strong impact on the size of the space. If it's a very busy design, you can expect the room to shrink in size. One way to avoid this would be to limit your use to two or three walls and leave one area to be decorated with paint in a pale but matching colour. However, if you like the idea of creating a smaller space, go the whole way and run your design up and across the ceiling too. I have seen this done with a very pretty floral print in a bedroom and it does create a really cosy, country mood.

Another visual trick is to use stripes to run up the wall when the ceiling in the room appears to be quite low. It will instantly change the proportions of the space.

Because of the sheer diversity of designs you can use wallpaper to cheat different finishes on your walls. A leather paint effect would take some considerable time to achieve while putting up a 'faux' leather paper is a much quicker option. Covering your walls with fabric might present a considerable expense but a damask-look paper will be considerably cheaper. And there are the *trompe l'oeil* designs that are available. If you want a country scene in your living room search out a toile de Jouy design. If you'd like Doric columns in the dining room, you'll easily find a paper that you can use to cheat the look.

Have a look at IDEA 12, *Decorative effects for a designer home*, if you are interested in paint effects.

Try another idea...

'Family love is messy, clinging, and of an annoying and repetitive pattern, like bad wallpaper.'
P. J. O'ROURKE

Defining idea...

'The whole point of camouflage is to deceive the enemy's eye, making it as difficult as possible to perceive the outline of a tank. The same is true in a papered room. For the most part, straight lines, angles and intrusive architectural lumps such as chimney breasts can be quite successfully obliterated by the pleasing distraction of pattern.'
LAURENCE LLEWELYN-BOWEN, *BBC Good Homes Magazine*

Defining idea...

How did
it go?

Q **I've used a border to create panels around the walls in my dining room. Now I am not sure whether a picture in each one is going to look right as the pictures are different sizes but the panels are all uniform in layout.**

A *Often it's better to space the pictures out so that you have one or two empty panels in between each one that you fill. Try limiting the number of pictures that you hang rather than filling every panel.*

Q **But what about the different sizes of the pictures?**

A *Lay your pictures out. Put the biggest one down first and then try and collect together two or three others that when put in a group together equal the size of the largest. Then hang this group in a panel two or three away from the big picture.*

  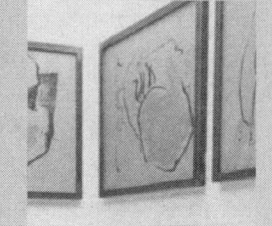

47

Have you wasted that loft space?

Look up to your roof if you need to expand.

There's a great way to avoid moving house if your reason for leaving is because you have outgrown your home — make use of the space at the top of the house.

I was tiny when we had the loft converted in our family home, but I do remember that there was an awful lot of mess. Now that might be enough to put you off the idea, but if you consider the pain of packing up your house and finding somewhere else to live, then the thought of a few weeks of chaos might not seem so bad.

A loft conversion is the most sensible way of getting an extra room (well that and adding on a conservatory, but you may well have done that already).

PUT PLANS IN PLACE

First, with some basic questions…
- What is your budget?
- How will the room be used?
- Where are you going to put the extra staircase that you will need?

Here's an idea for you... **There are loft conversions and then there are loft conversions. If you have a really good budget then why not put an extra bathroom or shower space in the room? If you are worried about it taking up a lot of space, you'll find plenty of bathroom suites designed with space saving in mind. This might be the ideal space to use glass bricks as a room divider so that you are not cutting down on light in either space.**

■ How are you going to lay out the space to accommodate the slopes and awkward shapes that the roof creates?

Knowing your budget is vital. That's not just what you wish to spend on the building work but also the furnishing and decoration of the room. There's no point in having all the work done if what you are then left with is plaster walls and bare floors. You need to decide on whether you are going to be putting another bed up there, if it will become an office or if it is just going to be the kids' playroom. Any of these scenarios will call on you to spend money furnishing the space.

Another reason for defining the budget is so that you can decide whether you can afford a dormer window which projects to the outside to form a full-height area in the loft with a vertical window or whether you will have to settle for a cheaper roof window which is set into the slope of the roof. Planning regulations in your area may also affect this choice.

You need to have a good idea of the ultimate use of the space because if it is going to be an office you'll need a telephone point, lots of electrical sockets for all of your computer kit, and light fittings to illuminate the work area.

See the ideas for a home office in IDEA 8, *Work that room*, for and bedroom storage in IDEA 42, *It works like a dream*.

Try another idea...

Consider up-lighters rather than a pendant fitting because they will throw light up towards what will probably be a reasonably low ceiling. If that doesn't worry you, then halogen spots set into the ceiling are a good option.

If it's going to be a spare bedroom or playroom, these things may not be of such importance to you and you may be able to save money by not including all of the above.

'The sky's the limit if you have a roof over your head.'
SOL HUROK, Russian-born impresario

Defining idea...

If you are converting a loft space for teenagers, then soundproofing has to be a priority and that may up the costs. Depending on the size of the space you may want to add a false wall inside the structure. Use timber battens to support a layer of plasterboard around the room. Think about where the TV and stereo are going to be placed. For starters make sure that the TV is not positioned against a party wall. Music can be muffled by hanging the speakers instead of standing them on a solid surface, or by positioning them on foam.

'Men of lofty genius when they are doing the least work are most active.'
LEONARDO DA VINCI

The reason for deciding on the position of the staircase is because you are going to have to lose space from somewhere on the floor below. If you are worried about it encroaching on a bedroom, then maybe think about a spiral staircase. As long as the children who may be using this are not too young it can be a space-saving solution. Another option, if the builders can work it in, is to make the flight quite steep. Use open treads to allow light into the area.

EXTRA TOUCHES

If you can afford it, think about including built-in storage in the room. It will work around the slopes of the ceiling making the maximum use of any awkward areas in the room. Because the room that the conversion creates is unlikely to be huge, you want to avoid cluttering it up with lots of different pieces of freestanding furniture wherever possible.

Also, consider what type of heating to put in the roof (and make sure it is well insulated whatever you choose). Check with your builder whether it is possible to include underfloor heating – this is by far the best solution because you won't have to worry about losing wall space to radiators.

Careful planning is the key to a successful conversion, so take time to get everything right.

Q   Do I need to get any approval for the job?

A   There is no doubt that you will need to check with your local authority or council before getting on with the job, and your builder should know which local officials you need to speak to. If you employ an architect they may take on the job of getting approval for your conversion. You will also have to comply with local fire regulations at every point in the construction of your loft. Some properties may not require planning permission, provided the loft conversion is the first extension to the house and it doesn't exceed a certain size.

Q   If I do go through with this, is it true that it will add value to my property?

A   If the job is done properly a loft conversion will increase the value of your house considerably. Make sure that you have done everything legally required for the work as a future buyer's surveyor will check on the permissions for the conversion, and its compliance with the relevant regulations.

How did it go?

213

48

A night on the tiles

A fantastic range of looks are made possible with tiled floors. You can lay down all sorts of patterns and even include pictures when you put down a tiled floor.

You can arrange insets to add extra colour and your choice is limitless. If you like the idea of a hand-made design, then it's there for the taking.

If you require a reclaimed floor to fit in with a renovated building, it's just a quick tour of France, Spain or Italy away. Well actually no, someone will have imported it for you, but those are three of the countries from where they are sourced.

The finish on tiles varies enormously. There are matt, unglazed surfaces, high gloss finishes and various sheens caused by the application of different glazes. If you love a particular look, then make sure before you buy your tiles that the finish will not be affected in the sealing process, as some tiles are pre-sealed before they are sold while others are sealed once they have been laid.

There's no question that tiles are hardwearing. But anyone who's walked across a stone-cold floor in the middle of the night might be wondering whether a carpet

When you are deciding on which colour of tile to choose, consider how they will work with other elements in the room. If you're planning to put down some rugs, will they complement the colours in the weave? If you have already bought curtains or blinds for the windows, will the tiles pick up on a colour in the print or design of the fabric that you have chosen?

would offer more comfort. If you can afford it, the best solution to that problem is to install underfloor heating.

The sheer variety of tiles on offer might be a little confusing so let's address a few specifics. For a rustic touch with a grand history turn to terracotta. Colours may vary. You'll find yellow and ochre tiles from Tuscany and rich red designs from Mexico, but one quality that most share is the rough and ready finish to these tiles. Don't be surprised to find slight pitting and areas that have been eroded in the surface of the tiles. You are getting a product that looks like it has lived a little, even if it was only recently manufactured. This of course makes it ideal for areas of heavy traffic where there is nothing better than a surface that doesn't show the dirt. But it also means that if you want the colour of terracotta but with a smoother finish you need to search out very specific extruded designs. These are sometimes confused with quarry tiles but in fact the two are made from different clays. The manufacturing process means that quarry tiles are much harder then terracotta and also less porous.

Ceramic tiles are the first choice for most bathrooms, most kitchens and a mix of other spaces where you want to add colour and pattern to the floor. Because they are made in moulds, they offer a uniformity that makes them easy to work with. Not only can you guarantee straight lines, but they are also simple to cut so can be worked into all sorts of nooks and crannies, curving around pedestals and butting up against waste pipes without too much difficulty. Just a point to bear in mind: if you know that some tiles will need to be cut you should allow for extra when you measure up and order them. If you break some, then go back a week later to the shop for a few extras, these may come from a different batch and you won't be able to guarantee an exact colour match.

Mosaic tiles can be used to stunning effect. Use different colours to create borders in a room, or lay an oblong in a contrasting colour in the middle of the floor or beside the bath to create the illusion of a mat. The different types, including ceramic, marble and stone, can be combined in a floor but it really is best to stick with one type for a uniform finish. You can be as adventurous as you want in creating patterns but you'll need a very patient fitter for a highly detailed design. In fact you are probably better employing the services of a mosaic artist if you are looking for something very decorative.

Part of the attraction of a mosaic floor is the contrast in texture between the tiles themselves and the grouting that holds them in place. This gives a pleasing, slightly rough feeling underfoot which also helps to make it less slippery than a floor covered in larger tiles. That's one of the biggest benefits of choosing it for the bathroom.

Bear in mind when buying mosaics sold by the sheet that the colour and tone of the stones may vary across each sheet. Make sure that if there is a mix of pink and brown tints in the mosaic, for example, that you don't end up with 80 per cent brown sheets and 20 per cent pink. You want to be able to have an even mix across the room, which is pleasing to the eye.

For information on wall tiles, see IDEA 45, *A taste for tiles.*

Try another idea...

'**Scrubbing floors and emptying bedpans has as much dignity as the Presidency.**'
RICHARD M. NIXON

Defining idea...

'**The finest workers in stone are not copper or steel tools, but the gentle touches of air and water working at their leisure with a liberal allowance of time.**'
HENRY DAVID THOREAU

Defining idea...

How did
it go?

Q   **I've put down unglazed floor tiles and I am aware that these need to be sealed. Are there any particular things to bear in mind?**

A   *You must be sure that the tiles are completely dry. If you seal them and any are damp you may well ruin them. Also make sure that the room is clean and free of dust or you will be sealing that into the surface too. You may need to test an area to see how porous the surface is: you don't want to use too much or too little sealant and it could be that your tiles will require two or three light coats in preference to one heavy one. If sealant is pooling on the surface you are applying too much.*

Q   **And when should I grout them?**

A   *With unglazed tiles you want to apply a seal first, allow that to dry, then grout and then seal again. You really do need to make sure that the surface is dry before you apply the grout and also that the gaps between the tiles are free of any dirt or debris. There are various different types of grout so check with your supplier which type would be best for your tiles.*

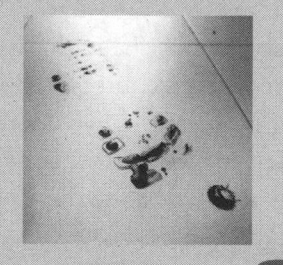

49

An organised mind

Nothing in the world beats brilliant storage. If you think that makes me sound rather sad and probably a compulsive obsessive, you may be right. I can't imagine how I would live without good storage in every room in my house.

I am not someone who can bear to be encircled by mess. Without being too dull about it, my view is that if you live surrounded by clutter, you will always feel slightly disorganized about your life.

Please don't turn the page if you think this is insanity. Just try a bit of organisation in your home and see how pleased you are with the results.

In most rooms in the house, built-in cupboards are worth their weight in gold. Now here I would suggest that you don't attempt a quick DIY job – find a craftsperson and pay them good money to put in cupboards that fit any wasted space. Obvious places to consider are at either side of a chimneybreast, in a recess caused by the juxtaposition of two rooms and under the stairs. If you aren't in a position to fund that kind of work, then go out and get a second job. Sorry, that's harsh. It's just that when you see a room with storage that has been built to perfectly fit a particular space, then other options often come a poor second.

Here's an idea for you...

Try and store all of the electrical items in your living room in one or two dedicated units. There is nothing more unsightly than the spaghetti mess of cables from a video and TV, which are just put on tables or on stands. A unit that houses these two items will keep all of the electrical wiring together even if it's just a trolley. Also be logical – try and store CDs in a unit with the player, and the same for DVDs.

BREAK IT DOWN

The key to good storage is to consider the room first and the storage second. Don't just go out and buy a cupboard that you think might 'fit in somewhere'. You want to be clear about the room it will work in, the purpose it will serve, and whether it is going to offer the maximum possible storage space for the room. My advice is to approach it on a room-by-room basis, as your requirements for the lounge are very different to your needs in the study. Apply a critical eye to each room, breaking down your possessions into groups. Which items need to be within easy and accessible reach? Are there certain things, which only get occasional use? Most importantly, is there anything that you can get rid of? Also apply a bit of lateral thinking. Not all storage has to be positioned on the floor and sometimes the best solutions are concealed from the eye.

I know from personal experience that the more space I have, the more I fill. And the longer I live somewhere, the more clutter I accumulate. What this means in practical terms it that your storage needs may well change over time, but start with the best of basics.

Concealed storage has real appeal. It could be a table that has drawers hidden underneath or it could be a footstool with space beneath when you lift the lid. The more items like this that you can find, the less you will need to rely on cupboards that take up valuable floor space. Of course there are some items that you want to see and have easy access to, like books. Consider if there are any wasted spaces in the house where you might put a bookshelf – the landing is often an area that is left clear of any furniture but if you think about it, might there be room for a full-height set of bookshelves?

Every hall should have somewhere to deposit coats and shoes (umbrellas, school bags and gym kits too). Look for a unit that has a mirror at the front and shelves concealed behind. These are widely available from stores like Ikea. Failing that, think about putting a chest or settle in the hall which has storage space beneath the seat.

The bathroom can be a real challenge if you have a fairly small room. There are units available that fit over the top of the toilet providing shelves or a cabinet above your head for keeping all your necessary bits and pieces. And that is a good example of clever use of space, which is what good storage is all about. A large, mirrored and lit bathroom cabinet can be pricey, but what you lose in the initial outlay you will gain over time from having a dedicated space in which to put toiletries.

Now the office is a challenge, but I would recommend that you invest in a filing cabinet and buy a desk that has plenty of drawers. Or, look out for old shop fittings – units with stacks and stacks of drawers or industrial shelving with plenty of open racks for slotting in baskets.

The secret of good storage is adaptability and versatility, so spend time researching dual-purpose pieces and practical items that fulfil all of your needs.

Try another idea...

Before you embark on your storage voyage, it's worth spending time decluttering your home, IDEA 15, *Keep it tidy*, has some great hints.

Defining idea...

'Search the true order Blunted by wind-blown thoughts. And to every Fall-hurled leaf a place.'
LEO TIFAL, Canadian poet

How did it go?

Q   I can deal with all the large objects in my home but what about the little things that litter each room?

A   *I suspect this is a problem for many people. Where do you put magazines in the lounge? How do you store the washing-up brush and scrubber in the kitchen? What do you do with the pens and pencils in your office? These are all small scale but they need a home just as much as larger things. Often these types of items are really dull so try and be decorative with the storage. A neat little jug is ideal for the kitchen ephemera, a kilner jar perfect for pens in the office, and I would recommend a purpose-built rack for your magazines but consider a wall-mounted one that won't clutter up the floor.*

Q   Sounds very bitty – isn't that what I'm trying to avoid?

A   *Yes, it may be, but unless you are going to put absolutely everything away behind closed doors (and yes, I would love to recommend you live like that), then you do have to have certain items out on the table top or sink surface and within easy reach. That's why I recommend that you try to choose decorative items for the storage.*

50

The pattern rules

Here's how different motifs can work to the good of your home. Of all the things that can upset the eye when you walk into a room, an excessive use of patterns must be one of the most common.

It's a visual nightmare when there are so many different things going on in a space that your eye has no idea on which to focus.

That's not to say that there is any reason why you shouldn't employ different patterns in the same room, but there is a way of using them to their best advantage. The rulebook that says you cannot combine paisleys with stripes or checks with florals has not been written – and quite rightly. Using patterns is a great way of brightening a colour scheme and adding visual excitement and interest to a space, but it just needs handling with some care to make any combination work to its best advantage.

Whether they are on patterned fabric or accessories, patterns can be used to make a statement about the style of the room and emphasise its personality.

Tartan, for example, immediately makes a room feel warm and cosy – amazing really when you consider that Scotland is hardly the warmest place on the planet. I suspect that it is more to do with the association with cosy fires and highland hunting lodges. It can be used to add a quirky touch to townhouses.

Here's an idea for you...

When you are making up items from lengths of fabric be aware that a very busy design should be used with care. If the fabric has a hectic pattern, keep the item it is being made up into quite simple, for example if you are making up a highly decorative material into a bedspread, avoid frills and flounces to trim your design.

Simple floral patterns suggest spring. They are the optimists in the fabric family symptomatic of new starts and fresh beginnings. Walk into a room where these designs have been used and even the most dedicated of minimalists will enjoy a lift to their spirits. Choose florals for a conservatory or south-facing lounge.

Stripes have the effect of making a space seem quite 'grown up'. There is something about the regular nature of this pattern that makes people sit with straight backs and sip their tea without slopping it into the saucer. It has a formal quality to it that can be usefully employed in period houses.

Geometrics could be seen as the juveniles in the group. From squares and circles to lines and squiggly shapes, these patterns evoke a mood of careless enjoyment. Slightly cheeky and reminiscent of the 50s, 60s and 70s when women were liberated and music became rock and roll, they are perfect for modern flats and new conversions.

Now that is just a few examples of the designs you can work with. There are hundreds of other options from classical scenes to animal prints and oriental flowers to ethnic motifs, each one evoking a different mood.

So how do you combine them in a space? It used to be the norm that you would use the largest motif on the biggest available surface, so huge flowers would end up on the curtains and you would graduate patterns down according to the scale of the area that they would cover. Medium sprigs would be used to upholster sofas and small buds spent their days covering cushions. There is a better way. Start with a decorative pattern, be it a fabric, wallpaper or even a carpet. Next find a plain design that works with that pattern – it might be paint for the walls or a fabric to upholster a chair – and finally choose a smaller scale pattern in the same colourway to complete the trio. If it's a fabric this will be used to cover cushions but it could just as easily be a patterned throw that will go over the back of a sofa.

For more information on different types of fabrics, see IDEA 36, *Softly, softly.*

Try another idea...

Here are a few ideas to help you work with pattern...

- Avoid using lots of tiny motifs in the same space – it will look much too busy.

- Think about using large designs with care: if the motif on a wallpaper is very big, how many complete designs will fit in to the drop on the wall? If you can only see one or two, is it going to work?

'When patterns are broken, new worlds emerge.'
TULI KUPFERBERG, musician

Defining idea...

- Where your walls are plain, introduce patterns on cushion covers or lampshades. If your furniture is all relatively plain, use a patterned paint effect or wallpaper on the walls.

- Don't mix two very different styles – avoid teaming Chinese-influenced oriental designs and an African-style ethnic pattern in the same room, for example.

'A designer knows he has achieved perfection not when there is nothing left to add, but when there is nothing left to take away.'
ANTOINE DE SAINT-EXUPÉRY

Defining idea...

Make your colour choices with care when you mix up different patterns and you can create quite spectacular effects in a room.

Q I have never tried combining designs before. What patterns do you suggest I use?

A *Some of the best pairings of patterns team stripes with checks or with florals. These are really simple to make work together. If you imagine a blue gingham tablecloth and dining chairs with loose covers made from ticking you should be able to visualise what I mean. In the same way, picture a red chintzy sofa sitting in front of a wall papered with a pencil thin red stripe design.*

Q So what about the colour choices?

A *Keep the colours of your patterns as close to each other as possible. That way you are less likely to make any mistakes. It can help to put together a colour scheme if you start with a patterned fabric as your inspiration. This makes it easy to choose a colour for the carpet, because you can choose the same shade as the background of the fabric for the floor. And you can pick out one of the colours from the patterned design to use as the choice of paint for the walls.*

51

Wood looks

From bare boards to the finest finishes, choose wood for your floors.

There is something very appealing about walking into a room with bare boards. It has a pared down simplicity that can make other more exotic options seem a little extravagant.

Plain old oak boards allowed to gain the patina of old age, or pine bleached or limed to give a white finish have a simple appeal.

Now that is the most basic type, but when you add parquet, wood laminates, new beech and hardwood flooring, maple, walnut, ash, birch and cherry into the mix you get some idea of the rich variety of looks that are available to you if you opt for wood.

Wood works in every setting, from the oldest rustic cottage to the most loft-style apartment, and that is a great part of its appeal. It is cooler than carpet but much warmer than stone, makes the perfect background for rugs and will work with virtually any colour scheme. In fact if you can decide on nothing other than a wooden floor as part of your decorating scheme for a room, then at least you can be assured that you have made an excellent first step in the planning process.

Use paints or stains to achieve a mock-tiled appearance or a chequerboard effect. Painting alternate floorboards in two different colours can look stunning used across a large area. For the more adventurous why not choose an area, say in front of the fireplace, and add a *trompe l'oeil* rug?

Prices vary enormously, from very cheap products that you can lay yourself to top-of-the-range materials that call for a professional fitter. If you are lucky enough to have inherited a wood floor in your home, do think very carefully before you decide to cover it up with another flooring product as you may be wasting money and time.

AGE OLD

Old wood floors should be kept where possible. Sanding, stripping and finishing is within most people's range of expertise even if these jobs are time consuming and very messy. If you have just plain boards, then it is quite straightforward, however if you discover that you have parquet you need to approach it with a little more care. Any loose blocks, for example, should be refitted before you make any attempt to renovate the actual surface of the wood.

I have mentioned liming already. This relatively simple process should be employed when you have dark boards and you want to lighten the mood in the room. All you need to do is clean the surface and remove any varnish, then rub either watered-down white paint or a proprietary product into the floor. It really is that simple.

'My idea of superwoman is someone who scrubs her own floors.'
BETTE MIDLER

Should you wish to darken the wood, the range of stains, varnishes and waxes available to you will allow you to pick the perfect shade for your floor.

MODERN CHOICES

Consider the following, which are two of the most popular choices for a wood floor:

If you want to consider adding rugs in the room, see IDEA 43, *The best-dressed floors are wearing...*

Try another idea...

- Veneered or laminate flooring can be pre-assembled in long strips ready to clip together. It comes in several different grades and is impact- and scratch-resistant.

- Hardwood floor can come in either square-edge or tongue-and-groove planks and can be supplied to you either finished. It also comes in a range of different patterns, including maple, ash, cherry, oak and beech.

If you want a new wood floor, then for the ultimate in durability choose a solid hardwood floor: it'll gain character with age and will last you for decades. Because you are going to live with it for years, and it won't be cheap, start out right and get it fitted by a professional. This type of flooring is at the top of the price range. For less expensive options consider laminate strips, many of which can be laid by even an incompetent DIYer. Bear in mind that laminate flooring may have only the thinnest of veneers on top of the wood facing and it won't be as durable as some of the more expensive options.

Wood doesn't need much maintenance. Regular vacuuming will keep down the level of dust in the room if you have old floorboards or just use a broom to sweep up when you feel the need. New products will benefit from a light mopping – make sure that you are not soaking the floor and you may want to wax them from time to time, but as long as they have been properly sealed in the first place they are relatively maintenance-free. If an area is in bright sunlight you can get some discoloration over time, so it may be sensible to move furniture around occasionally and place rugs in different parts of the room according to the seasons.

How did it go?

Q   **If I choose wood instead of carpet, how long can I expect my floor to last?**

A   *Solid hardwood flooring will be around long after your grandchildren have walked across it for the last time, if properly looked after, kept dry and protected with polish. Laminate flooring will last anything from 10–20 years and good fitting is key to prolonging its life.*

Q   **You have mentioned mopping and sweeping, but what if I get a scuffmark on the floor?**

A   *Dirty marks should be ideally cleaned up immediately before they have time to dry. The best approach is to use a sponge which you have dampened with a solution of very dilute washing-up liquid and warm water. Do not use too much water as it might cause surface discoloration. Do remember that gravel and dirt are the main enemies and, if worked into your floor, will stain and scratch the surface. Use a heavy-duty mat both inside and outside the front and back doors. Avoid dragging heavy items across the floor as they might gouge it.*

52

Inspiration for your home

Straight-talking advice about planning and completing your interiors.

Sometimes it's almost impossible to see the wood for the trees. However much you try to focus on one particular aspect of design, it is all too easy to get bogged down with all the details.

It's all very well for trained interior designers to tackle a room, but what about us mere mortals who approach the task with a little fear and considerable trepidation?

There are so many sources of inspiration for colour schemes that just deciding on the theme can take some considerable time. But once you have taken that first tentative step, what are your priorities?

Planning is the key. You want to arrange an order of work for the room so that each task fits in logically with the next. Make a checklist of all the jobs that will need to done, allocate each an estimated time from start to finish, and then work out how you are going to co-ordinate all the different tasks.

Here's an idea for you...

When you are working out the budget for your room, always leave a float outside of the overall budget. There is always an extra cost that comes up and you don't want to have to find money that you haven't got. Make sure that you've got a detailed quotation from everyone involved in the job; costs can sometimes mysteriously escalate if you don't keep an eye on your purse.

Any structural changes have to be completed first. If the chimneybreast is coming out or you are removing a wall, get these jobs out of the way before you proceed any further. This would be the right time to get any rewiring done, or to sort out additional lights and sockets. Just think a little bit ahead if you can bear it. Would it also be worth having cabling for your house alarm or the wires for wall-mounted speakers for the stereo system sunk into the wall? If you are going to have to replaster, then you may as well get everything done in one fell swoop.

Next, make a decision on your flooring and get the order in. If the supplier is not going to lay the floor, then you need to marry up the arrival of the flooring with a fitter. I would add a note of caution here: certain types of flooring need to acclimatise to the room in which they will be laid, so you may need to allow a period of time between the delivery of the flooring and the date that you book the fitter. It's much easier to bring fitters into a reasonably empty room than to have to shift out all the furniture or have them move it around while they work. It will cut down on stress levels if you can get the flooring in place before anything else that you have ordered arrives.

If you are going to have pieces of furniture upholstered in a specific fabric rather than buy them off the shop floor, then find out how long the job will take. You don't want to be left with a completed room and then have to sit on boxes for three weeks. Once you have worked out delivery dates (and try and get all the furniture delivered within a few days of each other) you can arrange to decorate the room.

If you are going to use decorators make it very clear that you have a start and finish date in mind. All too often I hear of situations where the job is half finished but then workmen are called off to another site which is allegedly more pressing. It may be to someone else but it most certainly isn't to you. I can't stress enough how important it is that you make this clear. It causes so many problems when you have to try and drag people back to finish a job. It's much more relaxing for you to watch decorators work in a room without the finished floor, and it is much easier if you are doing the work yourself to function in a space where you are not worried about drips of paint or blobs of paste marking a new carpet – so ideally you should get this out of the way before the floor goes down.

Unless you are buying ready-made curtains or blinds you need to be aware of how long it will take for these items to be made up. And also be sure that they can be hung after all the decorating is completed. Painting window frames is much more straightforward when there is no fabric hanging in the way. Once you have chosen all the elements for your room and decided on which professionals you are going to use, do impress on them the importance of your own schedule. That way there can be no misunderstandings further down the line.

With the plans in place you should be able to relax and enjoy it as your scheme slowly comes together.

If you are having difficulties planning your room, see IDEA 2, *You've got the look*, for ideas on setting styles.

Try another idea...

'*Interior design is a travesty of the architectural process and a frightening condemnation of the credulity, helplessness and gullibility of the most formidable consumers – the rich.*'
STEPHEN BAYLEY, design critic

Defining idea...

'*Always design a thing by considering it in its next larger context – a chair in a room, a room in a house, a house in an environment, an environment in a city plan.*'
ELIEL SAARINEN, architect and designer

Defining idea...

233

How did it go?

Q **I've made a list and created a rough plan of the timing but I am struggling to co-ordinate all the different aspects of the job. How do I go about it?**

A *It can seem like a monumental juggling act but I would suggest that you take each element and give it a priority so that the larger jobs are completed first and any small finishing touches dealt with at the end. Don't underestimate the importance of this part of the job. It may drive you to distraction but it is the most valuable thing that you can do.*

Q **What do I do if the decorators fall behind schedule?**

A *Unfortunately this can have a knock-on effect so it may be worth you warning people further down the line in advance of any delay. If this is going to cause too many more problems with your original plans, then consider revising the schedule of works involved.*

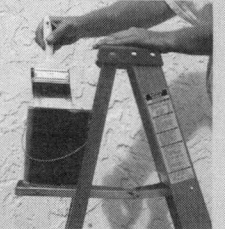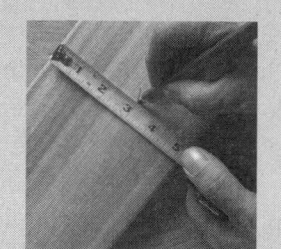

The end...

Or is it a new beginning? We hope that this book has inspired you to redecorate a room, change the layout of a space or clear the clutter from your home to make it a relaxing and enjoyable place to live. When visitors walk through the door, we hope you knock them sideways with your inspirational use of colour and clever design tricks in every room. Let us know if that's the case. We'd like to be amazed and impressed in just the same way as your houseguests.

So why not let us know about it? Tell us how you got on. What did it for you – what helped you create your ideal living space? Maybe you've got some tips of your own you want to share (see next page). If you liked this book you may find we have more brilliant ideas that could help change your life for the better.

If there is another aspect of your life that you want to work on, whether it relates to your fluctuating finances, your desire to lose weight and get fit, or even how you relate to your kids, you'll find lots more informative guides online at www.infideas.com

You can contact us via this website, or if you prefer to write then send your letters to: *Create Your Dream Home,* The Infinite Ideas Company Ltd, Belsyre Court, 57 Woodstock Road, Oxford OX2 6JH, United Kingdom.

We want to know what you think, because we're all working on making our lives better too. Give us your feedback and you could win a copy of another *52 Brilliant Ideas* book of your choice. Or maybe get a crack at writing your own.

Good luck. Be brilliant.

Offer one

CASH IN YOUR IDEAS

We hope you enjoy this book. We hope it inspires, amuses, educates and entertains you. But we don't assume that you're a novice, or that this is the first book that you've bought on the subject. You've got ideas of your own. Maybe our author has missed an idea that you use successfully. If so, why not send it to info@infideas.com, and if we like it we'll post it on our bulletin board. Better still, if your idea makes it into print we'll send you £50 and you'll be fully credited so that everyone knows you've had another Brilliant Idea.

Offer two

HOW COULD YOU REFUSE?

Amazing discounts on bulk quantities of Infinite Ideas books are available to corporations, professional associations and other organizations.

For details call us on:
+44 (0)1865 292045
fax: +44 (0)1865 292001
or e-mail: info@infideas.com

Where it's at...

Create your
dream
garden

brilliantideas

one good idea can change your life...

Create your dream garden

Tips and techniques to make
your garden bloom

Jem Cook, Mark Hillsdon
& Anna Marsden

Copyright © The Infinite Ideas Company Limited, 2008

The right of Jem Cook, Mark Hillsdon, Anna Marsden and Lizzie O'Prey to be identified as the authors of this book has been asserted in accordance with the Copyright, Designs and Patents Act 1988

First published in 2008 by
The Infinite Ideas Company Limited
36 St Giles
Oxford OX1 3LD
United Kingdom
T: 01865 514 888
E: info@infideas.com
W: www.infideas.com

A CIP catalogue record for this book is available from the British Library.

ISBN 978-1-905940-33-2

Previously published as *Create your dream garden* (978-1-904902-24-9) and *Create your dream home* (978-1-904902-03-4).

Brand and product names are trademarks or registered trademarks of their respective owners.

Text designed and typeset by Baseline Arts Ltd, Oxford
Cover designed by Cylinder
Printed and bound in India

Brilliant ideas

Brilliant features

Each chapter of this book is designed to provide you with an inspirational idea that you can read quickly and put into practice straight away.

Throughout you'll find four features that will help you to get right to the heart of the idea:

■ *Here's an idea for you …* Take it on board and give it a go – right here, right now. Get an idea of how well you're doing so far.

■ *Try another idea …* If this idea looks like a life-changer then there's no time to lose. *Try another idea …* will point you straight to a related tip to enhance and expand on the first.

■ *Defining ideas* Words of wisdom from masters and mistresses of the art, plus some interesting hangers-on.

■ *How did it go?* If at first you do succeed try to hide your amazement. If, on the other hand, you don't, then this is where you'll find a Q and A that highlights common problems and how to get over them.

Introduction

OK, so you know one end of a spade from another, vaguely remember something your Grandma told you about deadheading roses, and love the idea of a pond in your garden, just like the one you saw on the telly.

Your garden intrigues you, yet scares you at the same time. You love the idea of growing your own vegetables but worry about using chemicals to keep the pests off. And as much as you love them, why exactly do some clematis insist on having their roots in the shade?

Starting any new hobby – and let's face it, to most of us that's exactly what gardening is – can be a steep learning curve. And as you gaze out of the back door and realise you can only confidently name half a dozen of the plants growing away in your borders, it can be a struggle to know where to start.

Take heart. You just need to follow a few simple rules, keep an open mind about learning new things and, most importantly, be realistic about what you can achieve in the spare time you have. Plants do grow, and often with the minimum of fuss and effort if you get a few basics right.

It used to be that gardening was something you took up in retirement, muddling through with a few evergreens until you hit sixty, when an overwhelming urge to grow everything in shades of pink takes over. Not so today, as the boom of interest in growing things and 'living' in the garden has spawned a new generation of gardeners keen to replicate what they see on the telly.

The joy of gardening is not just the huge array of plants you can propagate, pamper and prune, but that there are so many different levels at which to do it. It could be as simple as scattering a few seeds or planting up a window box, or as complex as planning an orchard or growing something exotic.

Gardening can also be a microcosm of life, full of successes and failures, packed with highs and lows. It can also be a chance to get fit, develop your creative skills and get closer to wildlife.

Throughout the book there is an unapologetic bias towards organic gardening. We believe it's the best way to tend your plot, working with nature rather than against her, encouraging nature to keep the balance, not chemicals. But you'll be glad to know we don't just pontificate and leave things there. From dealing with common diseases to creating your own compost, this book is a checklist for how to garden organically.

It's also big on getting the basics rights. Do that, and the rest will follow. Good soil, regular watering, plants in the right place, the correct way to prune – it may sound a bit daunting, but it really does become clear with practice. And if you do get it wrong, you'll know what not to do next time.

Some of the chapters will give just a taste of what can be achieved, whetting your appetite for finding out more. Others are our take on old favourites like pergolas, plums and pansies. Oh, and there's also a bit about gnomes too.

As well as fruit and veg there are ideas about how to get the best from some of our most popular flowers and shrubs, and how to achieve that horticultural nirvana, year-round interest.

Every gardener needs a project, and we've come up with a few ideas that should keep you busy, from building structures with local, recycled materials, to digging a pond and choosing a greenhouse.

But ultimately, everything links back to your soil. Improve the soil and you'll improve the chances of your plants reaching their true potential.

What you won't find in this book is a crash course in garden design, a quick fix to the perfect garden makeover. Of course not everyone can spend as long in the garden as they would like. We all have other demands on our time. The answer is to accept that a garden is an evolving thing and that, although there are certain times when it's best to do specific tasks, it's largely forgiving and there's always next year.

Next time you pull on your gardening gloves and reach for your secateurs, remember the words of that gardening doyenne Gertrude Jekyll: 'There is not a spot of ground, however arid, bare or ugly, that cannot be tamed.' Just make sure you tame it organically.

Jem Cook, Mark Hillsdon and Anna Marsden

1

Did the earth move?

Not knowing what sort of soil you have in your garden is like guessing between sugar and salt in the kitchen – a recipe for disaster.

Hands up who knows what pH stands for? No, we didn't have a clue either but apparently it's vital to how your garden grows.

The old saying *'the answer lies in the soil'* is invariably true. Get to know your soil and you can add the right stuff to improve it, and grow the types of plants that will enjoy it. Hardly anyone gardens on rich, light loam but each soil type still has its own distinct merits.

THE ACID TEST

To find the pH (read on, dear reader, read on) of your soil you need a soil-testing kit, available at any garden centre. This will help you find out what kind of soil you're gardening on. And with this small yet vital snippet of information, you'll know how to feed your soil and what plants you can grow.

It pays to take three or four samples from the outer edges of the garden as you may have more than one soil type, each favouring different plants and treatments. The test will show whether your samples are acidic (below 7), neutral (7) or alkaline (above 7).

Raised beds may be a solution if you have particularly difficult soil and want to grow a range of vegetables and herbs. Build them approx 1.5m square so they can be worked from the sides without standing on the soil. Edge the beds, to a height of 30cm or more, to keep the soil in place. Use old railway sleepers, woven hazel, reclaimed bricks, galvanised steel, whatever takes your fancy. Fork over the soil to improve the drainage and then dig in as much compost as possible, adding a fresh layer of compost each time you replant.

Most garden plants favour soil that is slightly acidic at 6.5, but there's still a good selection of plants for neutral and alkaline soils.

With your pH sorted, discovering your soil type is even easier. Just pick some up. If it's tightly packed, squeezes into a sticky ball and hangs about on your boots – it's clay. If it feels gritty, and water runs through it easily – it's sandy. If you discover the white cliffs of Dover under the surface – it's chalk.

Clay soil is hard to work. It's wet and cloggy in winter and bakes rock hard in a dry spell. But it is full of good things and the nutrients your plants need to grow, so don't despair. You do need to improve its drainage though, so mix in some horticultural grit or coarse sand when planting. Clay soil is usually neutral to acidic too so add lime – ground down calcium – especially if you're growing brassicas. Turn unplanted ground over in the autumn and leave the frost to break up the big lumps.

Dig in or spread as much compost as you can, whenever the conditions suit. Timing is crucial but it's the soil and the weather that set the time, not you! As soon as it's dry enough to stand on without it turning into a mud bath, get to work.

'Soil is rather like a lucky dip – you only get out of it what you put in!'
Traditional saying

Success on sand will depend on how you can help the soil hang on to food and moisture.

Adding in compost will help retain water and fertiliser long enough for it to do some good. But this will need to become a regular chore so you may wish to just focus on parts of the garden where you are growing hungry, thirsty plants such as the veg.

Compost, compost, compost! Having mentioned it so many times you'd better turn to IDEA 7, *Sweet smelling brown stuff*.

Try another idea...

Because any fertiliser will pass through the soil quickly, spread it a little and often. Sandy soil can be acidic and will benefit from a light application of lime (250g per square metre – half that for clay soils). A bonus is that the soil is easy to work on and quick to warm up in spring, so grow early crops that will mature before things get too dry.

Chalky soil can be stony, or sticky and thin, but it's well-drained and you can work on it most of the year. Bulk it up by adding organic matter. Horse manure, which tends to be full of straw, is good for sticky chalk. As it breaks down relatively quickly, spread it on the surface and leave the earthworms to do their bit. Dig in any left-over straw in the spring.

Remember, chalky soil is alkaline and certain plants won't like it a bit. You can give plants a helping hand at the start of the growing season by sprinkling in bonemeal or blood, fish and bone, to compensate for the lack of phosphate and to help roots develop.

'The health of the soil, plant, animal and man is one and indivisible'
LADY EVE BALFOUR, founder of the Organic Soil Association

Defining idea...

Just to recap, most plants like clay soils, drought tolerant plants are for sandy soils and plant lime-lovers on chalk. This means that azaleas, camellias, rhododendrons and heathers

(except the winter flowering *Erica carnea*) will not grow on chalk but plenty of other plants, and most herbs, love it.

Oh and pH, that'll be potential hydrogen. Nope, I'm none the clearer either.

How did it go?

Q   Can I dig out some of my chalky soil and replace it with more acidic compost to grow some camellias?

A   *You can, but acid loving shrubs (camellias, rhododendrons and azaleas) might look odd amongst a garden of chalk loving plants. It would be better to plant your camellia as a freestanding specimen in a pot, where it can be admired in all its splendour without looking out of place. And enjoy azaleas by visiting gardens where they flourish.*

Q   My beautiful blue hydrangea has turned pink. Is this because of my soil?

A   *Blue hydrangeas are a sure sign of acid soil. If your soil is neutral a regular iron tonic should help recover its blue rinse. Some suggest burying nails around the plant but modern nails often aren't rusty enough!*

Q   Any suggestions for dry, sandy beds?

A   *Plants that cope well in dry conditions often have narrow or furry silver/grey leaves. Succulents and many grasses do well.* Try Artemisia, Verbascum, Cistus, *lavender,* Eryngium, Senecio cineraria *and wisteria.*

2

Top seed

Every seed is a gardening miracle, a small, dried-out husk that a few months after planting bursts into flower and brings new life to the garden.

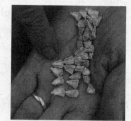

At least this is what it seems like when they actually sprout. But of course, as with everything in the garden, there's a flip side, and the euphoria of a growing seedling is easily dampened by the sight of a tiny shrivelled stem, or bare patch of earth that once promised so much.

Whether you've harvested your own or bought a packet, sowing them indoors can certainly give them a head start, as you've much more control, not just over the temperature but also over the pests that will chew off a shoot quicker than you can say slug pellets.

The first rule of successful sowing is to read the packet! It should tell you all you need to know. For instance, do your seeds need soaking before you plant them? This can soften the outer husks or remove chemicals that prevent them from

Here's an idea for you...

Growing from seed is an excellent way of raising unusual plants that you can't always buy in a mature state. You can also select your own colour combinations rather than put up with those more commonly available.

germinating. Are they suitable for sowing in trays or pots, or should you sow them directly into the ground?

Cleanliness is, of course, next to godliness, and while scrubbing out seed trays with hot soapy water is akin to rubbing down paintwork before you open your tin of gloss, it's still a crucial if somewhat laborious task.

Defining idea...

'One of the healthiest ways to gamble is with a spade and a package of garden seeds.'
DAN BENNETT

While the professionals use all kinds of weird and wonderful 'growing' mediums such as rock-wool, a good-quality seed compost is probably best for the amateur. Try to get one that contains sterilised loam and a peat substitute, which will be finer and more moisture retentive than either a general-purpose compost or home-grown humus, which will be too rich for the seeds.

Making sure the compost is firmed down is also important. This helps to avoid any subterranean air pockets which, just as it looks like the seedlings are taking hold, can cause sudden subsidence with the whole lot suddenly disappearing down a gaping chasm.

Defining idea...

'Seedsmen reckon that their stock in trade is not seeds at all ... it's optimism.'
GEOFF HAMILTON

Bear in mind too that some seeds such as Canterbury Bells (*Campanula medium*) need light to germinate so sow them on the surface.

As a rule of thumb, the larger the seed the easier it is to grow. Big buggers like lupins and sweet peas are best sown individually in pots, which means they can develop a good strong root system before you disturb them and plant them out. Or better still in this environmentally conscious age, why not use a biodegradable pot. Used for larger seeds, you can miss out the pricking out stage and just plant the whole thing, pot 'n all, into the ground.

If the thriftiness of getting something for nothing appeals, then check out IDEA 4, *Don't pay the nurseryman* for more tips on stocking your garden for free.

Try another idea...

Unless you particularly enjoy surprises you need to be disciplined when it comes to labelling, and as soon as you've finished one pot or tray, get it labelled or you'll spend the next few weeks wondering ...

'A good gardener always plants three seeds – one for the bugs, one for the weather and one for himself.'
LEO AIKMAN

Defining idea...

If you have a greenhouse, or a heated propagator, then lucky you. For the rest of us it's time to reclaim those window sills with homemade propagators using clear plastic bags, sticks and a seed tray.

If you have a propagator remember to use square pots simply because round ones waste valuable space.

'Think of the fierce energy concentrated in an acorn! You bury it in the ground, and it explodes into an oak! Bury a sheep, and nothing happens but decay.'
GEORGE BERNARD SHAW

Defining idea...

As they develop, your seeds will need differing levels of light, warmth, air and moisture and, once that shoot appears, nutrients as well. Read up on what you have to do so that you aren't caught on the hop.

7

As a general rule, the trick is to make sure the compost is damp but not waterlogged; the atmosphere is humid but not dripping. A watering can with a fine rose will help and you can improve the overall drainage by part filling the bottom of the pots with gravel.

Next you need to prick them out by gently prising out each seedling by its leaves (not the stalk) using a dibber, and move it on to a pot of its own, before growing them on, hardening them off, and planting them out. Then you can enjoy them. Nobody said it was going to be easy!

How did it go?

Q My seedlings have just shrivelled and died. Why?

A *Sounds like damping off, which is caused by a fungi that thrives in moist, warm conditions. It can be caused by too many seedlings too close together, and too much water, which makes them rot on the surface.*

Q How do I know if the seeds I've collected are viable?

A *The best way to test them is to put them in a jar of water. Those that are dead float, those that are viable sink.*

Q Success! My seedlings have germinated but now they won't stop growing and are starting to flop over. How come?

A *While you should always keep seedlings in a light, airy place, this can cause them to get leggy. With a bit of luck though, if you plant them deeply enough when you prick them out, so that a good portion of the stem is under the surface, they should pull though.*

3

Doing yer nut

A nut tree in your garden? You must admit it's an enticing proposition, but how do you go about wetting your walnuts and harvesting your hazels, without providing a free feast for Squirrel Nutkin and his chums?

The British Isles is not exactly famed for its nuts. For decades the hazelnut, which has nuts that stay fresh for several months, was a mainstay of the Navy, and its close relative the cobnut was once a popular crop down in Kent. But many of the great walnuts that once graced our parks and gardens were plundered during the Napoleonic Wars, when walnut became the musket makers' wood of choice.

Other factors such as their size, slow growth rate and the fact they are fussy pollinators have also seen the nut tree decline as a garden tree, but new varieties and growing methods could see their stock rise again.

Here's a project that should keep you interested for years to come! To grow sweet chestnuts, collect plump, ripe healthy-looking nuts in autumn. Remove the spiky casings and then float them in water. Only the nuts that sink are viable, so pot them up immediately but give them some protection from both frost and the squirrels.

NUT CASE

Traditionally grown in an orchard or 'plat' the cobnut is probably the easiest nut tree to grow. It's also frost tolerant to a degree, although it won't withstand a heavy hoar. Multi-stemmed and smaller than the walnut, the best yielding trees are pruned back to around 1.8m (6ft) between winter and spring.

Crucially cobnuts must be planted in pairs to encourage cross pollination. If you live in the countryside with indigenous hazel nearby, that should be enough to do the job, otherwise you will need to plant two different varieties. Recommended cultivars include the Kentish Cob and Gunselbert, and nurseries will be able to tell you if a variety needs a specific pollinator (some varieties, such as the Kentish Cob, are biennial).

The trees prefer sun or light shade, with their roots in a poor to moderately fertile soil. And while feeding isn't needed, certain varieties do relish a good hard pruning. The cobnut is also a favourite with wildlife and may entice nuthatches and even dormice to your garden.

VENEER OF RESPECTABILITY

Not for the walnut any minimalist chic or waif-like posturing; the walnut is a real tree. Handsome, noble, majestic, these are the words that describe this tree, with a stout and sturdy trunk which supports a broad spreading crown of mid-green leaves, festooned with catkins in the spring and rich in nuts during the autumn.

As a seedling, a walnut can take up to 15 years to fruit, but grafted to root stock, will usually crop in three. Getting them through the first few years is the tricky bit. The key is to plant them in deep, fertile soil, in a sheltered place with as much sun as possible. They also love nitrogen so no skimping on the manure.

Unlike cobnuts, some varieties of walnut are self fertile, including both Broadview and Buccaneer, while others need a partner to ensure cross pollination.

As for yield, the new cultivars are better croppers than traditional varieties, and from the last week of August you can get picking.

BITTER SWEET

For the ambitious, an altogether trickier proposition is growing a sweet almond, which can grow up to about 6.7m (22ft), with delicate pink or white flowers that bloom in early spring appearing before the long serrated leaves. The trees can be trained up a wall or left to become thick and bushy, and cross pollination is essential.

IDEA 43, *Small trees for small gardens* goes into more detail about how to choose and plant trees. And for other fruiting trees, IDEA 17, *Oranges are not the only fruit* tickles the taste buds with some pointers about apple and pear trees.

Try another idea...

'I got to wondering where they [the squirrels] are putting most of the [wal]nuts. It would obviously be close to the trees they collect from and in softer soil rather then harder. So I started building up leaves and mulches underneath the trees, making it softer and deeper.

'Now I happily let the squirrels bury the nuts. I come along and rake vigorously and deeply, working outwards from the base of each tree and soon unearth enough for me.'
BOB FLOWERDEW

Defining idea...

Originally from the Mediterranean, frost and almonds don't mix, but they can be grown in a conservatory. Outside, the best spot is a sunny, south-facing wall, with well-drained and loamy soil. Containerising any stone fruits isn't easy, and watering is crucial. Cultivars such as Ferradual come grafted to root stock, and will crop in four to five years.

As well as delicious fruit, the other great boon of nut trees is that with the exception of a touch of peach leaf curl on almonds, they are largely disease resistant.

How did it go?

Q   I'm at my wits end with squirrels! What can I do?

A   *Public enemy number one with nut growers is the grey squirrel. Their introduction into Britain at the end of the 1800s had a devastating effect on nut harvests, and even a lone squirrel can strip a hazel quicker than you can say cross pollination. Short of trapping or shooting, one way of protecting cobnuts is to hard prune so you can actually house them in a steel fruit cage. Alternatively, certain brands of animal deterrents keep the critters at bay. For walnuts beat the squirrels by picking the nuts before they are ripe and then pickle them.*

Q   I've heard that the walnut sap is toxic. Is that correct?

A   *True, it acts as a natural weedkiller, so it's worth remembering that few plants are hardy enough to grow underneath a walnut tree. And instead of composting any leaves and clippings, burn them first and then add the nutrient-rich ash to the compost heap.*

Don't pay the nurseryman

From dividing to layering, taking cuttings to swapping with friends – here's how to stock your garden for free.

It's extraordinary how many ways there are to make your own plants. Some methods are simple, others involve a little technical know-how and a bit of practice. But let's face it, we all like getting something for free, so clear some space in the greenhouse and get to grips with the art of propagation.

LONG DIVISION

Forget the calculator, this division involves a little bit of persuasion, and a pair of garden forks. Perennials can be teased apart to form three or more smaller plants.

Simply dig up dense clumps of border plants and insert two forks, back to back, into the middle of the clump. Lever the forks back and forth and the plant should give way and separate. The oldest, middle bit is best thrown away, as it's the younger,

There are several ways to increase your chances of success with your cuttings:

- **When taking a cutting put it into a plastic bag until ready to use.**
- **Try dipping semi-ripe or hardwood cuttings into rooting powder to get them started – tap off excess and don't return used powder to the pot.**
- **Place cuttings around the edge of the pot – this seems to work best although there is no scientific evidence!**
- **Label all cuttings.**
- **Always add grit or sharp sand to the compost to ensure it drains well.**

more vigorous outer growth that will yield new plants. Make sure you plant them straight away.

Clumps of hostas, more than a few years old, can be sliced through with a sharp spade.

CUTTINGS

Having conquered division we're onto multiplication. Cuttings can be taken from soft, semi-ripe or hard wood, as well as from the roots and leaves, all at different times of the year. Different plants respond to different methods so a bit of reading up is required but here are some general rules:

- Soft wood cuttings (taken from the top of the stem) work for perennials and most shrubs, and should be taken in spring. The cutting needs to be up to 7cm long. Cut just below a leaf node (the bit where the leaves form) and remove the lower leaves. Root these cuttings first in a jar of water and move to small pots of compost once the roots have formed.

- Semi-ripe cuttings (using wood that is soft at the top and firmer at the base) for trees shrubs and roses, should be taken in mid-to-late summer. Ease a shoot, about 12cm long, from the plant so that a 'heel' of the parent plant remains attached. Leave the top foliage on and put the bare part into the compost. Place several cuttings into one pot, moving each onto individual pots once a good root has formed.

- Hard wood (strong, hard stems from the current year's growth, with soft top removed) for shrubs and some fruits, taken between mid-autumn and early winter. Take pencil-thick cuttings, trim to 20cm long, making a straight cut at the bottom, just below a leaf node, and a slanted cut at the top, above a leaf node. Place cuttings in an outside trench or potted in a cold frame and leave for up to a year.

- Root cuttings, taken from the roots of trees shrubs or herbaceous plants, should be taken when the plant is dormant in the autumn. Unearth some of the root and remove a piece about the width of a pencil and as long as possible. Cut this into pieces of at least 5cm. To ensure you plant them the right way up, cut the end that was severed from the plant straight, the other end at an angle. Place them in a pot with the straight end showing just above the surface, cover with 1cm of sharp sand and leave out until the spring

- Leaf cuttings, from healthy fully developed leaves, work especially well with begonias and African violets. Either carefully remove

IDEA 2, *Top Seed* **looks at ways to ensure your seeds do exactly what they should.**

Try another idea...

'If you take cuttings of tender plants before spring arrives, it will make all the difference to the summer show. Pot them on frequently and not only will they produce big buxom plants but there will also be time to take further cuttings to swell the ranks in the same year.'
CAROL KLEIN

Defining idea...

the whole leaf, complete with stalk, and inset into a shallow hole in a pot of compost, or nick the underside veins of a leaf and lay it topside up on the compost surface. Cut sword-like leaves into sections of 5cm long and insert each upright into the compost. Once plantlets develop pot them on.

Layering sometimes takes place naturally, when a branch from a shrub or climber roots in the soil while it's still attached to the plant.

You can give nature a helping hand by selecting a flexible stem, bending it to the ground, nicking the underside and pegging it in place with a staple (bent wire or wooden peg). Cover with soil. Once a good root has formed, sever the stem from the parent plant and pot it up.

Budding and grafting is challenging stuff. Ask an expert to show you how or enrol on a short Royal Horticultural Society (RHS) or adult education course.

While it's only natural to try and save money and do it yourself, we should of course remember that good nurseries are needed to supply fine plants in the first place, so it's well worth supporting them where you can.

Q **I got lucky with my cuttings and now have too many to cope with. Lobbing them on the compost heap seems so brutal! What's the alternative?**

How did it go?

A *Why not share your success with your friends and neighbours, offering them the spare plants? If you have friends who also propagate their own plants, get together and decide who's growing what, so there is no duplication or waste. Sometimes whole communities get organised and hold 'Plant Swap Days'.*

Q **When my mother-in-law saw my withered seedlings she said I obviously hadn't heard of hardening off. I hadn't ... Should I have?**

A *Once a plant – either grown from seed or a cutting – has plenty of roots and shoots, and is ready for planting out, it will need to gradually get used to the outside temperature, especially at night. This is known as hardening off and can be achieved by placing the pot in a cold frame, leaving the lid open at night after the first few days. If you don't have a cold frame, place the pots in a sheltered spot against the house and bring them in at night if a frost threatens.*

17

Indian summer

Why let your borders flop at the end of July when with a bit of TLC and a sharp pair of secateurs you could be enjoying a second show of colour?

It stands to reason that you want to get as colourful and as long-lasting a display as possible from your flowers, especially given the effort that's gone into getting them to bloom in the first place.

Clipping plants back after flowering can seem drastic but in a week or two fresh leaves will provide the perfect foil for other plants yet to perform.

CRUEL TO BE KIND

The lungwort (*Pulmonaria*) is one of those harbingers of spring that gives you faith in the new season to come. Its blue and pink flowers (there are varieties that have just blue or white flowers too) are a welcome supply of nectar for early bees, but when they've done their bit be ruthless, and cut them off, together with most of the leaves. Water well and feed with a handful of bonemeal, and fresh dappled leaves with their 'spilt milk' markings) will soon appear.

Here's an idea for you...

Once they've flowered, shrubs and climbing roses could do with a bit of a lift. Plant the freely wandering, late flowering Clematis tangutica or some colourful climbing nasturtiums to ramble through and brighten things up.

You can be equally brutal with poppies (*Papaver orientale*) and also Lady's mantle (*Alchemilla molis*), once its lime green flowers show the first sign of browning (this will also prevent self-seeding, which this plant is particularly keen on). Hold back with the secateurs, and the leaves of these early performers will fade, rust and crumple by midsummer.

Plants that start flowering in the early summer can also benefit from a haircut to encourage a second flush of colour. Cat mint (*Nepeta*) and the pink flowering geranium (*endressii*) are two useful front-of-the-border fillers that respond well to this treatment. And if you cut them back just half at a time, you keep a succession of flowers and prevent the pudding-basin haircut appearance.

If you cut centaurea, delphiniums, anthemis and salvias back to ground level after flowering they may surprise you with a second flush too.

REGULAR SERVICING

Midsummer is the time when you can really get to know and enjoy your plants, learning things about them that you can put into practice next year. There are often no big or laborious jobs that need doing – this is the time to potter. A bit of deadheading, a touch of cutting back and your border will keep its shape for weeks to come.

Deadhead once a week if possible – unless you want seeds for next year. Cutting off the spent flowers helps the plant put its energy into flowering again, instead of producing unwanted seeds.

When plants begin to look sad and need cutting right back, gaps may start to appear which can spoil the overall effect. While neighbouring plants may spread into the space, you can also strategically place the odd pot or container, submerging them out of sight. Alternatively, use some late flowering annuals, such as cosmos or lavatera. And, if you're organised, now's the time to send in the reinforcements, those spare plants grown from seed that you couldn't squeeze in early in the year but can now get in amongst them and play their part.

The real key to prolonging the border's display is succession planting. With a bit of thought and a season or two's experience, you'll soon become a dab hand. Try to think ahead. Group your plants together so that they not only complement each other in colour, height and leaf shape but also in flowering season. This simply means including some later flowering perennials close to your early performers.

Especially useful from midsummer until the first frosts are the Michaelmas daisy (*Aster*) and other daisy flowers (*Rudbeckia, Helenium, Echinacea*), the thistle-like *Eryngium* and *Echinops*, Japanese anemone and dahlias. Intersperse these next to plants that are in bloom in spring and you'll have a blooming border right through to late autumn.

Staking your plants well but discreetly is important to maintain the shape of your border. IDEA 10, *Support network* will take you through this.

Try another idea...

Defining idea...

'*Around mid-July, another change starts to come over the garden as the early cast of summer shrubs and perennials dies away... Presenting this next wave of shrubs and perennials well means maintaining some sense of order and design amid the burgeoning growth. Serious sessions with shears and strimmers are de rigueur, and work wonders. I am like a gunfighter with my left-handed secateurs, whipping them out of their holster at the slightest provocation.*'
STEPHEN LACEY, in *Real Gardening*

21

How did it go?

Q **My dahlias look fantastic from midsummer onwards but looking after them sounds such a pain. Is it as bad as it sounds?**

A *True there is more to dahlias than just cutting them back, unless you live in a very mild area, where you could try leaving them in place, cutting them down, and covering them with protective mulch. Otherwise you need to lift and store the tubers. The key to it is keeping them dry and protected from frost.*

Dig up the dahlias once the foliage has been blackened by the first frost, leaving on about 10–15cm of stalk. Gently remove as much soil as possible and put them in the garage or greenhouse to dry off. Once completely dry remove any remaining soil and find a frost-free place to store them until spring. You can put them in shredded paper to ensure they keep dry. In early spring replace the paper with compost to encourage them to start growing. Once healthy shoots and the first leaves appear, and there is no further threat of frost, plant them back in the border, putting plenty of compost in the planting hole.

Q **I've tried deadheading but get confused between newly opening buds and shrivelling flowers. How can I tell the difference?**

A *I know what you mean. It's not always easy to tell and petunias are particularly tricky. As a general rule if you can see a seed head forming in the centre of the flower it is time to snip it off. You'll soon get the hang of this, noticing too, the position on the stem of old flowers as opposed to the new ones. Persevere as the rewards are great – longer and fuller flowering.*

Design without the despair

You don't need a degree in landscape architecture to give shape to your garden – just a bit of inspiration and a rudimentary knowledge of elbow grease.

Starting from scratch is both daunting and exciting. You're about to invest a lot of time, and quite a few quid, into turning your weed-strewn plot into something with a little more structure, style and sophistication. So from the start it pays to have some vision or picture of how things are going to look when you're finished.

You need to get a feel for the site, thinking about what could go where and then working out whether it really should. Where are the garden's sunny spots? Where's the shade? Does anywhere tend to get waterlogged?

But at the same time don't get bogged down in detail because there's a lot to be said for seat-of-the-pants design. In other words go out and make a start. Keep standing back – even viewing from an upstairs window – and you'll soon get a feel

Here's an idea for you... **Take your inspiration from other gardens, whether big or small. And you don't necessarily have to visit Sissinghurst to glean ideas. Many villages organise garden strolls – not to mention the National Garden Scheme, which lists gardens open for charity in its famous *Yellow Book*.**

for shape and proportion. The best advice at this stage of the proceedings is to leave the tape measure in the tool box.

SETTING YOUR SITES

The first essential is to establish which direction your garden faces. On a suitable day follow the path of the sun across your garden noting the variations in light and shade, because while you may be basking in the reflected glory of a south-facing plot, it could sit under the canopy of the neighbour's spreading chestnut tree for most of the day.

Apropos neighbours, it pays to learn a little of their own gardening ambitions too. Is their newly planted leylandii to remain at a clipped 4 feet or allowed a free rein? And would neighbours on the other side mind if your clematis peeps over the top of their lapped larch fence?

Now, we all like our privacy but it's easy to become a bit obsessive about screening our gardens from the rest of the world. This is the difference between the British and Dutch gardening philosophies. We hide behind walls, fences and the densest hedges known to man, while the Dutch open their gardens for everybody to view as they pass by.

OK, now the fun really starts. Armed with small stakes or pegs mark out certain areas, such as the herbaceous border, rose bed and vegetable patch. A hosepipe is a great help in doing this. Being both light and flexible it will give you an immediate outline on which you can pass judgment.

At this stage, don't even think about any permanent structures like brick walls – their role and positioning will become more obvious as the rest of the garden takes shape. Shifting a few barrow loads of misplaced soil is one thing – reconstructing a wall or concrete path is another.

If you don't have the space for a pergola, IDEA 10, *Support network* explains how hazel rods can be used to create temporary support structures for a variety of plants.

Try another idea...

OFF THE STRAIGHT AND NARROW

Unless you have a plot the size of Versailles, try and upset the symmetry of your garden, or at best confine any rigid formality and straight lines to the vegetable plot.

If you want a water feature, fine, but remember it doesn't have to be a lake if you only have a few square feet to play with. You could always confine yourself to a mini fountain or birdbath while the children are young and unaware of the potential dangers of a pond.

No matter how small your garden, you can still make use of existing rises and falls too, or create new and different levels. They help give the impression of more space and give you the opportunity to make a new patio or seating area.

'I uphold Beatrix Farrand's sentiment (Gertrude Jeykell's too) that the design should always fit the site; the site should not be bent to the design.'
ROSEMARY VEREY

Defining idea...

25

The idea should be to create mystery! Try not to open everything up at once. Add fences, a winding path, a trellis or pergola smothered in climbers, which will tempt visitors to find out what's going on behind.

And treat permanent buildings as assets too. Cover garage walls with a cotoneaster; grow a wisteria on a south facing house wall; take advantage of a porch with a climbing rose. Even log stores or coalbunkers can look aesthetically pleasing given the right treatment. Cover up manholes or drain covers with a pot.

How did it go?

Q **You say throw the tape measure away but I have access to computer technology. Can this help me design a garden?**

A *Certainly. Computer buffs score well here as you can create a three-dimensional picture. However, I'd only use it as a very basic guide as Mother Nature can play nasty and deceitful tricks even on the most sophisticated electronic plans.*

Q **My original concept was to make as natural-looking a garden as possible. I have few straight lines and no symmetry yet it still looks too organised and slightly twee. Where am I going wrong?**

A *Your gardening philosophy sounds perfect and I'm sure the effect will come as your garden matures. Let plants intermingle and drip and flow over the edges of paths. You know how French women, having spent hours in front of the mirror, achieve that look of studied dishevelment. Adopt that concept in your garden by having a plan without being too exact.*

7

Sweet smelling brown stuff

A garden without a compost heap is like a car without an engine – it ain't going anywhere.

Although there may be a tendency to get a bit self-righteous about one's compost heap, you can't really consider yourself a true gardener until you've mastered the art of turning potato peelings into black gold.

Many of us have childhood memories of a mound of dark, sweet-smelling black stuff somewhere in the garden. It was a breeding ground for small red worms that were perfect for fishing. You may also remember a chemical-ridden, toxic heap of grass cuttings that oozed a black slime and smelt like a chemical works.
It's not hard to work out which one is more likely to make your roses grow.

HEAP OR HYPE?

First attempts at a compost heap can soon turn into a dumping ground for any garden waste (but never, ever dog waste). This system also means the heap might grow to a size more suited to a small National Trust property. So the first rule of composting is to know what goes on the heap and what goes on the fire.

Here's an idea for you... **Befriend your local greengrocer. They discard sackfuls of perfect composting material every day. If you're not already doing your ecologically friendly bit make a start here.**

For starters, perennial weeds and anything diseased should be burnt, while anything too woody, unless finely shredded, should be bagged up and taken to the local tip. And only add cooked foodstuffs if you want to attract a family of rats to your garden.

Now for the good bits. Kitchen waste is perfect and if you're serious about this (which you should be) set up a separate bin for your peelings and pods, and train the family to use it.

The autumn clear up, particularly of the herbaceous borders, will also give you plenty of raw material.

Defining idea... **'A fool looks for dung where the cow never browsed.'**
Ethiopian proverb

Grass cuttings are a permanent source of controversy. Use them by all means but layer them between other fibrous material, to avoid the black, nourishment-free slurry mentioned earlier.

Dead leaves can also be tricky if just dumped on a heap. But they are worth persevering with, so store them separately in punctured plastic bags or, better still, in chickenwire cages. They will compost, but in years rather than months.

The other perennial question is whether a compost heap should be wet or dry. The advice is neither. Yes, it needs to be covered with something like an old piece of carpet, as this helps build up the heat and accelerates decomposition. But it pays to leave it exposed occasionally to rain, as it shouldn't be allowed to dry out.

One friend also regularly adds his own urine, although whether he's on a mission to boost its nitrogen content, or just too lazy to go to the upstairs loo, is another question completely.

IDEA 8, *Tools of the trade* deals with self-mulching grass cutters.

Try another idea...

The ultimate prize is horse or cow manure, and you'll be surprised how easy it is to get hold of the stuff, even if you live in town, with it's riding schools and city farms. However, don't be tempted to spread fresh manure as this will scorch your plants. Leave it for at least six months, until it no longer resembles dung and is more like crumbly soil.

In an ideal world you need three bins. Leave a full bin for approximately three months before turning it into the next one. Then repeat the process and you should achieve the ultimate crumbly brown compost within six to nine months.

'Earth knows no desolation. She smells regeneration in the moist breath of decay.'
GEORGE MEREDITH (novelist)

Defining idea...

There are two schools of thought as to the best time to spread it, either late autumn or early spring. In spring the compost has had that bit longer to reach a state of readiness, and the ground is at its hungriest. But spreading in the late autumn is fine as well, as long as you don't cover frozen ground.

Compost can be used to regenerate poor soil, helps break up heavy, clay soil and enables light soil to hold on to water and nutrients. On chalky soil use it as a mulch, spreading it on the surface for the worms to carry down. With other soils, dig it in.

'Money is like manure – it's not worth anything unless you spread it around.'
UNKNOWN

Defining idea...

The compost bins themselves play a vital role but needn't cost the earth. To construct three bins that have an air of originality, take eight 10cm × 10cm posts, 1.5m tall and either plane a groove the length of the posts or nail strips of wood to form the grooves. Having set the posts in the ground, cut planks of wood to the required length and slot them in. The rougher the wood the better – offcuts from sawmills are great, especially those showing bark as this will help them blend with their surroundings, unlike the ubiquitous green plastic bins.

The timber's irregularities also allow air into the compost to encourage the decomposing process.

How did it go?

Q I've done it! I've made tons of fantastic compost and I've been spreading it everywhere. But I've got a lot left. What else can I do with it?

A *When putting in new plants or moving those that are already established, line any hole with your compost. The same applies to shrubs or young trees. Before you plant sweet peas or runner beans dig a trench two spits deep (a spit is a spade-depth of earth) and line the trench with layers of sodden newspaper, which helps prevent water loss. Cover generously with compost before returning the soil.*

Q The compost I made seems great but how come I've got more slugs than ever?

A *Immature compost is slug friendly. They thrive on it. Make sure the compost is well rotted before spreading.*

8

Tools of the trade

From the unusual to the indispensable, here's what you'll find in all the best garden sheds this year.

Your garden shed is the bulwark of the garden, the quartermaster's stores. But what you keep in it is worth some serious thought because if there's one aspect of gardening where you mustn't skimp, this is it.

The basics haven't changed much in the tool department for years, although modern refinements in design and materials have increased efficiency and made the gardener's job a little easier. Simplicity is still key, though, and the more complex the tool the greater the chance of it breaking down.

Before deciding on which brand of tool to purchase try out a few. Borrow from family and friends, or spend time handling them in the shop. Compare several and get a feel for their weight and balance. Imagine using the tool for half an hour or more. Only you will know what feels right in your hands. Check for quality of finish and the firmness of the handles.

Here's an idea for you... **Invest in an adjustable rake. In recent years there have been few non-mechanical tools that have come onto the market that have revolutionised any aspect of gardening – but this is a notable exception. A simple lever on the back of the rake head allows you to narrow or widen the gaps between the prongs. This makes it a real all-rounder, allowing easy raking between plants in the borders or prize specimens in the shrub bed, but also strong enough to scarify the lawn in autumn, as well as gather fallen leaves.**

ACE OF SPADES

First and foremost buy the best spade on the market. It should be made of stainless steel – it's rust free, easy to clean and will slide through even the stickiest soils.

Take care too over your second in command, the garden fork. Buy a cheap one and the tines will twist or the shaft split at the first sign of hard work. Here the choice of handle and how the stem is secured to the prongs are most important. Select the size you feel comfortable with, one that will suit the jobs you have in mind – a heavy-duty fork for digging and turning the compost heap or a smaller border fork for areas full of plants.

UNUSUAL SUSPECTS

But I'm reserving pride of place for three unlikely and certainly unheralded tools: the pickaxe, the builder's barrow and the sack truck, a trio which, on the face of it, would probably be more at home resurfacing the M4 than making life easier in the garden.

The pickaxe has many obvious uses such as lifting stones or breaking heavy, compacted soil. But what about getting under obstinate tree roots, moving shrubs and digging holes for fence posts? If you garden on stony chalk you will need one to dig your bean trench too!

There's one type of wheelbarrow worthy of special mention, which is based on the builder's barrow design. They have a strong but light frame with comfortably spaced handles, ample capacity in a galvanised steel bin, a pneumatic tyre and a tipping bar. Wooden barrows may win in the aesthetics stakes but can be heavy enough to lift even when empty. As for plastic versions, they're fine if your garden waste is confined to vegetation but no good for the rough stuff.

A sack truck is another must. Why risk your back heaving around bags of compost, heavy stones, pots and containers, when you can slide a sack truck underneath and wheel it along like a doll's pram? Its versatility will amaze you.

Another rarely mentioned tool is a besom. Traditionally used for removing worm casts from manicured lawns, it's hard to beat when it comes to general sweeping. Make it yourself if you have access to a bundle of birch twigs and a hazel rod for the handle.

A good pair of secateurs is vital. Buy the best, look after them and you'll be well rewarded. But only use them for the job for which they were intended – which is cutting stems no more that 1cm thick. Anything bigger, and you'll just blunt them. Be patient, and fetch a small pruning saw or loppers instead.

IDEA 19, *To prune or not to prune*, talks you through the tools needed for pruning.

Try another idea...

'**But remember there are no flowers without tools and no tools without a garage to keep them in.**'
From *The Accidental Gardener's Almanac* by MICHAEL POWELL

Defining idea...

MAN AND MACHINES

If you are gardening acres of land, then machine tools have to be a priority. However, in most gardens they're an indulgent luxury and a one-off trip to the tool hire shop is more sensible.

But where needs must, invest in one top-of-the-range item that will last and actually get used – more about that in a moment.

Garden machinery tends to begrudge being disturbed, but in early spring it's time to drag your mowers and your strimmers coughing and spluttering out into the open.

As for that one serious investment, if you have large areas of grass, then the latest ride-on self-mulching mowers are heaven sent. Under normal mowing conditions – that's regularly mown, dry grass – there really is no sign of grass cuttings left lying around at all and, contrary to expectation, it produces less thatch than more conventional mowing methods. And because of the constant fine mulching, which acts as a feed, your grass will stay greener for longer.

A strimmer – petrol driven, electric or battery operated – will complement the magical mulcher above, getting into all those nooks and crannies. The battery model is the quietest and you can strim away happily for at least half an hour before recharging.

Clean your tools regularly but, come the end of the autumn, clean, oil and – where appropriate – sharpen them, because as all responsible gardeners know, garden tools are for life, not just for Christmas.

Q   What hand tools do I need to go with my fork and spade?

How did it go?

A   *Simply a hand fork, trowel and some shears. In practice you may need more than one trowel as they do seem to like hiding amongst the plants! When choosing shears make sure they have good buffers between the handles – less jarring for you.*

Q   Where does my hoe rank in the usefulness league?

A   *About half way down. A hoe is at home in the veg patch. (Hoeing flowerbeds has to be done more carefully, lest you behead a young plant.) Use the Dutch hoe to chop off weed seedlings, the draw hoe to make seed drills and earth up potatoes.*

9

Grass roots

There's a moment in *Asterix in Britain* in which a gent is seen tending his immaculate lawn one blade at a time. 'Another two thousand years of loving care,' he says, 'and I think it'll make quite a decent bit of turf.'

We're obsessed with lawns. Perfect carpets of emerald green are the aristocrats of gardens, a symbol of horticultural class and the hallmark of stately homes the world over.

This obsession can sap your energy and take up precious time and money. But with a bit of seasonal savvy you can transform rough turf into something that at least resembles centre court at Wimbledon – albeit at the end of the fortnight, rather than the start.

The first step is to know when and how to cut your grass. Regular cutting helps to invigorate the growing tips so, for this reason, mowing the lawn should be seen as a year-round job – including winter, when just a couple of cuts can make all the difference come spring. There's more to master mowing than meets the eye. Cut it too short, and the grass won't retain enough water; too long, and it will bend over and stop new shoots from getting any sun. Consistency is the key. If you do let the

Here's an idea for you...

Try sowing wildflowers like field poppies (*Papaver rhoeas*), cornflowers (*Centaurea cyanus*) and Ox-eye daisies (*Chrysantheum leucanthemum*) where the grass has given up the ghost. Or you could plant a camomile lawn – a favourite for hundreds of years. It forms a dense mat of foliage, which releases a heady smell when trodden on. Non-flowering varieties are best.

lawn grow too long then don't cut it right back in one go, as this will cause scalping. As a general rule never remove more than one-third of the leaf in any single mowing.

Watering is as crucial as it is easy to overlook. Hose pipe bans permitting, don't leave it too late to give your lawn a good soaking as turf that's already turned yellow or brown is unlikely to be revived, and only new shoots that manage to grow through will save it.

Of course lawns are for living with, so if you share your lawn with children, let alone dogs, then you need to accept that it's going to take a battering. Give your grass a chance to bounce back by over-seeding it during autumn, when the seed has most chance to get established. Simply sprinkle small amounts of seed over the whole lawn to thicken up thin areas.

For larger, bald patches turfing may be more suitable, and is quicker but more expensive. But don't throw your money away by letting it dry out – just lay it! For reseeding, fork the whole area, re-level the soil, and sow at the full recommended rate. Easy!

As for grass type – seed or turf – the current vogue is for dwarf perennial rye, which offers all the traditional toughness of rye but the added attraction of ornamental leaves. It's a creeping variety of grass, which spreads underground before sending up new shoots. It's quick to establish, and quick to recover from damage, which is why it's favoured by the sports industry.

For a more delicate effect you may want to look into clump-forming grasses such as fescue or bent. It's true that their resistance to constant wear and tear, and to disease, is limited, but on the other hand you can cheer yourself up with a chuckle over their names.

For more ideas about how to make your garden child-friendly – and child resistant – see IDEA 29, _Danger – children at play_.

Try another idea...

DO WALK ON THE GRASS

It's also important to aerate an established lawn by forking it in both spring and autumn. This helps to alleviate compaction and helps drainage, but it can be an arduous task. Alternatives include mechanical aerators which you can hire, or specially spiked overshoes which do the job as you simply walk up and down. Drainage can be further improved by applying a top dressing of six parts sand to three parts soil and one part peat substitute. This can then be brushed into the holes.

Scarifying is also a crucial part of your new routine, and removes dead grass and moss. This allows air to reach the new shoots and gives them a chance to grow. Scarifying is the best treatment you can give a lawn and you can do it at anytime of year (except the depths of winter) by using a spring-tined rake. It will also give you a workout as satisfying and intense as anything you'll get in the gym!

Spring is the best time to feed your lawn and, whether you choose a quick- or slow-release product, don't stint on quality and always check the label for any risk to children or pets.

'Until man duplicates a blade of grass, nature can laugh at his so-called scientific knowledge.'
THOMAS EDISON

Defining idea...

So, just to recap – keep cutting all year, scarify when you fancy it, feed and weed in spring, and get to grips with those bare patches in the autumn.

How did it go?

Q **We've got kids and we want them to enjoy the garden but their toys aren't really compatible with a lush lawn. Any tips?**

A *Leaving a paddling pool or sand pit in the same spot for as little as two days can kill everything underneath it. It's also a good idea to move swings and slides on a regular basis – or you can designate an area that you are prepared to let suffer, and then deal with it later.*

Q **Other than flagstones and decking, what are the alternatives?**

A *Whisper it, but artificial grass is becoming popular. It's made from polypropylene, and is available in a choice of colours. But while it may save on the mowing, it's pretty unforgiving when it comes to small elbows and knees.*

Q **Where's the best place to buy seed?**

A *Avoid paying for seed that comes ready packaged with pretty pictures of a perfect lawn. Far cheaper to buy in bulk from a nursery that supplies it not only loose, but for different types of conditions too.*

10

Support network

Do your delphiniums droop as soon as you look at them? Your lupins lean at the first breath of wind? Then you need support.

We all have our down days, lackadaisical days, when everything seems too much trouble. Plants are no different. Turn your back for a minute and they can come over all floppy and limp as they search for something to lean on. And that's where the keen-eyed gardener comes in, armed with a range of natural and man-made structures and gizmos that will give trees and plants a bit of backbone.

BOLSTERING THE BORDER

If your border is to keep its looks throughout the summer, herbaceous plants need staking. This needs to be done in April or May when the plants are still young and stout, and also to give the plants' lush new growth the chance to smother their crutches.

Here's an idea for you...

If you've got enough space, think about cultivating your own clump of hazel. It's a fast grower, produces long straight rods, and its early spring catkins are an added bonus. If cut around March, when the sap is rising, it's extremely pliable and can be put to endless uses in the garden. It's particularly good for sweet pea tripods, and used together with thin, flexible pieces of willow (whips) woven through the uprights, you have a natural frame, just made for the creeping, curling tendrils of the sweet pea.

Tall plants with heavy flowers such as delphiniums, sunflowers, and hollyhocks, need individual supports – usually bamboo canes. Tie them in when the plant is 10–15cm high, supporting it loosely with garden string. Keep doing this as the plant grows until it's about waist high, and then by the time it flowers the plant will be tall enough to hide the cane.

But remember to put something over the top of the cane, such as an old yoghurt pot or cork, otherwise you run the risk of resembling your black-eyed Suzy.

Other strong performers like monkshood (*Aconitum*), daisies, peonies and dahlias, benefit from the all-round support of metal hoops, link stakes or a personal favourite, pea sticks.

The real beauty of pea sticks is that they look natural because they allow the plants to grow through them, and cut out the need for any string or ties. Felled or fallen trees and forest trimmings are a great source, but failing that your own garden prunings will do. Choose twiggy bits with a strong central stem, and cut at an angle to make them easier to push into the ground. They last for years, so you can keep a selection of different heights for different-sized plants.

Look at a mature tree, with its stout trunk and majestic spread, and it's hard to imagine it ever needed any kind of support. But in its first few years hugging and

kind words will have been no substitute for a good staking. This will have helped it survive high winds and blustering storms while its stabilising roots took hold.

IDEA 5, *Indian summer,* **features other 'things to do' to keep the border looking good.**

Try another idea...

How to go about staking a tree, however, is the subject of some horticultural debate. Should the stake be straight or slanted into the prevailing wind? Should it be short, to make the tree do some of the work itself, or tall, to give maximum support? It's worth experimenting to find the method that works best for your situation but there is one key rule that all arboriculturists agree on – stake as you plant, sinking the post (a strong one that will last for a couple years) into the planting hole before the tree. Do it the other way round, and you risk driving it through precious roots.

A tree is a big investment, so two more things to remember. Tie the tree to the stake with a special tree tie – one with a spacer between the tree and the buckle – and place the buckle against the stake, not the tree, to stop chafing. And don't forget to check the supports at least twice a year, loosening them when necessary.

FRUIT AND VEG PROPS

Most veg grows happily without support but runner beans and peas must have a framework.

Defining idea...

'Go 'n get some more sticks,' ordered Selina, '... Look here, in the kitchen garden, there's a pile of old pea sticks. Fetch as many as you can carry, and then go back and bring some more!'

'But I say,' began Harold, amazedly, scarce knowing his sister, and with a vision of a frenzied gardener, pea stickless and threatening retribution.

'Go and fetch 'em quick!' shouted Selina, stamping with impatience.
From *Dream Days,* by KENNETH GRAHAM

Beans need canes or hazel stems, and peas, strangely enough, need pea sticks. If neither are available a nylon, wide-mesh net can be strung between supports 2m tall for beans, and 1.5m for peas.

Runner bean frames, whether arranged in wigwams or rows with cross support at the top, should be firmly tied and well grounded. Given the right amount of compost and water, these climbers put on tremendous growth and provide a ready-made sail for any strong winds gusting through.

Raspberry canes need help staying upright and in line – two characteristics which make them much easier to pick. They need a strong frame of end poles 180cm high with cross wires spaced at heights of 50, 100 and 150cms. Place cross slats at the top to take the net and you won't have to share your fruit with the birds.

How did it go?

Q   Do I need to support my fruit trees, or can I let them get on with it?

A   Free-standing trees can be left unsupported once they're established but you should keep an eye out for a particularly heavy crop. There is nothing more frustrating than a bough full of fruit breaking under the strain. A cracked branch can be propped up to allow the fruit to ripen but it will have to be severed cleanly at the end of the season.

Q   Can you use plants to support other plants for a more natural look?

A   Yes, this works particularly well with climbers. A rambling rose or Clematis montana wandering up and through a mature tree (perhaps one with little summer interest) can look spectacular.

Gnome-free zone

Not all garden ornaments need have pointed hats and fishing rods, especially if you take the time to design and make your own.

Sir Charles Isham has a lot to answer for. Not for this Victorian a great scientific discovery, a great invention, or even a great expedition. No, this 'eccentric spiritualist' as he is often called, was the man responsible for introducing the garden gnome to Britain in 1847.

Over 150 years later and while the imps are still popular, there are plenty of more ingenious ways to bring a touch of mystery to your borders. Here we look at how to acquire a work of art for nothing – your own Hepworth or Epstein. But don't reach for the chisel just yet, as it's your powers of observation and improvisation that matter.

Here's an idea for you...

Inspired? Well, fashioning a garden seat from a branch of fallen willow will take all of ten minutes to make. A 2m length sits on two shorter pieces, with the supports cut with a slight hollow to house the seat. It's neither nailed nor glued. The weight of the seat is sufficient to hold it securely.

SET IN STONE

There are many types and shapes of stone from shards of flint to massive sandstone boulders called sarsens. And while it's unlikely prehistoric man built Stonehenge or the Avebury Circle with gardens in mind, he was heading in the right direction. So where do you source your raw materials? Building sites, where old barns, mills or cottages are being restored or converted, are havens for smaller pieces of sarsen. Farmers churn up a good number each year too and would welcome a willing pair of hands to help move a few.

Flint is another great resource and again any farmer will cheer you on as you rid him of the cause of many a blunted ploughshare. Flint comes in all sizes and colours, from white through to beige, burnt orange to black. As a result, its decorative uses are endless. The bird bath, *on the previous page*, was made some fifteen years ago from flint. A piece of old piping was used as a mould to make the stem, and a round plastic basin for the bath itself. By removing the moulds before they are totally set, you can wash off some mortar with a fierce hose to expose the flint.

SYLVAN BAZAAR

Of course, the key to this rural foraging is to ask first. Dismantling a dry stone wall, or taking other pieces of natural stone that obviously serve a practical purpose, is not only illegal but stupid.

A few years ago, one of us discovered a large stone that turned out to be an old gatepost, half buried next to the wooden post that had replaced it. The farmer was

only too glad to root it out with a digger and place it under a French window, where it has become a formidable seat. And not only was it free, but it's also sustainable, eye-catching and will no doubt outlast anything that could have been bought from the local DIY superstore.

Being much lighter than stone, wood is often more easily available. Who can honestly say they haven't been taken by a smoothed piece of driftwood washed up on the tide line, or a gnarled bough, recently crashed to earth? Garden designers love them and import them from far and wide – which rather negates their recycled value, but that's another story. They can be seen dried, cleaned, even polished and for sale at mortgage-threatening prices.

But you don't have to reach for the cheque book, and even beachcombing isn't necessary, particularly if you live some way from the coast. Forest floors, particularly in autumn and better still after a storm, are a virtual sylvan bazaar. Use recently fallen material only. Dead or rotten wood should be left well alone to provide a haven for insects, especially stag beetles.

The hornbeam log shown overleaf was discovered in the Belgian Ardennes that was brought back in the boot of the car. The ends have been sawn parallel and it's been cleaned and polished. That's all. It's a wonderfully tactile piece and has a human's muscular form. In the summer it's used as a garden table, in winter it is taken indoors and looks perfectly at home. Eat your heart out Henry Moore.

There are more joinery skills to be had in IDEA 40, *Structurally sound*, while in IDEA 46, *Up the garden path*, patios and paths are laid to rest.

Try another idea...

'*We demand that garden gnomes are no longer ridiculed and that they be released into their natural habitat.*'
Statement by the Garden Gnome Liberation Front

Defining idea...

47

How did it go?

Q **I've tried making my own bird bath but just mention the word water and it starts to leak. Any tips?**

A *Skim mortar over the inside of bath, allow this to dry thoroughly and then paint with at least two coats of yacht varnish.*

Q **So you don't like gnomes?**

A *No, not particularly. But that's not to say that some stylised ornaments, such as animals, aren't attractive, if not more so than a perfect replica of an animal. The photo below shows stones with black metal painted heads and legs (an idea of Dutch artist Cees van Swieten). The stones have been selected for size only and at first didn't appear especially appropriate as sheep. Add the head and legs, however, and the whole flock was brought to life.*

12

Slugging it out

There's more than one way to defeat gardener's number-one foe.

Slugs and snails, like weeds and aphids, are something that gardeners have to learn to live with. Even those who declare chemical warfare on the critters will soon discover that it takes more than a few pellets of metaldehyde (the active ingredient in most slug pellets) to defeat these malevolent molluscs.

But that isn't to suggest you should simply throw in the trowel and accept that your hostas will be shredded and your delphiniums decimated.

Your garden is likely to be home to several kinds of slugs and snails, but it's the grey field slug that does most damage, closely followed by the chestnut and garden slugs. And while the large black ones may be the easiest to pick off, they probably do less damage than the other three.

Snails are said to be less destructive, particularly the banded ones, although large, grey common garden snails, and smaller strawberry snails, with their flattened shell, have voracious appetites.

Every gardener has a favourite way of ridding the beds of slugs and snails, from best bitter to copper tape, but we would like to take this opportunity to denounce barrier methods once and for all! We've tried the lot, from broken egg shells to grit, gravel to ash, even used coffee grounds. But it's not long before the buggers have decided that a dish of young lupin shoots is well worth a little discomfort.

Copper tape is more effective but, as with copper-impregnated slug mats, is only suitable for pots and containers.

KEEPING THE BALANCE

Officially the jury is still out on whether slug pellets really do harm wildlife by killing off the thrushes and frogs that eat the poisonous cadavers. But until there's concrete evidence to the contrary, surely it makes sense to use a more wildlife-friendly aluminium sulphate-based pellet instead. Also effective are beer traps, sunk into the ground and filled with

Here's an idea for you...

With delphiniums choose good strong plants in the first place and grow them on in pots, where it's easier to deter the enemy. Cutting back the main growing shoot will allow the plant to grow more shoots and gather its strength. Plant out when it's about 25cm high and it should be robust enough to fight off an attack.

For extra peace of mind, remove the top and the bottom of a plastic bottle and then place over the plant. Smear a layer of petroleum jelly round the rim for a bit of extra protection. If you can get your delphiniums through one year, they're likely to be strong enough to win the fight in future years.

your least favourite brew. Half a grapefruit does just as well but these devices are indiscriminate and will take out ground beetles too, an important slug predator.

Other tips include keeping your garden free of leaf litter and plant debris, which gives the slugs somewhere to chill out during the day. Others, however, argue that weeds, especially dandelions, can entice slugs away from your blooms, while one prize-winning hosta grower claims to plant 'sacrificial hosta seedlings' as a way of saving his best specimens.

The best form of defence is, of course, attack and although pricey, nematodes certainly work. These naturally occurring parasites eat the slugs and you can boost the numbers in the soil by mixing a packet of the microscopic bugs with water and applying as per the instructions. You'll soon notice a lot less devastation in your borders.

But by far the best way to beat the molluscs is to hunt them down yourself at night. Yes, the neighbours' curtains may twitch as you crawl around, torch in hand, but as well as fostering a much closer affinity with your plants, catching the little bleeders at work is extremely rewarding.

Once caught, how to dispatch them is up to you. Under foot, in a bucket of salty water or for the truly beneficent, bagged up for later release into the countryside.

But be aware that nature maintains a certain number of snails in any one garden, so clearing them away is a bit like painting the Forth Bridge, and there's always a clutch of baby monsters waiting to take their place at the table.

IDEA 35, *Wildlife friendly*, goes into more detail about how to attract wildlife to your garden.

Try another idea...

'Slug-resistant plants are a myth.'
PAULINE PEARS, Henry Doubleday Research Association

Defining idea...

51

LET THE WILDLIFE WORK FOR YOU

The trouble with all these remedies is that you need to mount a continuous campaign, renewing the treatment after rain, or setting the alarm clock for the middle of the night to search out the offenders. For a longer-term approach, try encouraging some allies into the garden.

A pond will enhance the frog population, while a pellet-free garden is more likely to attract nesting birds. And if you don't feed birds after June, they'll be more likely to seek out the pests in your garden instead.

A cool, damp place, such as the bottom of a stone wall or behind a water butt will encourage toads to set up residence, and if you live near water, then encourage ducks and moorhens into the garden – both thrive on slugs.

How did it go?

Q   **Any more suggestions about what to do with my hostas, which are still taking a battering?**

A   *The best solution is to choose the right type of hosta. The family* Hosta sieboldiana *is the one to grow. Its large, spectacular leaves are on the whole too tough for slugs and snails. If an adventurous creature does have a go one bite seems enough.*

Q   **Any plants that slugs and snails don't seem to like much?**

A   *Foxgloves, euphorbia, astilbe and sweet peas seem to be pretty low down the pecking order.*

13

Growing under glass

Whether you're pottering in a top-of-the-range greenhouse or hunched over a cold frame, growing under glass can deliver miraculous results.

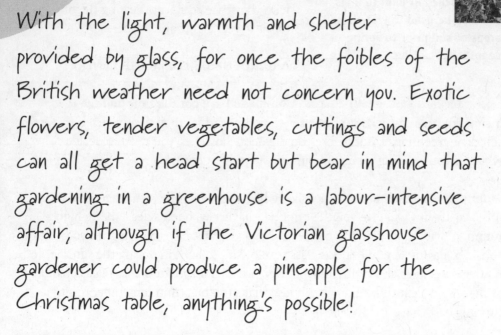

With the light, warmth and shelter provided by glass, for once the foibles of the British weather need not concern you. Exotic flowers, tender vegetables, cuttings and seeds can all get a head start but bear in mind that gardening in a greenhouse is a labour-intensive affair, although if the Victorian glasshouse gardener could produce a pineapple for the Christmas table, anything's possible!

You first need to ask yourself what you're interested in growing and how much time you can set aside to grow it. If you're working full-time or have a young family, investing in a free-standing greenhouse with all its accessories and accoutrements could leave you fraught and frustrated, and with no time to do your investment justice.

Here's an idea for you... **If you don't have space in your garden for a greenhouse then buy a cloche. This is a portable frame covered with glass or plastic which can bring temporary shelter to delicate plants and early flowers. Large cloches or mini tunnels can also be used to warm small areas of soil prior to spring vegetable planting.**

Instead think about a cold frame or mini lean-to greenhouses, which are cheaper and much less demanding. These can still give plants like fuchsias, pelargoniums (the large-flowered geraniums grown outdoors in the summer), dahlias and trendy cannas the winter protection they need, as well as providing you with the space to start preparing the blooms for next year's pots and borders.

A GARDENER'S COMMAND CENTRE

But if you have got the time and the inclination to get stuck into some serious propagating, then treat yourself to a free-standing greenhouse. But before you dig deep, however, you need to decide whether you're going for an aluminium or wooden frame.

Aluminium is light and less expensive, while a wooden one (usually red cedar) is more costly but will give you the option of having wooden sides a metre high all round, providing insulation on very cold and very hot days. You might also want to consider leaving one full side as glass to allow more light in during the summer for tender vegetables and fruit. But whatever you decide, go for one as big as possible, as there's no such thing as a greenhouse that's too big. (And remember to site it running east to west if possible.)

Aluminium greenhouses usually come in a pack for 'easy' self-assembly, but will need to be erected on firm ground or concrete slabs. A wooden greenhouse is trickier and will need footings (concrete underpinning) and a course of bricks, which needs to be dead square because the panes of glass have been cut to fit and don't bend easily! At

this stage it's worth setting a pipe or piece of hose through the footings too, so that the electrics can be threaded through later.

With average DIY skills this is a project worth attempting – after all, all gardeners need a project and what better one than this. But if the intricacies of plumb lines and stretcher bonds are beyond you, then best call in the professionals.

To see what's involved in propagation and to help you decide on the type and size of greenhouse that suits, see IDEA 4, *Don't pay the nurseryman.*

Try another idea...

LIFE ON THE INSIDE

Even if you aren't growing directly into the soil, it's still a good idea to have soil beds along either side of your greenhouse. They help the humidity and allow you to 'dampen down' when things get too dry and hot. But you'll need to change the soil every couple of years.

And toasty as your greenhouse may sometimes feel, without a little help a greenhouse is not 'frost free'. A lean-to has the added advantage of the warmth from a house wall, but an unheated greenhouse is only a degree or two warmer than outside. Basic protection for overwintering plants can be provided by bubble wrap, pinned or clipped on the inside of the glass.

As with any hobby, gadgets and gizmos are vital, and one accessory no self-respecting greenhouse should be seen without is a self-opening vent. These miraculous contraptions work of their own accord, keep an eye on the temperature for you, and open or close mysteriously when things get too hot or cold.

'After working in a greenhouse for a year I grew nine inches.'
Noted by ALAN TITCHMARSH in *Trowel and Error*.

Defining idea...

Staging and shelving are also a must and can be bought as a kit or homemade. Then, in order of importance, come a radio (well, you don't want to become totally isolated from the outside world!), propagators, heating and a watering system. Heating will not only keep you warm but a minimum night-time temp of 4–5°C will be sufficient to satisfy the needs of a wide range of plants. And, on sunny days, shading may be necessary. While blinds are widely available, special shade paint, applied to the glass and then washed off in the autumn, is a much cheaper option.

How did it go?

Q Greenhouses seem expensive and complicated to put up. As my garden is out of sight of any neighbours I was thinking about a polytunnel, is this a good substitute?

A   *A polytunnel is a good alternative and much used by commercial growers. However, plastic doesn't let in as much light as glass, especially as it ages. Also remember to secure the tunnel well against the winds and make the frame tall enough to work in it with comfort.*

Q How important is it to clean the greenhouse – can I leave it to the rain?

A   *A clean greenhouse lets in more light and keeps disease to a minimum so it's a good idea. Give the glass a thorough clean in October/November, washing off any shade paint applied in the summer. Give the inside a good clean once all the spring plants are safely bedded out; wash and sterilise all pots, trays and propagators before use.*

Your own little powerhouse part I

Bulbs and corms are just packed with energy. Treat 'em right and you can enjoy years of colour.

From hyacinths to tulips, crocuses to snowdrops, bulbs are one of the safest bets when it comes to guaranteed spring colour. There are also more varieties than you can shake a stick at, but whether you're a devotee of daffs or addicted to alliums, there are a few general rules to follow.

YOU PAYS YOUR MONEY...

It pays to buy your bulbs early as the condition in which they're stored is just as important as the soil you eventually plant them in. They need to have been kept cool and dry, not hot and bothered on a shop shelf.

Planting crocuses in the grass works especially well. Try mixing mauve and purple C. tomasinianus. But make sure you choose an area of lawn that you're happy to leave unmown until all the foliage dies back. This will encourage them to carrying on flowering each year.

You also need to avoid the temptation of buying a job lot. Of course, they look good value but with bulbs the biggest really are the best, as they tend to be the ones that produce the best blooms on the strongest stems. The other bonus about buying them loose is that you can check each one, making sure they're not soft or diseased.

The difference between bulbs and corms, by the way, is that bulbs, like an onion, are a mass of fleshy, food-storing leaves, enclosing a bud. A corm, such as a crocus, is a swollen stem that usually only lasts one season, to be replaced by another underground.

COLD STORAGE

Bulbs need the winter's cold to get them going in spring which is why there's always such a rush of activity in the autumn, as gardeners are faced with a heap of the scaly brutes to intern.

With daffs and crocuses, get them planted early, before the end of September if possible, as they're already set to send out their roots. Leave tulips until November, and most of the others can be fitted in somewhere between, spreading the load on your back and knees at the same time.

Plant them at roughly three times their own depth, unless otherwise specified. That's about 25–30cm for your average daff or tulip, while smaller ones, such as chionodoxa and scilla, should go in a hole roughly 10cm deep. As for spacing, with

all bulbs it's a good idea to plant them in clumps, and while theoretically you should leave up to 15cm between the bigger bulbs, let's face it, when you've got a few hundred to plant, who's measuring?

Bulbs enjoy free-draining soil, so if you garden on clay add some grit to the planting hole, and the more random your planting, the better the overall effect. Drop a handful of bulbs on the ground and plant them where they land.

Certain bulbs, notably the snowdrop (*Galanthus*), snowflake (*Leucojum*) and winter aconite (*Eranthis*) need to be planted 'in the green', which means just after flowering, with the leaves still intact. (You should be able to buy them like this from the garden centre.) Make sure they don't dry out.

Once in the ground, bulbs need little maintenance but will appreciate a handful of bonemeal after flowering to store up energy for next year.

LEAVE THE LEAVES

Once they've done their bit, resist the urge to cut back the dying leaves too soon, as you'll weaken the bulb and reduce its flowering potential for next year. Yes, deadhead them, but only cut down the foliage once it starts to yellow.

Tubers and rhizomes may sound like a medical conditions, but there's more colour to be had from these crusty little customers in IDEA 39, *Your own little powerhouse part II*.

Try another idea...

'*Bulbs are cheap, so we should refuse to feel guilty about splashing around quantities of them in our mixed borders. Most can stay where they are planted for years, either increasing or gradually petering out. That said, I have to admit to spending more on bulbs, annually, than on any other kind of plant.*'
CHRISTOPHER LLOYD

Defining idea...

59

If you choose to leave your bulbs in situ all year (which seems to us the eminently more sensible option!), it pays to dig them up and separate them every few years to prevent overcrowding. And if you've got any particularly expensive varieties in the ground, such as one of the giant alliums, mark their position so you don't inadvertently disturb them when they're dormant.

Daffs look their best naturalized in grass but if planting in the spring border choose dwarf narcissi as a good way of avoiding the perennial problem of daffodils with withered foliage. Varieties such as *N. cyclamineus* and *N. pseudonarcissus* (Lent Lily) have much smaller leaves that are easily concealed by other plants. Complement them with a blanket of blue grape hyacinth (*Muscari*).

Alliums are true show stoppers, particularly the giant varieties such as *A. giganteum*, with its fabulous 12cm spherical heads. There are hundreds of other varieties of this common onion genus, from the small, yellow-flowered *A. moly* (golden garlic) to the medium size *A. cristophi*, with its metallic pink flowers.

Tulips are in a class of their own – not so good in subsequent years but fabulous in year one, so you should treat yourself to fresh bulbs annually. Planted in November, in bold groups or containers, their form and intensity of colour can't be beaten. There's a shade and shape to suit every taste, from the frilly pink parrot tulip 'Fantasy' to the lily flowered 'Red Shine', and the almost black Darwin variety 'Queen of the Night'. Flowering from March to May, they really do match their pictures in the catalogues!

There are hundreds of summer, autumn and winter flowering bulbs too, as well as those that have been bred specially for fragrance, foliage or floristry.

Q   Why do so few of my bulbs ever flower?

A   Chances are they're overcrowded and starved unless they have been eaten by mice! They (bulbs not mice) don't mind being close together as long as they've got plenty of light and you give them some feed as soon as the leaves show. What they hate is dry dark spots under trees or a dense hedge. Bulb blindness is easily cured by lifting and replanting in well-fertilized soil.

Q   Any suggestions for bulbs that work well underneath a tree?

A   The hardy cyclamen is great for naturalizing underneath trees. You'll be amazed by the ability of the delicate pink flowers and marbled foliage to push through the ground in autumn (C. neapolitanum) or December to March (C. coum).

How did it go?

15

Small but perfectly formed

You don't have to own a plot the size of a football pitch to make vegetable gardening worthwhile.

The crunch of a home-grown runner bean, the sweetness of a pod-fresh pea, the sheer productivity of a simple potato. This is how the vegetable gardener measures success.

Growing vegetables is all about getting back to basics: the sowing, the nurturing, the eating. It doesn't matter what you grow or where you grow it. You can devote a whole plot to curly kale if that's what takes your fancy. And you really don't have to grow broccoli if you don't like it.

ROTATION, ROTATION, ROTATION

But it's not all anarchy down on the allotment and there are some simple rules to follow. Think about how labour-intensive your crops are going to be for a starter; are they an add-on to the other, more pleasurable, pursuits in the garden, or your *raison d'être* for pulling on your wellies in the first place?

Here's an idea for you... **Growing veg from seed is time consuming, so why not buy some young vegetable plants at the same time as you buy your summer bedding. Go for healthy, stocky plants but don't buy until the frosts have passed, unless you've a greenhouse to protect them.**

Will you be able to freeze your veg at the end of the day? While it's tempting to cram in as much as possible, have you thought what you're going to do with armfuls of runner beans and sackloads of potatoes come harvest time (friends and relatives can only take so much, you know)?

Then there's crop rotation – sounds serious but it's a proven way of maximising production and minimising pests and diseases.

Vegetables fall into three basic groups and the idea is that you move these groups around your patch each year.

- Brassicas include cabbages, broccoli, sprouts and cauliflower (the latter notoriously difficult to grow). They all prefer alkaline soil, so you'll need to add some lime if yours is on the acid side. This should also help prevent club root.
- A second group – the roots – includes carrots, parsnips, beetroot and potatoes, and needs a balanced, high-potash fertiliser (no manure) adding to the soil a few days before sowing. Carrot fly are attracted to the smell of carrot leaves (especially when crushed) as well as recently dug soil, so try to introduce some scented, ornamental plants nearby to keep the pests at bay, and keep the soil around your carrots firmed down.
- All the other veg, from legumes (beans and peas), to leeks, spinach, corn, courgettes and onions, fall into a third category, and all respond well to plenty of manure or compost, dug into the ground in autumn or winter.

If you decide to grow a selection from one group only, say runner beans, leeks, courgettes and spinach, then you don't need to worry about rotation. Just keep adding loads of muck. Plant lettuces around the edge of the well-manured bits, and water all the vegetables regularly, especially when getting them started.

You can get better acquainted with the concept of companion planting in IDEA 32, *Alright mate*.

Try another idea...

Broad beans are toughies, so sow these outside in the autumn. Other beans and courgettes can be sown straight into the ground (once it has warmed up) but they'll get off to a quicker start if sown in pots under glass, in early spring. Sow leeks in a metre-long piece of plastic guttering. Once they've germinated, slide the whole lot off into the veg patch to grow on until big enough to handle. Plant out by sinking each seedling into a 25cm hole, made by a dibber or trowel handle. (You may want to trim the roots and tops a little to make this easier.) Fill each hole with water to secure the seedling in place.

Spinach and all root crops don't like being moved, so sew these directly into their final growing positions.

EYES BIGGER THAN YOUR STOMACH?

Don't try to fit too much in, and remember to leave enough room to work. If your soil is easily waterlogged, build in some paths or raised beds, so there's no excuse for not working in wet weather. Vegetables that grow upwards are useful in a small patch, runner beans especially. But do start picking them when they're young and slim, and not when they've become thick and coarse.

'A cauliflower is a cabbage with a college education.'
MARK TWAIN

Defining idea...

Defining idea...

'To get the best results, you must talk to your vegetables.'
PRINCE CHARLES

You can also grow veg that you just keep picking, such as perpetual spinach (fantastically healthy and it will re-grow easily if kept well watered) and cut-and-come-again lettuce.

If you haven't got room for a vegetable patch, don't dismiss the humble tub or container. Although this is small-scale veg growing, it's still a viable alternative. Potatoes in pots work particularly well, and one chitted seed potato in a 25-litre pot should produce 45 plus new spuds.

You could also try tomatoes, aubergines or peppers, courgettes, lettuce, onions, carrot or peas. Use plastic containers or line terracotta ones with plastic to keep from drying out. If possible, set up a watering system – a hose with outlets to each container – that will trickle water easily to each pot.

Letting vegetables loose throughout the garden is another way of overcoming space restrictions. Their lush green leaves, brightly coloured flowers and stalks certainly don't look out of place. Grow runner beans on an arch, edge beds with coloured varieties of lettuce, or add drama to the back of the border with globe artichokes. But try and remember what's been where, so you can move your veg around from year to year.

Q With the right soil conditions and frequent watering, can anyone grow monster veg for the show table?

How did it go?

A *Growing vegetables for show takes years of practice and bucket loads of experience (and manure). However, there's nothing to stop you having a go in your local garden club's annual show. All you need are a few straight runner beans or a group of courgettes or carrots the same size. If all else fails you can always enter the 'most unusually shaped vegetable' class!*

Q The 'other half' insists the garden's for flowers not veg. How do I go about renting an allotment?

A *Sadly nearly half the allotments in Britain were sold off to developers in the 1970s and 1980s. As a result, though, you'll probably have to join a waiting list. Contact your local council or wander along to an allotment and have a chat with the tenants.*

16

Living with the enemy

Some gardeners are obsessed with their destruction; others see them as an extra splash of colour. But whatever you think of weeds, you can't ignore them.

If you're happy to spray and blast chemicals around your garden, indiscriminately killing anything that gets in the way, then this chapter's not for you. If, on the other hand, you're prepared to take on the likes of the pernicious bindweed and the dastardly dandelion without threatening the existence of everything else that lives in the garden, then read on.

Many weeds are of course wild flowers that would be greeted with whoops of joy if spotted swaying on the edge of a cornfield, or growing amidst the hawthorn and the elder of a hedgerow.

Some weeds even have their uses. Horsetail is rich in silica, for instance, so a few handfuls crushed up and added to the watering can will give plants a good protective coating, making them much harder for insects to chew.
Cover a bundle of nettles in 10 litres of water and leave for a few weeks. Then strain off the liquid, add it to water in a ratio of 1:5, and you have an excellent liquid feed.

They are incredibly successful plants, usually natives that have had centuries to adapt to the environment in which they grow, making them extremely hardy and able to reproduce quickly and easily.

This makes them a tricky and devious enemy. But on the upside, thriving weeds are a sure sign that you have good, rich soil.

The best course of action when tackling weeds is some form of coexistence. Let nature take complete control and it won't be long before the whole garden is strangled by the most pernicious weeds. But become obsessed with uprooting them, and you'll be left with precious little time to do anything else.

Defining idea...

'There is simply too much that we do not know to carelessly chuck noxious chemicals at a superficial problem like weeds.'
MONTY DON

The other benefit of this leniency is that some wildlife thrives on weeds. Without stinging nettles, for instance, peacock, small tortoiseshell and red admiral butterflies would have nowhere to lay their eggs. Isn't that reason alone to leave a few growing away unobtrusively at the back of the border?

KNOWING THE ENEMY

There are two main types of weed, the annual and the perennial.

Annuals like groundsel and cleavers (also called goose grass and like caviar to geese!) can generally be cleared by decapitating them with a hoe. This is best done on a dry day, when you can leave them to wither away. When the soil's damp, just pull them out by hand, a very therapeutic way to get closer to your plants.

Perennials, like stinging nettles, docks and dandelions, require a bit more effort and need digging out with a fork, root 'n all. Try to pull up the entire root or they can grow back from the merest piece left in the ground.

Ground elder can quite happily smother several square feet a year, while the horsetail does a lot of its work underground, entangling its black roots with those of other plants, making it even harder to get rid of. Thorough and repeated digging is the best approach, although it can have even the most dedicated organic gardener dreaming of weedkiller.

With its white trumpet flowers, there are certainly uglier plants than greater bindweed, which is actually part of the convolvulus family, cultivars of which we quite happily grow in the garden. The trouble is it doesn't know when to stop and will just keep on climbing unless kept in check. Organically, this means getting to grips with the fleshy, underground stems in early spring.

In case you haven't had enough of garden nasties take a look at IDEA 47, *Common diseases*, which lists all in gruesome detail.

Try another idea...

'A weed is a plant that is not only in the wrong place, but intends to stay.'
SARAH STEIN

Defining idea...

71

Defining idea...

'Weeds are flowers too, once you get to know them.'
EEYORE in *Winnie the Pooh*

Perhaps the most invasive weed is Japanese knotweed, which has even been known to push up its shoots through thick concrete. Trying to defeat it is useless. You need to work round it, and just keep cutting it back.

UNDERCOVER OPERATIONS

In the absence of any organic weedkillers, mulching is also a good way of keeping the likes of bindweed and couch grass at bay. Remove what you can first of all and then spread a liberal layer of garden compost. This will starve the seeds of the light they need.

Other good mulches include grass clippings and straw, and although semi-permeable membranes look far from natural when exposed they do work, and fulfil the key role of letting in water but keeping out light.

Another way to keep weeds down is by planting plenty of ground cover plants. You need to do a thorough weeding job first, and keep going while the plants themselves get established, but the likes of *Heuchera*, creeping jenny (*Lysimachia nummularia*), hardy geranium, dead nettle (*Lamium*) and *Polygonum affine* – the friendly low-growing knotweed – should rise to the challenge.

Flame guns, or a hot-air paint stripper, are other ways to kill weeds that have sprung up in cracks and crevices on paths and patios. But beware of torching other plants nearby. To be honest, like leaf blowers and patio heaters, we don't really think they belong in the garden. Get down on your knees and do some proper weeding instead. It's good for the soul.

Q **I've done as you said and now I've got a pile of dead and dying weeds. Should I put them on the compost heap?**

How did it go?

A *Couch grass is a definite no-no, along with bindweed and horsetail. As for the others, it depends on your heap. If it's a hot one, which is often encouraged by adding in layers of grass cuttings, then the heat should be enough to kill any annual weed seeds. But if in doubt put them on the bonfire.*

Q **I've got a few packets of old weed killer left over in the potting shed. Surely it wouldn't hurt to just use these up and then go organic?**

A *Use them and you could burn a hole in your pocket as well as your garden's ecosystem. Many pesticides were recently banned and you could be fined for using them. Contact your local council to find out how to dispose of them safely.*

Oranges are not the only fruit

Picking fruit from your own tree is one of the ultimate horticultural highs. But before you can enjoy the sweet taste of success, you need to digest the bread and butter of growing fruit.

In the last thirty years, half of Britain's pear orchards and over 60% of its apple orchards have been destroyed. So what better time to start planting some of the fabulously named traditional varieties of British fruit, from the Kentish Fillbasket apple to the Vicar of Winkfield pear?

GOING PEAR-SHAPED

First up, always buy trees from a reputable supplier, who specialises in fruit and can answer the following questions.

Is the tree on the right rootstock? All fruit trees are grafted onto roots that have been specially selected for the size and shape of tree they will ultimately support. They are identified by the letter M followed by a number. The rootstock determines the vigour, resistance to pests and disease, and the eventual formation of the tree. Only buy trees on recommended rootstocks, as these are also the only ones guaranteed to be virus free.

- With apples, the stock ranges from M.27 for a small tree up to a couple of metres high, to the vigorous MM.111 that grows to 5m plus.
- Although there's no fully dwarfing rootstock for pears, Quince C is semi-dwarfing, and Quince A semi-vigorous.
- The rootstock for plums is St Julien A, a semi-dwarfing variety, which will pollinate with all other plums, damsons, gages, peaches, nectarines and apricots!

Here's an idea for you...

If you're really short of space but want a few different varieties in your garden, then try a 'family tree'. Two or three pears or apples can be grafted onto one rootstock giving different varieties from the one tree.

The second key question is: *How does the tree pollinate?* If the tree is a self-pollinator it will produce fruit all by itself. If not, it will need another tree, of a different variety, with which to 'mate'. Find out from a specialist book or nursery which varieties are compatible. It may be that one exists nearby in a neighbour's garden. If not, you'll need to do some matchmaking.

All apples need a compatible cross-pollinator, and while *Conference* and *William* pears are self-pollinators, they'll do better if paired off (ouch!). The cherry *Stella* and most plums are self-fertile, although planting two varieties of plum will improve the yield.

Finally, ask about growing conditions. Take account of the area you live in, the space and shelter you can offer the tree, and the soil type.

When planning where to put your fruit trees check out IDEA 15, *Small but perfectly formed*, to see how they will fit in with your veg patch.

Try another idea…

Apples are the least fussy and the hardiest of fruit. When planting, dig in plenty of manure and mulch, and feed in spring. There are hundreds of varieties to choose from, all of which will be different in some way whether it's in their taste, their resistance to diseases, or the time of year when they fruit. Some will even keep better than others.

Pears are for your heirs, as they say, and will take a few years before they start producing. They come early into blossom and late into fruit, so make sure they're not in a frost pocket, or be prepared to rush out with some fleece or net curtains if frost is forecast. They're not too fussy about soil but don't like shallow chalk and also enjoy a feed in spring.

Plums, liking rich moist ground, also blossom early and need a protected site. In heavy cropping years you may need to prop up their branches.

And don't forget the damsons! A neglected star of the fruit world, it needs virtually no pruning, is fully hardy and produces bucket loads of uniquely flavoured fruit, great for crumbles and pies – and don't bother removing the stones. If you're short of space grow one on your boundary as they survive in the hedgerows in the wild. *Merryweather* is a self-fertile variety.

Cherries are hardy and have lovely blossom but are only worth planting if you intend to employ a full-time bird-scarer!

'In an orchard there should be enough to eat, enough to lay up, enough to be stolen, and enough to rot on the ground.'
JAMES BOSWELL

Defining idea…

77

WELL-TRAINED FRUIT

Horticultural developments mean that you can now buy apples and pears that have been trained to specific shapes. Cordons grow at a 45° angle, while espaliers have a main vertical stem with horizontal tiers. Both are great space savers and can be grown against a wall or along a wire frame.

Step-over apples are espalier trees with the upward growth pruned out above the first set of horizontal branches, and provide excellent low 'walls' around the vegetable garden. Espaliers too can be used as decorative, productive screens.

Yep, there's a lot to take in with fruit trees, but just remember, there are few sweeter tastes than a ripe pear – except perhaps a ripe pear that you've grown yourself.

How did it go?

Q   How do I know when the fruit is ripe enough to pick?

A   *With apples and pears take the fruit in the palm of your hand and gently twist. If it parts company easily it's ripe. If it doesn't, don't force it, leave it for a few more days. With plums, pick one and cut it in two. If the flesh comes away easily from the stone pick all the plums that appear to be at this same stage.*

Q   My crop of plums has been great but how do I deter the wasps from enjoying it?

A   *A good tip is to throw any over-ripe or half-eaten plums well away from the tree so the wasps can feast in peace. Then pick the remaining fruit the moment it becomes ripe.*

18

Blow the raspberries

Whatever your age, juicy, sweet berries are a summertime delight, but which types and varieties suit which garden? And can you really grow a blackberry without prickles?

The beauty of berries is that they provide a quick return after planting, but while strawberries, raspberries and blackberries share some common ground, such as a preference for moist, well-drained soil that's mildly acidic, their growing habits and cultivation techniques are all significantly different. So sit up, and pay attention at the back.

STRAWBERRIES

For some, strawberries are the ultimate summer fruit, the king of the berries, with a big, bold crop just asking to be eaten. To get the best from strawbs, plant them in July or August to fruit the following summer. 'Honeoye' and 'Eros' are good all-rounders, while 'Cambridge Favourite' crops well, and is disease resistant.

If you can group all your berries together with other soft fruit then it may be worth buying a fruit cage to protect the whole lot. You can splash out on one with a metal frame, or build your own from wood. Then cover it with black or green nets, with a 2cm mesh, available from any hardware store. Remove nets in winter to prolong their life. It might sound a bit OTT but there can be few more soul-destroying sights than a fruit bush stripped bare before you've had a chance to harvest.

The plants prefer an open sunny spot with plenty of space between them, and need to be kept well watered, especially in spring when the fruits are swelling.

To keep the berries off the ground, where they can fall prey to slugs or rot, surround the plants with straw (one of many theories behind the plant's name) or strawberry mats, making sure the ground is moist first. As a final deterrent, net them to protect from the birds. To help your plants overwinter, remove the straw once they've finished fruiting, take off the old leaves, feed and mulch with well-rotted manure or garden compost.

Strawberries are thoughtful plants, providing not only a juicy crop but next year's plants as well. These come in the form of runners – those long stems with small plants attached that shoot off from the main plant. Choose the strongest of these – those nearest the plant – push them into the soil or small pots of compost, securing each with a bent piece of wire. Keep them attached to the parent plant for six weeks to allow the roots to form, before cutting them loose and planting them out. Sadly this free service doesn't last forever and the main strawberry plants will need replacing every 3–5 years.

RASPBERRIES

This prickly customer is relatively easy to grow, crops best in full sun and can last up to 20 years.

Before planting dig a trench, fill it with plenty of muck and mix in an all-round fertiliser. As the canes grow, cover them at the base with compost or grass cuttings to keep in the moisture, making sure the soil you're covering is already damp. But while they mustn't be allowed to dry out, water-logging can be just as harmful.

IDEA 10, *Support network,* will tell you what to do with raspberry canes that can grow to 1.5m, while for details on growing gooseberries see IDEA 52, *Currant thinking* – it may sound bizarre but read it and you'll see why.

Try another idea...

Plant summer fruiting raspberries in autumn, feeding and mulching in spring. 'Julia' is a good disease-resistant variety, while 'Tulameen' is a heavy cropper with few spines. This type of fruit grows on last year's canes, so it's important to only prune those canes that have just fruited, leaving the ones that have grown this year to bear next year's fruit. The autumn varieties, such as 'Autumn Bliss', produce raspberries on the current year's canes, so all the canes can be cut down to the ground after fruiting.

BLACKBERRIES

Blackberries are one of the most abundant fruits in nature's larder and throughout September blackberrying is one of those few pastimes that seems to transcend all ages. Octogenarians enjoy scrambling through the brambles just as much as eight-year-olds, often attacking the bush with a vigour unseen since they last attended the January sales, walking sticks thrashing wildly in their haste to bag a free lunch.

Blackberries have been around for over 2000 years, for eating, for hedging and for medicinal purposes – creeping under a bramble bush was long considered a cure for rheumatism, boils

'I am never so utterly at peace as when blackberrying or looking for mushrooms.'
ALAN BENNETT

Defining idea...

and blackheads. They enjoy the same rich, moist soils as the other berries but are a little less fussy. Plant in the autumn and immediately cut the stems down to just one bud. Each year, once fruiting has finished, cut down the stems that have fruited to allow new ones to develop. Make this easy by separating out the stems as they grow and training them against a fence.

They live for 20 years or more, and there are several varieties, such as the vigorous *Bedfordshire Giant,* the more moderate black butte, or the hybrid berry, boysenberry.

How did it go?

Q I like the idea of growing berries but I'm running out of space – what can I do?

A *Unlike other berries, strawberries are happy growing in containers such as strawberry pots, hanging baskets and even growbags. This has the double advantage of keeping the fruit well off the ground and saving space. Line the pot first with plastic to save it drying out, add a few drainage holes, and feed every two weeks with tomato feed once they start cropping.*

Q How can I make blackberrying more child friendly?

A *You don't have to plant those tough brutes you see in the wild, with their vicious, spiky thorns. Developments have resulted in thornless varieties too that still provide shiny, black fruit. These include 'Lochness' or 'Oregon Thornless', which also has attractive foliage.*

19

To prune or not to prune

How often have you purposefully strode out into the garden, secateurs in hand, intent on tidying up a headstrong hydrangea or mutinous mahonia, yet when you get within a few paces, the doubts kick in? Where do I start? Is it the right time of year? Will I end up killing it?

Pruning isn't just about chopping the top off a plant that's too big. Get it right and you'll be rewarded with a plant that produces plenty of flowers and fruit, has a good shape, and is a lot less prone to disease. So, take a moment or two to learn the whys, whens and hows of basic pruning, and who knows, you might find it so much fun you take up topiary!

WHY PRUNE?

Mark cut his gardening teeth pruning a forsythia hedge for his Grandma. The mass of yellow flowers seemed to come back year after year, so she was happy enough,

Here's an idea for you...

Fancy your hand at topiary? Shaping box, or the evergreen shrub honeysuckle (*Lonicera nitida*), into balls is a good way to start but turning a plain conical evergreen into a spiral is simple and effective. Tie a piece of rope to the top and spiral it around the plant to the bottom. Now cut alongside the rope to mark the line of the spiral. Remove the rope and trim further into the spiral until the desired shape is achieved.

and so was he, with the fiver it cost her for his dextrous shearing.

Pruning inspires plants; it's a chemical thing that makes them grow back in a different way. It may be a bit of an oxymoron but cutting plants back hard will stimulate rapid growth.

The basic pruning set should include a good pair of secateurs (for cutting stems and twigs up to 1cm thick), a pruning saw (for smaller branches), loppers for any hard-to-reach tough stuff, and garden shears for trimming soft growth. Try tackling everything with the same pair of blunt kitchen scissors and you'll be rewarded with mashed stems and a nice line in blisters.

WHEN TO DO IT?

Most plants need an annual prune to keep them healthy and productive. Just removing dead wood and any stems that are rubbing against each other (so letting in disease) can give even the most dishevelled shrub a new lease of life. And a cut in the right place, at the right time, can encourage side shoots, fruiting spurs and flowers. When to carry this out depends on the plant and when it flowers or fruits. There's no short cut – to do it properly you need to read up on the plant. But if it is done correctly, it's one of those jobs that brings on a warm glow of self-congratulation.

Many roses, soft fruits and fruiting trees need pruning in the dormant season – that time when they're asleep, from autumn through to early spring. Trained fruit trees

will need summer pruning as well to keep them in shape.

Shrubs, however, fall into two main groups and while it's not difficult, if you get it wrong, you'll have to wait another year to see any flowers. If the shrub flowers in spring, on branches grown in the previous year – forsythia is a typical example – prune it after flowering. If you mistakenly cut it hard back before flowering, you'll be taking out the stems that are covered in buds. (Sorry Grandma.)

The second group are shrubs that flower later in the year, on the current year's growth, such as buddleia. Pruning these in early spring will encourage them to produce fresh growth that will flower later that summer.

There is a third group – slow-growing shrubs that keep the same basic shape, e.g. magnolia, azaleas, witch hazel and the hardy hibiscus. Leave these alone except for the pruning out of dead or damaged wood.

Generally keep an eye on things and try to avoid drastic action where one minute your garden will be looking overgrown, the next bald! Again, the best approach is to consult a well-illustrated guide that demonstrates clearly the action you need to take. It needs to show the difference between end and side shoots, explain exactly where to make your cuts, and preferably have a picture of how the plant should look afterwards!

IDEA 22, *It's been a good year for the roses*, looks more closely at how to keep your shrub roses under control.

Try another idea...

'*All gardens, even the most native and naturalistic, benefit from the hand of an artful pruner. In this season, where the garden is poised for the green flood of springtime, remember that our gardens are co-creations, shared with mother earth. And like any good mother, she expects you to tidy up your room. Now get clipping!*'
TOM SPENCER (US gardening guru)

Defining idea...

Deadheading is a small job that makes a big difference. You'll reap the rewards in your containers and summer border, and if you're prepared to risk the odd mishap, it's a good way to get children involved too. Not only does it tidy things up but it also stops the plants putting their energy into producing unwanted seeds. Cut the flower back below the seedpod and you'll encourage it to concentrate its efforts on producing more flowers instead.

How did
it go?

Q   Some plants in my garden are looking leggy – the lavender in particular. Can I cut it down to the ground?

A   *Unfortunately lavender doesn't re-grow from old wood so trim these plants annually in March, cutting back to 5–10cm from the base where new shoots should be visible. Do not cut back into old or bare wood. If the lavender is really bare at the bottom dig it up and replant it in a deeper hole. Better still, start again with new plants, by taking cuttings from your existing plants in September, before throwing them away.*

Q   I have some tough pruning jobs ahead of me as several trees have got out of control. Will a pruning saw be strong enough for this work?

A   *A pruning saw is only suitable for the twiggy branches of shrubs and young trees. For major tree pruning, get the experts in. Don't attempt tree surgery or you may end up needing some yourself. But only use a bona fide company.*

20
Shrubs

The backbone of the garden – but are they really that interesting?

Without shrubs a garden would have no form. While trees provide the focal points, and perennials and annuals give that zip and zest in spring and summer, it's the much-maligned shrub that provides the structure, and the stage, for other plants to strut their stuff.

But that's not to suggest that shrubs just perform a supporting role in the garden. They come in a remarkable variety of shapes, sizes and colours. Some do their bit in winter, others in spring, summer or autumn. Some are spiky, others are feathery, and others still are broad-leaved. And most have showy flowers too!

WHAT IS A SHRUB?

In simple terms, it's a woody plant that doesn't die down in the winter. Bushy, unlike the tree with its single trunk, it may loose its leaves and look half dead for part of the year but rest assured, when the time's right, it will burst back into life again.

Shrubs also have many uses. Their chunky growth can act as a windbreak for more tender plants, while in a border of spring and summer flowers, they can provide structure and colour as the plants around them die down.

But are you brave enough to plant a whole bed of shrubs? No, not the 'motorway style' planting so beloved of town planners, where a mass of impenetrable *Pyracantha* suffices for 'landscaping', but a bed where leaf shape, colour and flowers are blended to change with the seasons.

Here's an idea for you...

In this day and age the humble shrub is also a weapon in our on-going war against crime. A well placed *Berberis* or firethorn (*Pyracantha*) is as effective a burglar deterrent as you'll find. Thankfully the evergreen firethorn has more redeeming features than just razor-sharp thorns, such as creamy flowers and vivid berries. The variety Orange Charmer is also less prone to scab and its orange berries will only be attractive to the birds once all the red ones have been eaten!

SHRUBS FOR ALL SEASONS

In spring, after the bulbs have done their bit, the faithful forsythia and flowering currant (*Ribes*) take over, followed shortly by stunning magnolias, sweet scented lilac and broom.

In late spring and early summer the selection grows. *Potentilla*, with its pink, flame, yellow and white flowering varieties, is worthy of a special mention. It's tough and uncomplicated to grow, and flowers all summer long on attractive feathery leaves. And, although it has no scent, you can easily fool the nostrils by planting something more heavily scented nearby, such as mock orange (*Philadelphus*).

Towards the end of summer the 'grow anywhere' buddleia, or butterfly bush, starts to flower. A true survivor, it's colonised building sites, railway embankments and even clogged up gutters the length and the breadth of the country.

For something more linguistically challenging, try *Ceratostigma willmottianum*. Of medium height and covered with intense blue flowers, it's a shrub that does well at the front of a bed, and looks good alongside the hardy hibiscus.

There's more on shrubs with winter interest in IDEA 30, *Winter wonderland*, and IDEA 19, *To prune or not to prune*, helps guard against giving your shrubs the unkindest cut of all.

Try another idea...

As the garden begins to shut down, the winter shrubs take over. Winter sweet (*Chimonanthus praecox*) and Sweet box (*Sarcococca confusa*) have small flowers but fabulous scent. *Garrya elliptica* is worth growing for its amazing long catkins, and if you have acid soil and a sunny spot, then squeeze in a Chinese witch hazel (*Hamamelis mollis*), with its eye-catching golden yellow flowers and beautiful smell.

Berberis is both beautiful and prickly. It comes in many forms, with leaves of bright yellow, deep green, scarlet or wine, as well as evergreen, deciduous, dwarf and large varieties. What they all share is some of the most vicious and spiky leaves in the gardening world. But with its spring flowers, autumn colour and winter berries it's a perfect all-rounder for the shrub border.

TREAT 'EM MEAN, KEEP 'EM KEEN

Still think shrubs are boring? OK, how about this as a selling point? A bed of shrubs is perhaps the most efficient area of any garden. In spring and autumn feed and prune (don't forget to check which shrubs should be pruned when), add compost to the soil and generally tidy up. Job's a good 'un.

'*Shrub is a lovely word, sliding between the teeth with a soft landing. Shrubs help to mould a garden, adding colour, shape, texture and fragrance, and complementing trees, bulbs, annuals and perennials.*'
From *Shrubs For The Garden* by JOHN CUSHNIE

Defining idea...

Mind you, neglect your duties and things will soon get out of control.

Unlike annuals and perennials, shrubs take a while to get settled and spread out. This is where a little planning comes in. It pays to check a shrub's estimated spread and height, and try to visualise what it will look like in three years' time. If you have planted your shrubs too closely together, then they won't mind being moved in autumn or spring, as long as there's a good layer of compost in their new hole, and you water them in thoroughly.

How did it go?

Q   I love the stunning colours of rhododendrons and azaleas but can I grow them with other shrubs?

A   *Yes, if you garden on acid soil. Try to imitate the conditions of a woodland glade and match them up with other woodland plants – bluebells, ferns, heathers and hellebores. Remember some do have tree-like proportions. Choose some of the dwarf azaleas if your site is restricted and a little more open.*

Q   How can I keep the shrub bed looking good throughout the year?

A   *By not forgetting evergreens:* Escallonia, Euonymous, Mahonia, Eleagnus, Skimmia japonica, *holly (*Hedera*) and* Pieris, *for example. In sheltered southern areas you could try* Pittosporum, Choisya *('Sundance' is the golden form),* Convolvulus, Cistus *or* Hebes. *Some varieties of* Vibernum, Berberis *and* Daphne *are evergreen too, and you have the full range of dwarf or slow-growing conifers to choose from. A sample of all these will help hold the bed together all year.*

And so to bed ...

Traditionally summer bedding was planted en masse but (thankfully) there are more subtle uses for these bright, vibrant and vigorous plants.

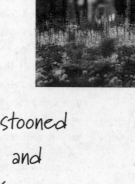

We won't beat about the bush — bad bedding can be frightening. A garden festooned in a pink and purple flurry of busy lizzies and pansies is the visual equivalent of GBH. Yes, we know some people love it, and will also throw in a few salvias and French marigolds for good measure, but please, there are more refined ways to use bedding.

After all, bedding is any type of flowering plant used specifically to give a few months display of colour, usually in spring and summer. They're not all annuals, they're not all tender, and they're not all pink.

Here's an idea for you...

If you're sowing your annuals directly in the ground try starting with what's termed a 'stale' seed bed. Cultivate the soil a good couple of weeks before you intend to plant it up and then leave it, allowing any weed seeds in the soil to germinate. Hoe these off and you can sow your annuals in a weed-free bed. Of course some weeds will return, but your seeds will have a head start.

Take your hardy annuals such as love-in-a-mist (*Nigella*) and nasturtiums. These can be sown straight into a prepared seed bed (the packet will tell you when) and can put up with the cold. In fact, you can also sow hardy annuals like the Californian poppy (*Eschscholzia californica*) and cornflowers (*Centaurea cyanus*) in late summer, to bloom early the following season.

It's a good idea to sow seeds in specific shapes on the ground, so you know what are seedlings and what are weeds when it comes to hoeing. And sow a couple of each plant in a pot too, label it up and then when they sprout, you'll know what your seedlings should look like.

Your half-hardy annuals, however, like cosmos and salvia, curl up and die at the first sign of frost, so these need sowing indoors from January onwards. Keep them warm, prick them out into biodegradable pots, and once you've gradually hardened them off, they can be planted straight into the ground, pot and all. This means you won't disturb those precious roots, and the pot will just rot away, enriching your soil at the same time!

Begonias, pelargoniums and cannas are also often classed as bedding although these can be treated as half-hardy perennials if overwintered out of the reach of frost.

Bedding also comes as plugs, usually via mail order, which will need potting on and hardening off before planting out, and of course you can buy bedding plants that are

already in flower. Buying petunias as plugs is a good idea as their seed is very small and tricky to handle.

But a word of warning: while trays of bright bedding may be on sale as early as April, resist the temptation to buy them. You can't plant bedding until the last frost has been and gone, which could be as late as early June in some places. And it's never a good idea to buy plants until you're ready to put them in the ground. Leave them hanging around in their trays and they'll get straggly and pot-bound.

When it comes to planting out, give your bedding a good watering first so the root ball gets really moist. And, while you might be planting them in optimum midsummer conditions, don't just plonk bedding in anywhere. You need to prepare the soil as much for a pansy as you would any other plant and most bedding grows best in well-drained soil in a sunny part of the garden.

When planting go carefully as annuals are delicate things. Make sure the roots aren't cramped or twisted, and plant them to the same depth as the original soil mark on the stem. Give them a good watering in, and then deadhead regularly to prolong flowering.

Now our idea of a good bedding is an impulse purchase used to fill a particular gap that's appeared in the border, or to invigorate a slightly forlorn hanging basket or tub.

Growing from seed is not only cheaper but also teaches you so much more about horticulture. IDEA 2, *Top seed*, should help you on your way.

Try another idea...

'*Bedding is apt to get a bad name because of the wretchedly mindless examples we see in public places. But at home, it gives us wonderful scope for variety. Lively and not so much with a song in its heart but an uninhibited shout of joy.*'
CHRISTOPHER LLOYD

Defining idea...

Bedding is an important part of succession planting and, personally speaking, looks so much better fitted into an existing border of shrubs and perennials rather than planted en masse, and on its own. It can take over where early flowering plants have been cut back, and shrubs and perennials have yet to do their bit. More subtle than the psychedelic carpet some gardeners prefer.

How did it go?

Q   Any suggestions for good bedding plants with a bit of height?

A   *Haven't you heard of sunflowers? Helianthus is just as much an annual as a low-growing lobelia. Love-lies-bleeding (Amaranthus caudatus) is a half-hardy annual that does well in borders, with its dangling flower tassels. The tobacco plant Nicotiana sylvestris is over 1m and Clarkia elegans and Sweet Williams (Dianthus barbatus) will reach 60cm plus, whilst half-hardy fuchsias and cannas provide bold upright features when surrounded by lower growing bedding.*

Q   What do I do with my half-hardy perennials once they've done their bit?

A   *You can cut back plants like pelargonium and chrysanthemums to just a few centimetres, dig them up, re-pot them, and overwinter in a frost-free place. But some experts say you'll get much better plants from cuttings taken in late summer. If you go down this route keep a regular eye on them, adjusting the humidity if necessary, to make sure they don't rot away.*

It's been a good year for the roses

Roses have made something of a comeback over recent years, although arguments still rage over their care, their cultivation and even their classification.

Now, in the interests of brevity and sanity, I'm not even going to attempt to cover the thorny area of rose nomenclature. Suffice to say the species behind this recent resurgence is wildly held to be the modern shrub rose.

Technically any rose bred after 1867 is considered modern, although given that the Crusaders were bringing back species from abroad as long ago as the thirteenth century, it does still make them reasonably novel.

What sets them apart from other roses is their breeding. It's their lineage that makes them so diverse, because not only do they draw on all the finer qualities of the older roses such as scent and vigour, but also characteristics of the modern species, such as long flowering periods (given some diligent deadheading), bright colours and disease resistance.

Here's an idea for you...

Don't fall foul of Rose Replant Disease! When replacing an old rose with a new one, make sure you dig out a good proportion of the old soil, to a depth and width of about 50–60cm. Replace it with soil that has never been near a rose. The reason for this is that all roses have a fungus on their roots and the soil around them, which seems to be harmless to the old plant, can be overwhelming for new plants, and weakens them before they get going.

Of course, roses are renowned for their beauty, the exquisite composition of their foliage, their scent and the velvety texture of their petals, but modern shrub roses are also wonderfully informal plants, which suits the current vogue for naturalistic planting. After all, what would you choose to complement your carefully planted border – a large flowered Hybrid Tea, pruned and clipped within an inch of its life, or the branching stems and dripping flower clusters of a modern shrub rose?

That said, they can be sprawling beasts, with some capable of forming mounds more than 2m high, such as R. 'Nevada', which produces creamy white flowers on arching stems.

Others make excellent hedges, such as R. 'Buff Beauty', with its large clusters of apricot flowers, and R. 'Cornelia', with apricot-pink flowers set against dark green leaves.

Defining idea...

'There has been a huge swing away from the sort of roses my grandparents loved, fancy Hybrid Teas and Florinbundas with names like 'Tallyho' and 'Gay Gordons'. In summer, borders glowed like Las Vegas, in winter they looked like the Somme.'
STEPHEN LACEY

As for colour, R. 'Ethelburga' is a new variety with highly scented pink flowers, while R. 'Autumn Sunset' is a deep yellow, with bright glossy foliage.

A few tips on planting roses in general. During the growing season they can be bought in containers. But buying them as bare-rooted plants, during the dormant season is generally a cheaper and healthier option.

IDEA 47, Common diseases considers some of the ailments that could strike your plants.

Try another idea...

You need to add plenty of compost or well-rotted manure to the planting hole, making sure that the soil has a neutral pH. They will do much better in a sunny site but mulch regularly to keep the roots moist.

Modern shrub roses don't need extensive pruning. In spring, remove any dead or diseased wood, and then cut back the main shoots by about a third and any side shoots by about two thirds. They do need staking, however, and tough metal rings are required to keep them shapely and their flowers off the ground.

As for diseases, modern shrubs are more resistant than many varieties to the usual suspects such as mildew, black spot and rose rust but, as with all roses, good cultivation is the best way to fend off pests and diseases.

'**What place, I often ask myself, should roses take in our gardens? A silly question, really, because each of us has to make up his mind about it for himself and each will reach a different conclusion, right for him, wrong for his neighbour.'**
CHRISTOPHER LLOYD

Defining idea...

OK, having said I'm not going to get bogged down in classifications, special mention is due to *R. rugosa*, or the Japanese rose. It's a close relation of the modern shrub and considered by some to be the healthiest of all roses, doing

well in most soils and vigorous enough to make excellent hedges. *Scabrosa* has unusual, velvety, mauve flowers and a flush of huge red hips in autumn, while for scent try the pure white R. 'Blanche Double de Coubert'.

How did it go?

Q Cut the wise cracks – but what's a sucker?

A *Most roses you plant in your garden have been budded or grafted onto rootstock from a wild rose to give it extra vigour, among other things. A sucker is any shoot that's growing from below where your cultivated rose has been added. Ignore them and the wild variety will soon take over. But don't prune them off, suckers need to be pulled off, moving some of the top soil to get at them.*

Q I know you don't want to talk species and classification but what's the difference between a climber and a rambler?

A *Ramblers are unruly but gloriously effervescent, clothing structures with rapid growth and showers of smallish flowers. Climbers are more restrained and dignified, featuring spaced out larger blooms on fewer but thicker stems. It's a question of horses for courses.*

If it's good enough for pandas

From the wild jungles of China to the elegance and solitude of a classic Japanese garden, the versatility – and occasionally the roots – of bamboo knows no bounds.

Mark remembers a bamboo in the back garden of the house he grew up in. And also how exotic it seemed to have something growing in North London that was surely more at home in the jungle. He even had fanciful ideas that a distant relative, a captain in the Merchant Navy perhaps, had brought it back from China. But it was more likely won at the local church bazaar.

ME OLD BAMBOO

While the bamboo may originate in far-off, exotic climes, there are over 200 temperate varieties that grow happily in the UK. After all, this is a plant that's perfectly at home in

Here's an idea for you...

One of the great benefits of a tall, mature bamboo is that it makes an instant screen, and can help blot out an eyesore that may otherwise ruin the effect of the garden. Although not cheap to buy, mature bamboo does establish well. When buying, generally the more canes on a clump the better.

the Himalayas, and laughs in the face of the worst Jack Frost can throw at it.

Bamboos are grasses with woody stems and lush, usually evergreen, leaves. They can grow to just 10cm – or to 10m plus – and have canes, or culms, that vary from gold through to black, forming tight clumps or spreading out over a huge area. Some can be used as ground cover, other as screens, and they're also popular for their swaying and constant movement.

Bamboo differs from other plants in a number of ways. For a start, when a cane emerges, it will, unlike a tree, retain the same girth and never thicken. It will also reach its full height in one year. New, thicker, more vigorous, taller clumps will flow as the roots get stronger. Branches and leaves grow from the nodes on the canes. But it's the roots or rhizomes that cause all the problems. Some species can grow up to a metre a day, but while you need to be cautious with bamboo, there are plenty of clump forming varieties that are easily kept in check.

That said, when planting all but the smallest clump forming varieties, it pays to surround the plant with an impenetrable barrier of thick plastic, or metal, buried two or three feet down. (This barrier needs a bottom to it as, if the sides are blocked, the rhizomes will grow downwards.) This will stop the roots running and taking over the garden. Most enjoy well-drained soil and a sunny site, and once planted, need very little care – bar the odd bit of pruning in spring to thin out old and dead canes. Old leaves and their sheaths should be left around the base of the plant as a mulch.

Of course, you don't grow bamboo for its flowers. As a result the best way to propagate bamboo is through division. If you do manage to coax yours into flower you could do the plant more harm than good, as producing the grass-like heads can exhaust them. This is why some species flower once every 100 years but incredibly, if one species does flower, it's likely to do so all over the world that year.

IDEA 44, **Whispering grass don't tell the trees**, and IDEA 50, **Frills and fronds**, will give you some inspiration for planting schemes using complementary leaf shapes.

Try another idea...

Here are four varieties, all with different habits, that you may want to try in your garden.

- **Dwarf white-striped bamboo** (*Pleioblastus variegates*). A good bamboo for the beginner that grows to about 75cm. It also spreads slowly, which makes it compact enough for a small garden or container. The leaves are variegated green and cream, and it works particularly well with other grasses or taller bamboos. Cut back the old culms in spring.
- **Umbrella bamboo** (*Fargesia murieliae*). This is one of the most widely grown bamboos and another one that suits the beginner. It grows to around 4m and doesn't mind heavy, clay soil. It produces tall clumps of green canes, which often arch under the weight of its own apple-green leaves. Perfect as a screen or wind break.
- **Black Bamboo** (*Phyllostachys nigra*). Very de rigueur at the moment but not the easiest to grow. Can reach between 3–5m, with slender canes that turn jet black after a couple of years. This is a great plant for round the pond (although not with its roots in water) as it produces some beautiful reflections.

'Bamboos are an easy way to mimic a garden Paradise.'
MONTY DON

Defining idea...

101

- **Fishpole Bamboo** (*Phyllostachys aurea*). This can get big and grow well over 5m, with grooved, and often distorted, brown-yellow canes and golden-green leaves. Where it really wins though is that it's one of the least invasive on the market.

How did it go?

Q   **Not very well, now you ask. I planted a bamboo a few years back and it's taken over the whole border. Help! What can I do?**

A   *Don't panic, and don't reach for the weedkiller either. Despite having rampant roots, the bamboo's rhizomatous roots are actually quite shallow. This means you can dig them out, although you need to get every bit to stop it growing back.*

Q   **Any varieties that should be avoided?**

A   *There are a few, such as* Sasa plamata, *which is particularly rampant, and you should think carefully before planting any of the* Pleioblastus *varieties, which will run wild!*

Q   **Can I grow bamboo in a pot?**

A   *Good idea but you've got to be prepared to keep potting it on and dividing it every few years, or it could burst out! Never let it dry out either, and a bit of slow-release fertiliser in the soil will help it along. Let its own leaves do the mulching.*

24

Oh I do like to be beside the seaside

Sand, salt and sea don't sound like a great combination when it comes to a garden but you'll be amazed at what you can grow beside the seaside.

There are two big problems with gardening on the coast: salt and wind. Salt dehydrates plants, while the wind will decimate what's left.

Yet despite this, there's a surprisingly large range of plants that can be grown by the coast, especially if windbreaks such as hedges or filter fences are used to reduce the force of the wind, and stop some of the salty spray hitting your plants.

First, a few tips. As a general rule, look out for plants with small leaves, which do better in a coastal setting. Equally, plants with grey, furry leaves such as phlomis are a good buy. These can withstand the salt much better than most other plants, as the small hairs keep the salt away from the surface of the leaf.

Another clue is in the plant's name. If it has *maritimum* or *littoralis* after it then it's a plant that comes from the coast, and one which should be happy in your garden.

One of the great benefits of a seaside garden is that the warming influence of the sea means it won't suffer from severe and heavy frost. So, with a bit of shelter, it's possible to grow perennials and exotics that wouldn't fare so well inland. These include many architectural plants such as cistus, cannas and cordylines.

'The artichoke outside my window has fourteen buds and is shoulder high, the huge thistles have filled out, the roses are in full leaf, the sages are in bud, the everlasting peas sprawl around lazily across the shingle. The gorse, which took a battering, is sprouting.'
From *Derek Jarman's Garden*

As for windbreaks, evergreen escallonias are a good choice, with dark, glossy leaves which are able to withstand the salt, while pink or red flower clusters brave the elements intermittently from early summer onwards. Hebes can also put up with the salt-laden wind, as can the feathery foliage of *Tamarix tetandra*.

Hedges have a bit more give than solid garden walls, which can actually channel the wind straight into the very beds you are trying to protect. You can also catch glimpses of the landscape through a hedge, or actually use them to frame a view.

And so to the plants. The Sea holly (*Eryngium maritimum*) throwing up spiny blue-grey bracts from June through to September, really is as tough as it looks and makes an excellent foil for other plants.

Red-hot pokers (*Khiphofia*) are another good seaside choice. Try growing a small variety such as Little Maid, which can stand up to the worst the weather can hurl at it. It's also long flowering with ivory blooms tipped with yellow from June until the end of August.

The tree lupin (*Lupinus arboreus*) is an evergreen perennial that thrives in sandy conditions. If it dies after a few years don't worry, they are short lived but it will be well worth investing in another. They have spikes of pale-yellow scented flowers, and are a great shrub for offering shelter to other more tender plants.

Supporting your plants in a windy garden is vital, so check out IDEA 10, *Support network*.

Try another idea...

Other candidates include sea lavender (*Limonium latifolium*), thrift (*Armeria*), chamomile (*Anthemis*) and the low-growing, mat-forming sedums, as well as Mediterranean herbs such as rosemary and thyme.

Cyclamen grow wild along the coast and are easily cultivated in the seaside garden, and the white rambling rose, Seagull, with its stiff, strong shoots, also does well.

One of the UK's most famous seaside gardens belonged to the late painter and filmmaker Derek Jarman. He turned a stretch of shingle beach in the lee of Dungeness power station, in Kent, into a magical space full of weird, spiky plants. One of his favourites was sea kale (*Crambe maritime*) with its fleshy blue-green, sometimes purple leaves. They die away completely in winter before sprouting again in March, the beaches' first sign that spring is on the way.

But, just like gardens in the city or the countryside, no two seaside gardens are the same. For every Jarmanesque homage to

'Isn't it better to produce a garden that looks at home in the reality of your climate, than to plant a garden full of flapping exotics and see them suffer? A garden full of war-zone plants, plants that are just getting by, is not a recipe for a relaxing garden, visually or physically.'
STEPHEN ANDERTON

Defining idea...

pebbles and stones, there's another plot hanging on to the top of a cliff, or another surrounding a bungalow in a small seaside town. What they do share is a setting which at times is all tranquillity and peace, yet at others foreboding and hostile.

How did it go?

Q   I fancy a tree in my seaside garden. Would I be wasting my time?

A   *Choose carefully. There are a few trees that will put up with a constant coating of saline spray, such as the tough old sycamore. Yew is tolerant of thin soils, drought and exposure and the ash is also good on exposed sites, although they're large hungry trees and little will grow under them. Sorbus aria, with its crimson berries, also does well.*

Q   Any ideas for introducing some much needed annual colour to my seaside garden?

A   *With a bit of shelter and a sunny spot, cornflowers, poppies and daisies all spring to mind. Echiums cope well with sandy, chalky soil, and have a range of colours from white through to purple. They also make a good plant for ground cover. The wild flower, viper's bugloss (E. vulgare), is the most recognisable.*

Red alert – with a touch of orange, yellow, amber ...

It's not just the trees and shrubs that add autumn colour to the garden; there are plenty of perennials and bulbs that can bring some seasonal dazzle to the borders.

Some gardeners disappear into their own terracotta shell as the leaves begin to fall. They may occasionally be seen shuffling around the potting shed or berating the postman when their seed catalogue still hasn't arrived, but generally they tend to enter the equivalent of horticultural hibernation.

Yet, should they dare to venture outside, there's a phenomenal range of plants that keep interest going in the garden until the first frosts and beyond. And they'd probably be surprised to hear that they're available in more than just shades of red.

Here's an idea for you...

Seed-heads can also add interest and colour to the post-summer garden, so it pays to leave on some of the more majestic. The Chinese lantern (*Physalis alkekengi*) looks good in the borders or in tubs, while a frosted thistle or teasel is a dramatic sight in the misty morning light. And don't dismiss the humble rose hip, either.

PERENNIAL PERFORMERS

Some of our most recognisable plants come into their own during the autumn. To get the most from them, you need to give a bit of thought to where you plant them, and what other flowers or foliage will be peeking up as they come through.

A great autumn stalwart is the aster, or Michaelmas daisy, which like many of the daisy-shaped flowers is an import from the North American prairies. The rivalry in aster circles reads like the plot from a 1980s soap, with the New York asters (*A. novi-belgii*) vying for top notch with the New England asters (*A. novae-angliae*). The latter tends to win out, with more flowers and paler foliage. Try the large mauve flowers of *A.* 'Mrs S.T. Wright', or the rose-pink *A.* 'Harrington's Pink'.

Asters like the sun, with their roots in well-drained, fertile soil, and should be cut back to ground level and mulched as soon as they've done their bit.

Another plant with its roots in the prairies is the rudbeckia. Again, there's a myriad of types, and it's easily grown from seed, as one of us recently found out with an innocent packet of *R.* 'Rustic Dwarf'. They just kept on sprouting and the mahogany, amber and gold flowers couldn't be given away for love or money in the end. A larger variety is *R.* 'Herbstsonne', with floppy golden petals up to 10cm across.

Sedums offer a completely different colour palate to rudbeckias, with pinks, mauves and purples. Also known as the iceplant because their leaves are cold to the touch,

they offer up flat flower heads much loved by any surviving autumnal bees, although they also pay a passing resemblance to some hybridised version of pink broccoli. This is another plant that likes a sunny, fertile, well-drained spot, but which also benefits from a bit of support come mid-summer. The rust-coloured 'Autumn Joy' (S. 'Herbstfreude') and the mauve S. 'Spectabile' are probably the most common and S. 'Purple emperor' with dark purple leaves and a mass of small pink flower heads is a welcome new addition. Iceberg is one of the most spectacular.

Other perennials worthy of a mention at this time of year are free-flowering hardy chrysanthemums, the dainty rose-pink South African lily (*Schizostylis*) and clump-forming Japanese anemone. The pink form looks great against a background of Firetail (*Persicaria amplexicaulis*), and the white on its own, or amongst dark-green foliage.

AUTUMN BULBS

There are plenty of autumn bulbs too, which should be planted in the spring. *Nerine bowdenii*, with its large clusters of pink lily-like flowers, is excellent in a sheltered sunny spot, at the base of a wall. Crocuses also pop their heads up in autumn, including *C. speciosus*, with its many hybrids such as the dark violet 'Oxonian' and the pure white 'Album', that look good

IDEA 5, *Indian summer* looks at how to get the most from summer flowering plants, while there's much talk of fiery foliage with IDEA 43, *Small trees for small gardens*.

Try another idea...

'As summer edges into autumn the oranges can mass slightly, chrysanthemums, dahlias, gladioli and red-hot pokers rudely milling in amongst the effete garden party.'
MONTY DON

Defining idea...

109

naturalised in grass. There are also colchicums, similar to crocus but with oval-shaped corms. These are ideally planted in groups in semi-shade among the shrubs. And for a burst of yellow in September/October, try *Sternbergia lutea*, which as you'd expect, loves full sun.

Add to all this a backdrop of reddening trees and shrubs, swaying grasses, frosted seed-heads and the odd shot of evergreen foliage, and even the most reclusive autumnal gardener will be forced to poke his head from underneath his shell.

How did it go?

Q **No sooner had I planted some Michaelmas daisies than the old chap next door starting going on about mildew. Is he right?**

A *'Miserable dark foliage, invariably adorned with mildew,' is how one learned gardening writer describes the New York asters. Try the New England varieties instead. They're more resistant. But mildew can also be a sign that your plants need more water, more feed and even dividing up.*

Q **I've got good autumn colour but nothing with berries on. Any suggestions?**

A *For a bold statement of intent try* Callicarpa bodinieri *with its fantastic violet berries. There's a wide range of cotoneasters that are heavily laden with berries, usually red, in the autumn, as well as the firethorn, Pyracantha, with red- and orange-berried varieties, and over 450 varieties of berberis to choose from, many festooned in seasonal berries. Those that are deciduous have stunning autumn foliage too.*

Cutting a dash

Some long leggy blooms were just made for the vase but how do you get your supermodels to look their best before their time in the spotlight?

Gardening is many things to many people. Some go in for monster veg, others see a perfect lawn as the pinnacle of their achievements, others decide to specialise in a particular species such as conifers or grasses. But for most gardening is about colour — and that means flowers.

The trick is to be able to provide fresh cut blooms for the house without denuding the garden. But don't ignore other garden highlights such as autumn fruits, striking leaves, coloured stems and even bare twigs, which all have their part to play.

A CUT ABOVE THE REST

Many plants do well when cut including wild hedgerow flowers, shrubs and tree prunings, but perennials and annuals are the showiest.

Here's an idea for you...

Bring spring forward a few weeks by cutting some forsythia twigs at the end of February. Choose branches that are covered in flower buds (although these will still be closed) and put them in a vase on a light windowsill. In a week or so they'll open and you can enjoy bright yellow blossom at least three weeks before it appears outside. Amelanchier branches will also do the business.

As a guide, in spring choose newly emerging blossom or the first spring flowers such as daffodils, bluebells and tulips. Try a few stems of lily-of-the-valley in a small glass too.

In summer you can select almost anything from the border, and use shrubs for a bit of bulk. The Peruvian lily (*Alstroemeria*) makes a great cut flower but can be tricky to get going. Buy them in pots with the leaves just beginning to show as it's difficult to get the bare roots into growth. Plant in full sun, in the middle of the border and don't move. Perhaps the best summer flowers for picking – indeed they should be picked every other day – are sweet peas (*Lathyrus odorataus*). Choose a scented variety such as Painted Lady or Fragrantissima. Dig a deep pit, add a generous layer of compost, backfill and plant against supports. Once the blooms appear pick, pick and pick again unless you want a tripod of peas instead of flowers!

There's plenty of colour in autumn too. Make sure you have dahlias and daisies in your border, such as rudbeckia, Michaelmas daisies and helenium. The vibrant and vigorous firetail (*Persicaria amplexicaulis*) grows like a weed throughout summer and autumn, but it's great for filling out large arrangements. And at this time of year you can add interest with rose hips, honeysuckle berries and clematis seed-heads.

Even in winter there are still plenty of possibilities for the vase. Catkins (*Corylus avellana*) and pussy willow (*Salix caprea*) are starting to show – as are snowdrops, which can tough out the most severe winter. Pick hellebores too – as they look great close up – but 'sear' the stems after picking to prevent them flopping. And

where would we be without holly (*Ilex*) and ivy (*Hedra*) for a touch of festive cheer. To ensure holly keeps its berries for the end-of-year celebrations, pick it early before the birds get to it. Stick the stems in a patch of soil and protect them with a plastic bag.

IDEA 2, *Top seed*, demystifies growing plants from seed, and IDEA 20, *Shrubs* may whet your appetite for flowering shrubs.

Try another idea...

Tempting though they may be, don't bring hawthorn or gelder rose blossom indoors as they smell of Tom cats, and wear gloves when cutting *Euphorbia* as the sap can cause irritation.

CUTTING EDGE

If you're really keen, and never want to have to buy in flowers again, then why not develop a separate 'cutting garden'. Include bulbs and favourite perennials, together with scented climbers and small flowering trees. If space is restricted, then pinch a corner of the veg patch.

Plant lots of annuals, choosing a mixture of colours and shapes, like cosmos, clarkia, marigolds (*Calendula*), snap dragons (*Antirrhinums*), cornflower (*Centaurea*), love-in-a-mist (*Nigella*) and tobacco plants (*Nicotiana*). Sow in seed trays in the spring and transplant once the last frosts have gone.

Prepare the soil well by adding compost and a sprinkle of bonemeal, and plant in rows or clumps for a bit of mutual support – but make sure you've room to pick them. Once the performance starts, add a bit more support, give some liquid feed and water well.

'There's nothing like going out into the garden and picking flowers for the house. It's the gardener's equivalent of collecting new-laid eggs from nesting boxes.'
SARAH RAVEN

Defining idea...

113

BLOOMING GOOD

To get the best out of cut flowers there are some simple rules. Cut at an angle, for maximum intake of water, remove lower leaves and place in tepid water as soon as possible. Crush woody stems and slit tough stalks to encourage them to take up water. Any flowers that leak sap or are flopping can be sealed and brought back to life by dipping the stems in boiling water for 20 secs. For a lasting effect add some 'cut flower food' to the water, or a teaspoon of sugar mixed with a few drops of bleach, and keep the vase away from heat.

How did it go?

Q When I cut roses for the house they either droop straight away or fail to open at all. What should I do?

A   *Not all varieties behave well when cut. Those that do include Iceberg (white), New Dawn (pale pink), Graham Thomas (yellow) or Charles de Mills (deep red). The old fashioned rose, Rosa Mundi (Rosa gallica vesicular), does well too and has stunning hips in autumn. Cut your chosen stems whilst still in bud and make a 2cm slit up each stalk, to increase the take up of water.*

Q Having grown flowers for cutting do I need flower-arranging classes?

A   *Although formal arrangements have their place, don't feel under pressure to create a work of art. A natural group in a jug will do fine. You'll need to collect a choice of containers over time but for starters a pale green vase, 25cm tall, will set off most flowers and branches well ... and you'll need a small glass container for the sweet peas.*

Hedging your bets

Hedges are a long-term project but there's a lot to be gained from planting a wall of box or yew.

Not too long ago farmers were ripping up hedges by the kilometre in an attempt to win ever more land for cultivation. Gardeners, whether consciously or not, appeared to follow suit, driven by the need to keep up with the Joneses and their latest in wavy lap larch board, classic picket, or rustic post and pole fences. Fortunately, the trend has been bucked.

Unless you've inherited a hedge that happens to be in the right place, establishing a new one takes some years. So why do you want a hedge? Is it purely a decorative feature, or are you looking to create a screen to ensure some privacy and cut out noise? Perhaps you want to establish a boundary, need a windbreak, or simply want to attract wildlife?

Here's an idea for you...

An unlikely candidate for hedging is buddleia, but if you're not a stickler for hedges clipped to perfection then create a 'buddleia barrier' for summer and autumn. Then it's great for that wispy, shaggy look, while its colourful, vibrant flowers are the perfect lure for butterflies.

A mixed, informal hedge covers most options (whisper it, but we're covering conifers later). Hazel, hawthorn, beech and hornbeam are some of the most common.

It's essential to plant up a new hedge in the late autumn, as the plants will need time to find their feet before the first growing period the following spring. Apart from the usual organic matter, some bonemeal will help them on their way. These first six months are the most critical period, so water at the first sign of a dry spell and resist the urge to clip them, however unkempt their appearance.

Should you be the proud owner of an already established but unruly mixed hedge, give some serious thought to laying it. There's evidence that this ancient country craft is enjoying something of a revival, so here's your chance to make a contribution. The end product provides you with a windbreak, screen and a haven for birds.

It's a job best done in the late winter or early spring, just as the sap is beginning to rise. If your hedge is on a slope start at the bottom and work up, otherwise start at either end. Use a billhook to chop the trunks almost through. This is lighter and sharper than an axe, and the chopping action will cut through any branch quickly and easily. Now more pliable, push them over, laying them up the slope at an angle of about 40°. As you move along, drive in rough-hewn stakes at 1m intervals, and then weave and intertwine the leaning branches between the stakes.

If you can, to give everything a bit more rigidity, thread willow wands and hazel rods between and along the hedge top. Both these and the stakes will rot away in time, and by then the hedge will have thickened enough to support itself.

You can trim the hedge when you've finished but not necessarily to spirit-level accuracy. Perhaps better to let nature take its course instead, with her characteristic undulations.

Bear in mind, though, that you need to let your newly planted hedge settle in for a few years before laying.

PINES NEEDLE

Ok, here we go, can't put it off any longer. The conifer: it's suffered in recent years, thanks largely to those leylandii innocently planted in the 1970s, which have now reached maturity. They're a suburban blight, and as a result the popularity of all conifers seems to have plummeted to such an extent that you're now more likely to read about them in the law courts section of your daily paper, rather than the gardening pages.

Privet will grow anywhere and if you want to discover the artist in you, use it for some topiary. See IDEA 19, *To prune or not to prune.*

Try another idea...

'*... shaping a hedge is the closest most of us will ever come to doing sculpture or erecting a monument, but I think the real reward is more mundane. Shearing is very empowering – it gives you an exhilarating sense of control and achievement. You can stand back afterward and say, "look what I've done".'*
From *All About Hedges* by RITA BUCHANAN

Defining idea...

In the right place, a conifer hedge does still have a lot going for it – all you need to do is monitor it closely and make sure it's kept at a manageable height.

There are two essentials you need to consider first. Proportion – if you've got 10,000sqm to play with then the sky's the limit, but in a small garden the last thing you want is a hedge soaring 20ft up in the air, blocking out all your light, with thirsty roots turning the ground beneath it into a dust bowl.

The other essential, if your hedge is part of the boundary between yourself and the neighbours, is to let them know first. It can avoid so much hassle in the future.

If time is on your side try yew, which is a relatively slow grower. Given acid to neutral free-draining soil it will add 30cm a year, but it does give the richest of greens and is one of the few evergreens that allows you to prune back into old wood. In a hurry? Cypress (especially *Chamaecyparis lawsoniana*) is a speed merchant growing at 1m a year!

Other shrubs not normally associated with hedges, but which perform perfectly well, are the ornamental plum (*Prunus cerasifera*) or the purple berberis (*B. thunbergii*) – the thorns of the latter will also deter intruders. The thick evergreen *Escallonia macrantha* will help maintain your privacy.

Of course, fences have their place but gardens are about living, natural things. And you can add more life and colour to your hedge by encouraging other plants to grow through it. Honeysuckle's the leading contender along with varieties of rose and clematis, while it's not uncommon for a blackberry bush to self seed and put in a welcome appearance.

Q   **Box – it's a bit overrated isn't it?**

A   *Box is at its best when given a short back and sides. Keep it low and smart, and it makes an ideal frame for vegetables, or to give shape to groups of annuals or perennials.*

Q   **I thought my plants would be protected in the lee of my new hedge, but they actually seem to be suffering. Why is this?**

A   *Hedges are greedy bruisers and consume all available surrounding water. Keep your hedge trimmed so it is narrower rather than wider at the top, and place your plants at least a metre away from its base, where they will seek their own moisture and still enjoy the shelter of the hedge.*

How did it go?

On the waterfront

Whether you're using the latest in toughened liners or an old washing-up bowl, ponds add a whole new aspect and lease of life to the garden.

In Europe the humble pond dates back to medieval times. The cloistered walks of abbeys and monasteries often included a well or fountain to aid meditation, while in Renaissance Italy they took on an altogether different look.

Along with fountains they became big, brash and ornate, the central feature of a wave of formal gardens sweeping across Europe. By the time Versailles was built in 1715, size was everything, and a fountain was considered inadequate if its jet was anything less than 100ft.

It took the sober British to bring things back down to earth, as the Romantic period took hold, and nature came back into vogue. But enough of the history. The point is that, while ponds are a fantastic addition to any garden, size really does matter.

Here's an idea for you...

Dig a shallow hole next to the pond and allow the pond's liner to extend into it and beyond. Refill the hole, and you've made yourself a bog garden. Keep it wet and add some moisture-loving plants. Many irises are happier in a bog than directly in water. The lady's smock (*Cardamine pratensis*) has a beautiful pale mauve flower, while the umbrella plant (*Darmera pelata*) has white or pink flowers and dark-green leaves which turn bronze. And no bog garden, especially a shady one, is complete without primulas.

DOWN TO THE DIGGING

It's very easy to allow a pond to dominate a garden. But if your aim is to attract frogs, newts and dragonflies, then the smallest wet area will do.

A few other things to consider:

- Formal or informal? Formal requires a lot more work, can look out of place in an otherwise informal garden and isn't much loved by wildlife.
- If the idea of running water appeals, then work this out carefully before starting on any construction.
- Ideally site your pond in partial shade, away from deciduous trees, whose leaves will clog it up in autumn.

When marking out the pond with pegs, take the time to make sure they're level. And although plants will help upset any symmetry, for an informal pond, avoid perfect squares and circles.

The size and depth is up to you, although 1m in the middle should be the max – it hardly needs saying that young children can drown in the shallowest of ponds.

IDEA 35, *Wildlife friendly*, identifies which birds and insects you can expect to visit your pond.

Try another idea...

Around the edge you need a shallow ledge to enable creatures to crawl out, with flat-bottomed terraces and shelves on which to lodge baskets.

Remove any heavy or sharp stones, and then line generously with soft sand before laying a single piece of butyl liner over the whole area, making sure it extends beyond the pond's edge. Cover the bottom with about 10cm of earth, again devoid of sharp stones, for direct planting or as a 'bed' for your baskets to sit on.

You can now fill with water – rain or tap – and then trim the excess liner.

THE WATER MARGIN

Having a pond opens a whole new world of planting possibilities, and if you're new to it, it pays to visit a specialist water plant nursery.

There's a huge variety of aquatic plants but first on your list should be the marginals, those plants that live in the shallow water at the pond's edge. The kingcup (*Caltha palustris*) has deep yellow cup-shaped flowers, while water irises (*Iris laevigata*) give you a tall, handsome foil and grow best in about 15cm of water. The yellow flag iris is best left to the wild except 'Variegatus', the yellow and green striped one. Also be careful with bulrushes and grasses as they are inclined to rampage.

'The still surface of the pool reflects the ever-changing patterns of the clouds, and the broad stone surround invites you to sit and let your tensions slip away.'
GEOFF HAMILTON

A pond wouldn't be complete without waterlilies (*Nymphaea*) and, as well as stunning flowers, their broad leaves help shade the pond and reduce green algae. N. *pygmaea* is ideal for small ponds, N. *alba* and the crimson N. *Escarboucle* are vigorous if you're looking for something bigger. They're best grown in baskets, which have been lined with an old sack to stop the soil escaping. Use heavy garden soil, top out with gravel and then sit them at the recommended depth.

Oxygenating plants are essential – but once established they can be invasive, so during the summer be brutal and remove plenty. *Elodea crispa* is the most manageable.

POOL MAINTENANCE

Shading the surface of your pond from direct sunlight with surface plants or overhanging trees will help the water stay clear and algae free. But net the pond in autumn to prevent dead leaves falling in and contaminating the water.

Installing a small pump will help keep the water aerated and grace your pond with either a fountain or trickle feature. Electrics are required here and must be handled by a professional. Clean and check the pump once a year.

Submerge a stocking packed with barley straw to combat blanket weed – believe us you'll experience this sooner or later. It may be an old wives' tale but usually has some impact. Pull the green cobweb-like weed out whenever you can too, and leave it on the side for a day so any small water creatures can crawl back into the pond.

Q   **I'm embarrassed to say that my butyl liner is showing – what's the remedy?**   *How did it go?*

A   *Assuming the top of the pond is level, and you really did use a spirit level during construction, try surrounding the pond, or just those exposed areas, with flattish stones. Lay them so they hang over the pond's edge to hide any lining. You can even firm them in with a few blobs of mortar but leave the occasional, strategically placed gap on the shallow side for frogs to escape.*

Q   **The pond freezes over in winter, sometimes for several weeks. Does this matter?**

A   *For that length of time, yes, as the water needs oxygen. When freezing weather is forecast leave an old football in the pond. It will help you create a breathing hole each day. But never smash the ice with an axe or sledgehammer as the shock waves will kill fish, frogs and newts.*

Danger – children at play

Children and gardens don't always mix, but there are ways of making a garden fun for kids without turning it into a council playground.

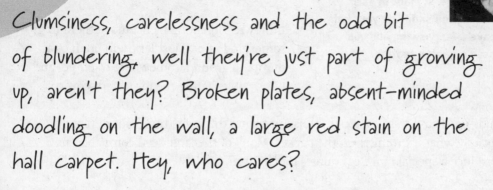

Clumsiness, carelessness and the odd bit of blundering, well they're just part of growing up, aren't they? Broken plates, absent-minded doodling on the wall, a large red stain on the hall carpet. Hey, who cares?

It's when this bungling is transferred to the garden that tensions can be strained, because while carpets can be cleaned and walls scrubbed, prize winning blooms are irreplaceable, for a year at least.

But if you're a gardener with kids then you'll want them outside, taking an interest in flowers, nature and the environment.

Here's an idea for you...

The stark A-frame of a swing can jar in a garden. But look again, and with some carefully positioned twine and the odd stick, you've got the perfect support for climbers like clematis, honeysuckle and sweet pea. A plant in each corner, and suddenly your kids have a leafy swing and you have a garden feature.

KINDERGARTEN

First things first, kids love to dig, so to avoid them excavating what to young eyes may look like a bare patch of ground, but which is actually a seed bed raked to a fine tilth, leave a patch for them.

If they're old enough, encourage them to grow something; if not, just let them use it as a dumping ground, somewhere to empty and bury things before the joy of rediscovery.

Kids need easy-to-grow, tough, resistant plants that, nine times out of ten, do exactly what it promises on the packet. Many of the large seed companies now produce a special range of annuals for children.

You can't go wrong with the bright colours of sunflowers – with the annual competition to grow the tallest – marigolds, cornflowers, campanula and pansies. They'll also love fluffy Lamb's ears and nasturtiums.

Edible things in the garden are also a plus, and can teach an important lessons about which plants can be eaten and which can't. Strawberries grown in hanging baskets make for an interesting and tasty treat, as do crispy green runner beans, sweet pod fresh peas and crunchy carrots (although these will need a wash). Herbs are a winner too – easy to grow, great to smell, and good to eat.

Attracting wildlife into the garden is another way of firing young imaginations. The more organic your garden, the more beetles, bees and butterflies that are likely to live there. And you won't have to worry about kids touching leaves sprayed with pesticides, or picking up intriguing blue slug pellets.

However, short of discovering a pride of lions behind the potting shed, even wildlife will only hold the attention for so long. Garden toys are also required.

The most avant-garde designer would struggle to find a place for sandpits and trampolines in a garden, but even these can be disguised with a bit of hard graft, that great gardening euphemism for digging. In this case you're burying the aforementioned toys: putting the trampoline into a pit, with the bouncy bit at ground level, and building a simple sunk brick pit with a lid for the sand. Out of sight, out of mind?

NATURE'S TOYS

There are countless other ideas too. You can use willow whips to make living wigwams and tunnels. Just stick them in the ground, where they'll root and keep on growing.

Mazes cut in the lawn or stepping stones weaving a magical path through the borders (watch out for prickly plants) are instant winners, and any large weeping

IDEA 9, *Grass roots*, will help you fortify your lawn in preparation for the summer holidays.

Try another idea...

'I conducted a wide-ranging survey and asked my three children what they most wanted from a garden. The answers were immediate: tree house, tree house, mountain bike course,'
From *Gardening Mad* by MONTY DON

Defining idea...

trees a perfect hideaway. Trees also offer the chance for some kind of tree house but, if your carpentry skills aren't up to that, a rope tied to a sturdy branch is an instant escape route for many a fantastical game.

Talking of which, if there is somewhere on your plot that screams out secret den, then check it's safe – remove things like stinging nettles and rusty nails sticking out of fence posts – and let the kids call it their own. You can even lend them a helping hand to put up something a bit more permanent.

SAFETY FIRST

There are a few other health and safety issues but most are common sense. Clear up dog and cat mess, watch kids around water, don't let them eat soil, wash cuts ASAP (and check kids' tetanus jabs are up to date) and make sure tools are stored safely so your toddler isn't suddenly let loose wielding a vicious pronged fork.

If you've got kids the garden should be their domain as well as yours. Flourishing cover drives and wristy backhands should all be applauded not decried, and even off-target free kicks that decapitate delphiniums should be a cause for celebration – albeit through gritted teeth.

But children should also be viewed as willing helpers, with an attention span of at least half an hour, if you're lucky. So get them to do a worthwhile job such as picking up leaves, sorting out flower pots or even, under supervision, a spot of weeding or deadheading.

Keep it basic though, as asking a six year old to prune every third shoot back to the fifth bud is only going to end in tears. And it won't be theirs.

Q   **I've heard a lot about poisonous plants in the garden. Are the dangers real?**

How did it go?

A   *Among the most common poisonous garden plants are laburnum, with its seed pods that look like peas, monkshood (Aconitum) which causes a skin rash and is extremely poisonous if eaten, and the foxglove (Digitalis purpurea) which can cause changes to the heartbeat. For more tips on child-proofing your garden, visit the Royal Society for the Prevention of Accidents (RoSPA) website at www.rospa.co.uk.*

Q   **What about tempting their nostrils too?**

A   *There's a whole range of plants that smell of chocolate including Chocolate cosmos (Cosmos atrosanguineus), while the climber* Akebia quinata, *with its purpley-red flowers, smells of vanilla. The curry plant (Helichrysum italicum) has curry scented leaves which give off a spicy aroma on a warm, sunny day and, who knows, a hint of lavender may calm them down when things get overexcited.*

Winter wonderland

Evergreens, dried seed-heads, berries and coloured stems are the secret to year-round interest.

A garden with winter interest makes work for idle hands and gives you the chance to enjoy those plants that actually look at their best on a cold and frosty morning.

SHAPE AND STRUCTURE

Winter lays the structure of a garden bare. But if you plant evergreens for interest, and train and clip trees to give shape, your garden need never loose its sense of form. Even the hard landscaping provided by paths, steps, paving and walls helps to keep the garden together, while a well-chosen trellis, support or arch can provide a new, seasonal focal point.

If you're not an over-tidy gardener, then leave border plants with unusual seed-heads – such as *Phlomis*, *Sedum* and *Echinops* – well alone and enjoy their frosted shapes. Similarly, soft brown grasses can look warm and mellow in the winter light. If you do go for this approach, everything will need cutting back in February, before the new growth appears.

Bare, needle-less Christmas trees dumped outside back gates, in the vain hope that the bin men will show mercy, are a sure sign the festive season is over. Much better, though, to recycle them, either to be shredded at the local tip or cut up, with the biggest branches used to protect tender plants such as *Osteospermum* and the crowns of a young *Gunnera*. Alternatively, you could recycle the tree by planting it back in the garden. A yew tree can be carefully dug up and planted again each year, and with a bit of root pruning should last ten years or more. Keep it in moist compost whilst indoors and when replanting make sure the planting hole – which can be the same each year – is well drained, and add a good helping of manure. Yew is, of course, poisonous but unlikely to tempt the kids.

The coloured stems of the dogwood (*Cornus*) range from bright green and yellow through to scarlet, wine red and almost black. They're a must for winter colour, while the vivid, violet berries of *Callicarpa bodinieri* look positively tropical, and last well into December.

It's staggering how many small flowers can survive the winter weather. Appearing in early January, the delicate snowdrops (*Galanthus*) reliably force their heads through the cold, hard ground and go well with aconites and hellebores. For the best chance of getting snowdrops to take, and then colonise, buy them after they've finished flowering, when they're still 'green', and plant them where they won't dry out in summer.

Without the more blousy competition of the borders, evergreens come into their own at this time of year. A low boundary wall, a clipped ball or spiral of box (*Buxus*) or yew (*Taxus*), can look stunning, whilst slim conifers such as the Italian cypress (*Cupressus sempervirens*) provide upright accents at a time when most other plants have been cut down.

FROST AND SNOW

IDEA 20, *Shrubs*, gives details of the many and varied shrubs with winter interest.

Try another idea...

Glimpse a snow-covered garden and you're immediately whisked off to a land of make-believe, amid comments of 'it used to snow so much more when I were a lad'. It probably didn't, but enjoy it anyway.

A topping of snow along the box hedges reinforces their shape, while a sprinkle around the low-growing black grass (*Ophiopogon planiscapus* 'Nigrescens') shows off its striking foliage. But if there's a heavy covering keep an eye on upright growing conifers, and shake off the snow before it bends or snaps the branches.

A delicate covering of frost is also to be enjoyed, as long as you've taken all the right precautions to protect your tender plants and pots. Those that need their centres guarding against the cold, such as the tree fern and cordyline, should be wrapped up with straw, surrounded by chicken wire. Pots of half-hardy plants should be taken into a frost-free, sheltered place, or covered in bubble wrap or hessian, and raised off the ground.

Other anti-frost measures include insulating the outdoor tap, placing footballs in the pond to prevent it freezing over, and feeding the birds. Add in a bit of digging, turning the compost heap, running repairs to fences and walls, and cleaning your tools, and you might just have time to look at that seed catalogue before the first daffodil appears.

'The flowers of late winter and early spring occupy places in our hearts well out of proportion to their size.'
Gardening writer GERTRUDE S. WISTER

Defining idea...

135

How did it go?

Q **You mention placing orders from seed catalogues but do I have to wait for spring before I start sowing?**

A *Winter is a good time to get certain plants under way (if you have a heated propagator all the better). For bedding, sow pelargoniums and begonias at this time, while on the veg front start off broad beans, beetroot and peas in pots. You can also take root cuttings from* Acanthus, Echinops *and perennial poppies (*Papaver*).*

Q **Can I plant shrubs and trees in winter or should I wait for spring?**

A *Planting shrubs and trees when they're dormant is a good idea. Just make sure the ground isn't waterlogged, and frost isn't forecast.*

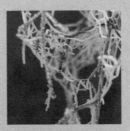

The sweet smell of success

Sit back in a deck chair surrounded by the heady fragrance of a well-positioned honeysuckle, or the calming scent of lavender, and suddenly all the hard work seems worthwhile.

Nature introduced scent to attract pollinating insects but it can also have a remarkable affect on Homo sapiens. Scent is evocative: smell hyacinths and you think of spring; sweet peas mingled with the aroma of freshly cut grass and summer holidays come flooding back; while bonfires and fallen leaves mean that autumn's approaching.

Fortunately, most types of plants come in scented forms from shrubs to climbers, perennials to annuals. But it's not just a question of choosing the right ones – you also need to place them where they will be truly appreciated.

It's a natural reaction to press your nose into a flower and take in its scent. Sometimes, though, you'll be disappointed and plants previously renowned for their perfume are now scentless, their smell bred out of them in favour of other features. So always check the label for a mention of fragrance if you are unable to sniff the flower itself. Sweet pea *odoratus* 'fragrantissima' is a dead give-away.

UNDERNEATH THE ARCHES

Arches, pergolas, even the porch are all crying out to be smothered in aromatic blooms. Honeysuckle is a traditional choice. The deciduous type (*Lonicera periclymenum*) is slightly less rampant than the evergreen version *L. japonica* 'Halliana' but both have delicious scent.

The romantics, of course, will choose roses, particularly climbers like the pink R. 'Mme Grégoire Staechelin', R. 'New Dawn' or R. 'Zéphirine Drouhin' (the latter is good for a north-facing aspect). You can prolong their interest too by combining them with a contrasting coloured clematis – sadly not fragrant – while the species rose R. *englanteria* will cover a fence with aromatic foliage and fill the air with the smell of fresh apples.

'Another hint of it as the summer breeze stirs, and I know that the place I should be off to is my childhood.'
MICHAEL FRAYN writing about the scent of humble privet in *Spies*

More vigorous are the ramblers such as *Rosa filipes* 'Kiftsgate' or R. 'Rambling Rector', which have one splendid flush of thousands of small, white-scented flowers, but they do need space and some ruthless pruning every three years.

And you can bring some of that scent indoors too, by using rose petals to make pot-pourri, or as environmentally friendly, biodegradable confetti at a summer wedding.

Freesias are less commonly grown but *F.* 'Yellow River' and *F. alba*, in particular, have good perfume. They grow from half-hardy corms, flowering late winter to early spring, if given a sheltered site. Dig up after flowering and dry them off ready to replant in the autumn.

IDEA 26, *Cutting a dash*, will give you ideas on cutting scented flowers for the house and IDEA 42, *The herb garden*, tells you how to grow these culinary companions.

Try another idea...

Another unusual plant worth growing for its scent, shape and pale yellow flowers is the tree lupin (*Lupinus arboreus*). Don't panic – it's only a 1.5m shrub and will not get out of bounds as, sadly, it is short-lived. Also include for scent, if your garden is not too cold, the deep purple-pink *Daphne mesereum* or the paler *D. odora*. Remember too, the sunnier the position the greater the scent.

SCENT AND SEATS

A wisteria wrapped round a garden shed, or hovering over the compost heap, smacks of bad planning. Its subtle clove-like scent will be wasted. Scented plants need to be close at hand – you need to be able to smell them as you take in the early spring sunshine. So, either move a seat near to them or, if that's not practical, plant up the area around a fixed seat with those fragrant plants that will wow your senses, like pots of lilies – the most fragrant are *Lilium candidum* (Madonna Lily) or *L. regale.*

Many plants release their scent in the evenings, when the fading light means they have to try harder to attract insects. So if you've got a particular part of the garden for alfresco suppers, make sure the likes of the tall tobacco plant (*Nicotiana sylvestris*), evening primrose (*Oenothera*) and night scented stocks (*Matthiola bicornis*) are within nostril range.

'It is a golden maxim to cultivate the garden for the nose, and the eyes will take care of themselves.'
ROBERT LOUIS STEVENSON

Defining idea...

For centuries lavender has been used in perfumes, bath oils and sewn into bags. Inter-planted with pinks (*Dianthus*) and you'll have a winning combination of colour and scent. Both like well-drained soil and a sunny site.

Cat mint (*Nepeta*) provides an alternative scented edging, and don't forget the sweet peas, which should be placed where you regularly pass by or need to stop, say en route to the vegetable patch.

How did it go?

Q   Are there any winter shrubs with scent?

A   *Surprisingly many shrubs provide scent in winter and at the beginning of spring.* Chimonanthus praecox *is not called 'Winter sweet' for nothing and the perfume of* Hamamelis mollis *is a real delight. (If your soil is chalky grow its lookalike,* Cornus mas *instead.)* Mahonia *is well worth growing for its dramatic evergreen foliage and delicately scented pale yellow flowers that bloom as winter passes.*

Q   Are there some plants to avoid for their nasty smell?

A   *Hawthorn blossom and the wild gelder rose have a foul smell when picked. Others, such as lilies and* Viburnum badnantense, *have a strong heady scent, which is lovely in the open air but too strong for some, in a confined space. The skunk cabbage (*Lysichiten americanus*) is an attractive bog plant with striking yellow flowers which, up close, smells (not unsurprisingly) of rotting cabbage.*

32

Alright mate

If you think the idea of plants ganging up on insects is more suited to a sci-fi plot than a vegetable plot, then you've not heard of companion planting.

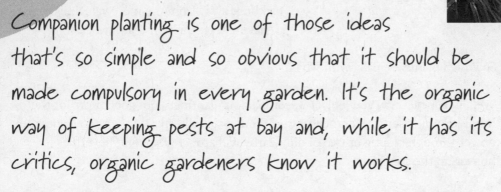

Companion planting is one of those ideas that's so simple and so obvious that it should be made compulsory in every garden. It's the organic way of keeping pests at bay and, while it has its critics, organic gardeners know it works.

And now they can back up this optimism with scientific fact, because boffins at a British university have proved that the marigold, a companion plant par excellence, really does contain an oil that repels aphids. The oil is released as a vapour which wafts around and deters bugs from landing on neighbouring plants.

BUZZ OFF

There are several different ways in which plants help each other. Many destructive insects locate their food by smell, so by interplanting possible targets with other plants that have a strong scent, you can confuse the enemy.

Here's an idea for you... **Buy a book on bugs, or borrow one from your local library. The vast majority of insects are actually beneficial to the garden, so it pays to learn what they look like before you inadvertently squash a friend not a foe.**

A second way is that some plants, through scent, colour and pollen, attract predatory insects into the garden. These predators will then seek and destroy the harmful insects which were about to have a good chew on your plants. And a third group virtually sacrifice themselves for the cause, luring the bad bugs away from the more valuable crops, to have a go at them instead.

So which plants are pally with which?

Well, whichever way you look at it, companion planting is not good news for the humble aphid. Garlic underneath roses is one way to keep greenfly at bay, but if any do get through, a sprig or two of dill nearby will attract wasps and hoverflies to hoover up the stragglers.

Aphids also turn their proboscis up at chervil, which is good interplanted with lettuce, and they don't care much for coriander either.

Yarrow (*Achillea millefolium*) is a fine flowering plant for the veg patch and another one that draws in the predators, including ladybirds, who love nothing better than an aphid picnic.

Try another idea... **For tips on getting the best from the veg plot try IDEA 15 *Small but perfectly formed*, and for more advantages of organic gardening see IDEA 34 *The good life*.**

One of the best vegetable combos is carrots and leeks, because while the latter repels carrot fly, the former gives off a smell offensive to the onion fly and leek moth (yes, apparently there is such a thing).

Another good double act sees tomatoes, with a bit of basil, deterring the asparagus beetles, while chemicals in the asparagus itself help prevent a harmful nematode attacking the roots of the tomato plant. Tomatoes are also one of the main beneficiaries of being mixed up with French marigolds

As you can see, this is all good stuff.

FRIENDS REUNITED

The trusty old nasturtium also has several uses. As well as a strong smell that keeps some aphids off the likes of broccoli and marrows, black fly love it but, being tough as old boots, it will rejuvenate after an attack, while other crops grow on unmolested.

Radishes can also be used as decoy, luring the likes of cucumber and flea beetles from their lunch of choice.

Of course you can help yourself by avoiding monoculture. If you offer up row after row of the same plant, with nothing planted between them, it's only a matter of time before the right pest flies past and tucks in. And, by growing aromatic plants that attract insects, you can give a helping hand to those plants that rely on good pollination to succeed.

'French marigolds are one of the best companion plants but they're of no culinary use whatsoever. Pot marigolds are not quite so good a companion but the petals are marvellous in soups and stews. Nasturtiums attract cabbage butterflies, so keeps them off the cabbages, and every bit of the nasturtium is edible. The flowers are wonderful in salads, and the seeds excellent pickled.
'But the best companion plant of all is the edible garland chrysanthemum, also called Shingiku in Japan and Choy Suy Green in Chinatown. It is particularly good with brassicas, keeping a lot of pests away, and attracting pollinators. You can use the young foliage in stir-fries, and the petals in salads. You can even use it as a cut flower. It couldn't be a better plant!'
BOB FLOWERDEW

Defining idea...

143

But companion planting isn't just about warding off insects. Plants can provide support for each other, act as windbreaks, create shade and act as ground cover – destroying weeds that would otherwise be fighting for valuable nutrients.

Yes, there's certainly an element of trial and error to companion planting. There are plenty of possible combinations and a few cases where the chemicals in one plant can actually inhibit the growth of another (see below). So it pays to keep a gardening diary to note down the combinations that work, and those that don't.

How did it go?

Q What's all this I've heard about nitrogen fixers?

A Now this is a really clever form of companion planting. The fixers are leguminous plants like peas and beans, as well as lupins, although a clump of these on the veg patch would probably only attract an army of ravenous slugs. A bacteria in their roots converts nitrogen into a form that can be more easily absorbed by other plants. When the legume dies down, some of this nitrogen is left in the soil as a free feast for nitrogen-hungry plants like sweet corn, spinach and the brassicas.

Q So are there any planting combinations that should be avoided?

A Apparently fennel is blackballed by most other plants – so if you do grow it, keep it in solitary confinement. Carrots are no fan of dill either, while beans and peas detest the company of onions.

33

From cabbages to kings

You've grown the basics, mastered the intricacies of crop rotation and shocked family and friends with your ability to put new potatoes on the table at Christmas. Well, now for something completely different.

We all love the challenge of growing something different, something new, something a bit unusual. Well it's not just flowers that throw up the odd horticultural challenge, the world of vegetables also has its own fair share of tricky customers.

But the effort involved in growing them is often rewarded when you serve them up for dinner. So, with salted butter at the ready, welcome to the molly-coddled, pampered world of asparagus and artichokes.

ASPARAGUS

Asparagus is a king among vegetables. It's a delicacy, and nothing else tastes quite like a freshly cut spear. And that is the key, because asparagus is a truly seasonal vegetable that should really only be eaten fresh in May and June, not shrink-wrapped for December. It's something that should be looked forward to, not devoured all year round.

Jerusalem artichokes are a perennial at the other end of the 'difficult to grow' spectrum. A member of the sunflower family, with attractive yellow flowers, they will grow just about anywhere, as long as it doesn't get water-logged. Simply plant the mature tubers in the spring and dig up the edible knobbly new ones as and when you want them, from autumn onwards. A nutty taste great for salads or boiled as a potato.

The best way to grow asparagus is by using one-year-old crowns planted out in March or April. Only male plants produce spears, and all-male varieties give a higher yield, such as Franklim F1 or Lucullus F1. And remember it's the newly emerging spears that you eat, not the stalks that follow on.

If you're lucky, and garden on sandy, well-drained soil, the crowns can be planted directly into the ground. If not, you need to prepare an asparagus bed. Now this certainly isn't easy but you are planting something that will keep on cropping for about 20 years. And, once established, asparagus only needs basic care to keep going.

How big an area you devote to asparagus depends on the size of your garden but bear in mind the plants need to be around 30cm apart. And, although it likes an open site, asparagus isn't fond of strong winds. The bed needs to be well dug, well manured and free of perennial weeds. To improve your drainage, add a liberal amount of horticultural grit.

Next dig a trench about 30cm wide and 20cm deep and build up a ridge, about 8cm high, along the bottom. The crowns need to be handled very carefully and kept moist. Lay them over the top of the ridge, with the roots hanging down over the side, and cover with another 8cm of soil. Water well and then, in autumn, top up the trench to soil level. Now the waiting starts.

It pays to give the plants two years to get established, cutting the fronds down in November when they begin to yellow. Then in May of the third year you can begin to harvest. When the spears are 10–12cm high, cut them about 8cm below the soil, but stop by the end of the month and let the spears develop into the feathery fronds that will feed next year's growth.

Check out IDEA 32, *Alright mate* for details about companion planting, while IDEA 42, *The herb garden* will tell you how to grow some herbs to accompany your veg.

Try another idea...

For subsequent years, June 21 is traditionally the last date of the season.

ARTICHOKES

This is a great plant, albeit one that's a little mixed up. Globe artichokes are perennials that can grow up to 1.5m, so don't hide them away on the veg patch, because as well as bearing a delicious crop, they're great architectural plants for the back of the border too, where they'll also get the shelter and fertile soil they need.

'You grow it [asparagus] because it gives you a supply of absolutely fresh spears, but also to spit in the eye of the seasonless "food" industry and its joyless inducements of year-round treats.'
MONTY DON

Defining idea...

They're also a bit on the fussy side, which is why there's a challenge in growing them. They're best grown from root offsets, or rooted suckers (success with seeds is far more variable). These you can buy first time round, but for successive years take cuttings from your own plants.

The soil needs to be well-drained and the offsets, which should be about 20cm long with their leaves still attached, should be planted 1m apart and about 5cm deep.

They need protection from full sun in the early stages and should be mulched and watered once they've become established.

Like asparagus, this is another plant that requires patience, and in the first year you should remove the edible flower heads to encourage more growth.

Cropping really begins in the year after planting. Allow around six stems to develop and then harvest the kinghead, the bud at the top of the leading stem, when it's still green and tightly folded. Leave it too long and it will open into a large purple thistle-like flower – very pretty but not very edible.

Leave about 5cm of the stem attached, and harvest all the secondary heads in June and July. They will carry on producing for up to five years, but as soon as they die down in autumn give them a good mulch and protect the crown from frost.

How did it go?

Q   How come my asparagus just never got going?

A   Lots of possibilities here but one of the most common problems is overzealous weeding. Asparagus has shallow roots that can easily be damaged by clumsy hoeing. And you really must stick to the harvesting regime if your asparagus is ever going to flourish.

Q   You've tempted me. Is there another tricky veg I can grow?

A   Cauliflowers present a real challenge and are fussy in the extreme, needing plenty of space and water. But there are some amazing new and tasty varieties such as 'Graffiti' with its purple florettes and the spiky lime green version, romanesco 'Celio'.

The good life

Gardening organically is as much about common sense as it is about being chemical free.

Gardening without chemicals takes a bit more thought, a bit more preparation, and a bit more effort. You need to be more vigilant with your crops and you need to understand much more about the wildlife in your garden, and how it can help you. Personally speaking, this is proper gardening. It's about rolling up your sleeves and getting your hands dirty, rather than donning protective goggles and pumping up your chemical sprayer.

DIRTY BUSINESS

Soil and its structure are at the heart of organic gardening. Get that right, so the logic goes, and strong, healthy plants will follow. And the best way to improve your soil is by feeding it with organic matter, which encourages the creatures living in it to do their bit, and will improve its structure and fertility.

Fed up with trying to coax some life into your lawn? Then why not turn all or part of it into a wild flower meadow. You'll only need to cut it a few times a year, and the wildlife will love it so much more than a close-cut turf. But remember, wild flowers like nutrient-poor soil, so it pays to skim off the top 15cm of topsoil before you start planting.

By using your own compost heap, you are effectively digging back in what grew in your borders the previous year, returning all those nutrients from whence they came.

With the soil improved, the rest is common sense. Buy disease-resistant plants where possible, make sure the pH of the soil is to their liking, and that the spot you've chosen suits their needs.

It's not just your use of insecticides and herbicides that you need to reconsider, but fertilisers too. Remember you're growing for the pot or the vase, not the show table, so do your plants really need all that feed? And there's plenty of evidence to suggest overfed plants are a lot more attractive to pests.

If you do carry on feeding, think about the organic alternatives such as bonemeal for adding phosphate, or dried blood for a quick fix of nitrogen. Liquid fertilizers made from comfrey or animal manures are also useful, especially for container-grown plants.

But gardening organically is about much more than avoiding pesticides and creating your own compost. It's a much broader concept that takes in issues such as conserving natural resources, avoiding pollution, and recycling.

Take peat for example. It makes our blood boil that so many gardeners and garden centres continue to use it. Peat is a finite resource and, to be quite honest, it's virtually knackered already. Peat bogs are some of our richest and most diverse

natural habitats, yet in the UK alone a staggering 2.55 million cubic metres is dug up for horticultural use each year.

There's much more on making sure you grow the right plants in the right soil in IDEA 1, *Did the earth move?*

Try another idea...

Yet some professional gardeners still swear by it, saying that it remains by far the best medium for growing a wide range of plants. And that may well be true, but the alternatives are improving all the time and where's the logic in destroying a natural habitat in order to create an artificial one?

Trials suggest that peat-free alternatives aren't as effective as the real thing, but that isn't really the point. This is a fantastic opportunity to experiment with your own mixes, using an alternative such as coir, bark chippings or a peat-free multi-purpose compost as your base. Then simply add your own measure of top soil, garden compost, sand and grit, and see what works with your seedlings, plants you've re-potted or your longer-term containers. OK, it may take a few seasons to get it right, but what's the hurry?

Recycling is also a key part of gardening organically, from making your own compost with kitchen waste to buying trugs and weeding buckets made from recycled car tyres. It's also about recycling water by using water butts; using prunings as plant supports; collecting and sharing your own seeds (but leave some for the birds!); even buying a kit to make your own biodegradable plant pots from newspaper.

'The chemical gardener goes to war on a daily basis and perceives his garden akin to a "battlezone", whereas the "organic" gardener tends to diffuse potential problems before they have the opportunity to escalate.'
PATRICK VICKERY, Gardening writer and nursery owner.

Defining idea...

151

Then there are all those things which are really just good gardening practice, such as rotating your crops, encouraging beneficial insects into the garden, and providing habitats and food sources for friendly predators.

Gardening organically is far from a panacea to all our gardening ills. You will still take losses (perhaps more at first), still have to face up to failures and still get frustrated as slugs engulf your delphiniums. But to most of us gardening is a hobby, a pastime, a challenge. And meeting this challenge by working with nature, not against her, is so much more rewarding than reaching for the bug buster.

How did it go?

Q   I've heard a lot about no-digging gardens. Is it organic?

A   *Undisturbed soil is a much better place for many beneficial bugs and organisms, and a policy of no-digging can also preserve soil structure and cut back on moisture loss. But it's only an option where the soil structure is already good and if you've got the time to really keep on top of the weeds.*
On the other hand, digging is the only way of incorporating bulky stuff into the soil – worms can only help so much! Breaking up the soil can also improve drainage, aerate it and improve root penetration. It also destroys weeds and exposes pests in the soil to winter weather and predators.

Q   Am I OK using John Innes compost?

A   *While there is a peat-free version, John Innes composts do still contain peat, albeit a small amount. And by the way, John Innes is a type of compost based on loam rather than a brand, and was developed by Mr Innes in the late nineteenth century. So now you know.*

Wildlife friendly

With intensive farming and the countryside fast disappearing under concrete and brick, our gardens have become a vital green oasis to many birds, insects and animals.

A garden without wildlife is a pretty sorry site. No bird song, no pollinating insects, no frogs or toads lurking behind the garden shed. No fun.

On a purely practical level, of course, by attracting hoverflies, tits and hedgehogs into the garden we're employing our own free, organic band of pest controllers.

But to become wildlife friendly doesn't mean you need to replant your garden from scratch, let it become an overgrown mess, or stop growing the plants you love. You just need to make a few adjustments, and employ some other organic methods of gardening at the same time. After all, it would be pretty pointless attracting song thrushes into the garden to help keep snails under control, while at the same time continuing to use slug pellets which could poison the birds.

There are four basics you need to provide to attract wildlife: food, water, shelter and somewhere to breed. But once they know these essentials for survival are all

Here's an idea for you... **To a toad, a drain is a des res. They love them, so hold off using bleach when you give them a clean. Instead, use one of the new 'green' bactericides that use naturally occurring bacteria rather than chemicals, and are harmless to wildlife.**

available in your garden, they'll come back time and time again.

So here are some suggestions on how to get the bees buzzing and the birds singing on your plot.

IT'S A FOOD THING

Try and find room in the garden for plants that wildlife enjoy, such as the seed-heavy teasels, sunflowers and thistles, or the berry-laden cotoneasters and hollies. They look great and birds will love them.

Grow plants that are rich in pollen and nectar too, such as *Verbena bonariensis*, buddleia, sedums, eupatorium and nepeta. As well as pollinators, these will also attract predatory insects into the garden, such as ladybirds and lacewings, which will lay their eggs on the plants. In due course these will hatch into larvae, which are the aphid-eating machines of the insect world.

In order to encourage maximum diversity, try and combine elements of a woodland area, wild flower meadow and a pond or boggy area in your garden.

The simplest of water features can make a difference – even an old washing bowl sunk into the ground in a quiet corner of the garden, part-filled with stones, will attract frogs and toads. And you can give nature a helping hand by asking friends with ponds both for a jar of bug-rich pond water, and any spare frog spawn they've got lying about. Bird baths are also important, both as a source of fresh drinking water and as somewhere to bathe.

GIMME SHELTER

Try to find an area of the garden you can let grow wild, where plants like stinging nettles can flourish. This 'weed' plays an important part in the life cycle of over 100 different species of insect, including several butterflies.

A great way of achieving winter interest in the garden is to resist the urge to cut everything back and tidy up in the autumn. Granted, some jobs need to be done but dead and decaying plants add an air of mystery to any border, as well as providing refuge for overwintering insects.

The likes of beech, blackthorn, hazel, hornbeam and hawthorn are excellent trees when it comes to offering wildlife shelter. And log piles are hotels with 24-hour room service to many bugs, hedgehogs and grass snakes. The insects and fungi that gradually eat the wood will, in turn, feed other creatures in the garden.

There's a whole range of purpose-built shelters too – from lacewing chambers to ladybird towers, nester kits for pollinating bees to butterfly houses. And the hedgehog house nestled under a forsythia in the front garden will certainly raise a few eyebrows.

Try another idea...

IDEA 28, *On the waterfront*, shows you how to attract some water-loving wildlife to your garden with your own pond.

Defining idea...

'Wildlife gardens have already saved the frog, the toad and the newt. Our bird population is enhanced dramatically by service station wildlife gardens which provide a lifeline every winter. Your garden, however small it is, can make a real difference.'
From *How to make a Wildlife Garden* by CHRIS BAINES

Garden birds, particularly nesting ones, devour caterpillars, leatherjackets and chafer grubs, as well as slugs and snails. So a few well-sited nesting boxes, out of the reach of your pet moggy, will work wonders.

This is just a taster of the simple changes you can make to ensure that local wildlife thrives and that your garden is with nature rather than against it.

How did it go?

Q   I've done all you said but still can't attract any animals into the garden. What am I doing wrong?

A   *It may sound obvious, but have you left them a way in? Birds and insects can fly in but most gardens are pretty much sealed off from the outside world at ground level, with brick walls, fences and gravel boards preventing hedgehogs and frogs from getting to the tasty treat you've so thoughtfully left out. Then again, do you have a cat or dog that is chasing the wildlife away?*

Q   If I keep putting food out for the birds, will it put them off their main meal, i.e. the pests on my plants?

A   *True to some extent. It probably pays to lay off refilling the bird table at the height of the summer, to encourage the tits and robins to forage in the border for their grub. If you do put nuts out for the birds during the summer, remember to put them in a mesh container so that the parents don't feed their chicks with chunks that are too big, and potentially lethal.*

36

Let there be light

From 500-watt security lights to a dozen or so strategically placed tealights on the decking, lighting your garden can be an illuminating business.

So why bother to light your garden? Well, it's a cliché but true all the same — many of us now see the garden as an extra room, an extra living space that we want to use and enjoy. So it stands to reason that we want to spend as much time in it as possible. Even when the moon's out.

There's a number of different ways you can go about lighting your garden and most of them you should be able to complete with only minimal (although vital) professional help.

Of course you could call in the professionals to do the lot. Mains-powered units are certainly impressive but installing them means a lot of upheaval and mess, as the

Here's an idea for you...

Whatever you do, don't dismiss the humble outdoor fairy light. They look great wrapped round the trunk of a tree or draped over a trellis, especially during the festive season. Ropes of lights are also effective, just twisting through your borders or lighting up the outline of a garden structure.

armoured cables need to be buried at least 60cm under your borders. There's the cost as well, and don't forget the impact it will have on the electricity bill.

Solar lights are a good choice and relatively cheap to buy. They're also a solution if you haven't got an electricity source for the garden, and useful too at the end of a long garden, where cables won't reach anyway.

Mounted on spikes, solar lights can be easily moved around the garden (best to site them in a sunny spot!) and, whilst they're not powerful enough to light up individual plants and walls, they're great used for lining paths or showing where steps are. For special occasions, flares look fantastic dotted amongst the beds – the citronella ones will also help keep the midges at bay – and lanterns with simple tealights are also effective.

But for a more permanent arrangement that can highlight the best aspects of your garden, go for a simple off-the-shelf number from the local DIY store. There are a number of kits where you just run the cable round the garden, clipping the lights on wherever takes your fancy. How many you'll need obviously depends on the size of your garden.

As for power, a 12- or 24-volt system uses a transformer plugged into the mains to reduce the voltage. Then plug the lights into the transformer. If you need an outside waterproof plug, this is where the electrician comes in.

So how to use them?

Spotlighting is used to highlight particular plants or garden features. It creates dramatic effects, drawing the eye towards it, and so works well when seen from a distance.

To find out how to build some of the structures you may wish to light up, see IDEA 40, *Structurally sound*.

Try another idea...

Up lighting involves placing the light below the plant, angling it so that it shines up through the branches or foliage. It's particularly effective used to light a tree or large shrub, and is a good way of adding a bit of extra height to a garden. Remember, you don't have to stick to white light. Create different moods with blues, purples or flame shades.

The reverse is down lighting, which is the best way to create pools of light. Fix the spotlights to a fence, pergola or tree, or on the wall around a patio or decking. They can then be used to pick out certain features, such as a garden ornament, or particular pots and containers.

'Filling anything other than your own private space with any kind of light is an intrusion and invasion of privacy. Garden lights must be personal and intimate. The light they throw must rest modestly within the shadows they create.'
MONTY DON

Defining idea...

The term 'grazing' refers to lights that are angled to show off a particular surface, such as a dry-stone wall, or the slats of a fence. It's also a clever way to bring out the colour on a painted wall.

You can use a hidden light source to silhouette plants or objects from behind, creating intriguing shadows and giving the garden depth. It's particularly good with architectural plants, such as yuccas and phormiums.

Waterproof lights in ponds or fountains are dramatic but can verge on the tacky unless carefully positioned. Use them to pick out moving water, rather than flooding the whole pool with light. There's also a range of solar-powered globes that float on water.

However, all this is not to say that darkness doesn't have a beauty all of its own, or that your neighbours want their lawn lit up by a badly positioned spot. There needs to be a touch of subtlety about any lighting scheme you install. In most towns and cities it's already impossible to escape the orange glow of a thousand street lights, but it's phosphorescence we really don't want to add to. So with gardens lights, less is certainly more.

How did it go?

Q I've never been happy using electricity in the garden. Any other safety tips you can pass on?

A If you're running cables up and down the garden, whether for lights or power tools, always use a residual current device (RCD). This circuit breaker will shut down the power should you inadvertently cut through the cable.

Q Will lighting up my garden put off the wildlife?

A Not necessarily so. A gentle white light fixed on the corner of your house will enable you to watch hedgehogs, foxes or badgers at night, if they frequent your garden in search of food. Turn your inside lights off for a better effect.

The can-can

All plants need water to survive, but how can we maximise its effect in the garden, while minimising waste?

Water is fast becoming one of our most precious natural resources, which is why, as gardeners, we need to use it as effectively and as sparingly as everyone else.

There are some basic rules that are well worth sticking to, in particular collecting it where you can. Don't just 'splash it all over' either, as this is one area where 'little and often' is the wrong maxim. A long and thorough soak is much better that a gentle sprinkle – once a week rather, than once a day.

WATER COURSE

For starters, only water when your plants need it and in summer never water during the day as it will have no lasting benefit and most of the water will simply evaporate. Best wait until the evening, so the water can do its bit overnight. With hosepipe in hand, it's a great way to relax after a hot day, and enjoy the garden.

Here's an idea for you...

To cope with the heavy demands of newly planted shrubs and trees, sink a piece of plastic pipe down to the roots after planting. Leave the top just above ground level. Angle the pipe towards the roots and you can water them directly. This has the added advantage of encouraging roots to grow downwards rather than upwards towards surface water. In between waterings, place a stone or cork in the opening to prevent mice or pests crawling in and feasting on your new investment.

Having got the timing right, how's your aim? Try and get the water straight to the plant's roots. A garden sprinkler pointing up in the air will refresh the leaves but unless left on for hours, its spray will never reach the soil. Use a hosepipe on low pressure instead and aim it on the roots. Count to a hundred (two hundred if you can bear it) for each shrub or climbing plant, especially those having to compete for moisture, say under a tree or against a wall. Mature shrubs and trees should cope with dry conditions in most summers.

Making your soil as spongy as possible will help retain the moisture, and you can do this by adding well-rotted compost in autumn or spring each year.

The final rule is to keep the soil cool. Covering it entirely with plants will help retain moisture and minimise evaporation.

The common garden hose is now quite a sophisticated beast with controllable flow, adjustable sprays and recoiling versions that can even wind themselves up after use. But consider all your options before simply leaving them on for long periods. In particularly dry areas a seep hose may be more economical, letting out water drip by drip and keeping the ground constantly moist below the surface. Connected to a timing switch these secret soakers can also be set to water at night.

But for the butts a lot of water would be lost down the drain. There's a sense of satisfaction in getting something for free, and collecting rainwater comes under this category. It's also coming straight from the heavens, so is free from contamination. Place two or three together with connecting pipes and the bulk of your watering needs will be met. Use green plastic butts where they're out of sight and old cider or sherry barrels for show.

Don't forget the greenhouse too. Fix guttering to a butt on at least one side, and it will mean an end to all those long trips back and forwards to the outdoor tap, saving time and effort, as well as water.

You can also use this supply to keep a watering can topped up at 'room temperature'. Cold water will be too much of a shock for seedlings and young plants. Invest in a can that has a fine wire mesh attached to the rose which prevents the holes in the rose from becoming blocked up – usually the curse of fine spray cans.

IDEA 7, *Sweet smelling brown stuff*, will help you produce all-important moisture retaining compost, and **IDEA 1**, *Did the earth move?*, suggests some drought-tolerant plants.

Try another idea...

'Water – its supply and its quality – is as an essential issue in our new world as it is everywhere else'
TIM SMIT

Defining idea...

HOLIDAY INSURANCE

All gardeners deserve a break but asking the neighbours to do the watering is a tall order. At least make it simple for them by setting up a self-watering system using capillary matting (readily available at garden centres). Place it on some polythene and cut a strip to act as a wick, running from under the matting to a covered container, set at a lower level. Place thirsty plants on top of the matting and let them gently sip away. All your neighbours will have to do is keep the container topped up every four days or so. Remember to water well before you go and don't forget to bring back a bottle of something, other than water, as a thank you.

How did it go?

Q   You say to be sparing with water so which plants need it most?

A   *Vulnerable plants include those with shallow roots, seedlings, young plants or those newly planted, leafy veg (like spinach and runner beans) and fruiting trees or bushes. Shrubs that form flower buds at the end of summer– such as camellias – will need a good drink in summer, to swell the buds.*

Q   Can I also recycle used water from the house?

A   *Yes, you can re-use bath or washbasin water, but not if it's had detergent mixed in it.*

38

Dear diary

Why keeping a record of your garden, and what you do in it, makes sense.

A garden is in a permanent state of evolution; it's never finished. That's what makes it so interesting and all the more reason to keep a note of its changing and maturing face. And make a photographic record too, because like a fisherman's tale, last year's crops, herbaceous borders and annuals were always bigger, better and brighter. Or were they?

By taking notes we learn where we went wrong as well as what we did right, so influencing future decisions. There are a number of ways of doing this but, whether in a notepad or on a computer, in the form of a full-blown diary or random scribblings, your jottings will act as important reminders and tips for next year and beyond.

Here's an idea for you...

Draw up a tree chart of your garden. Trees are major investments and should be around a long time. Make a plan and note the type of tree, where it was purchased and when it was planted. The chart will be an interesting reference point and vital information should you need any tree surgery. You could also leave it for the next gardeners, should you decide to sell up and move on.

FORWARD PLANNING

So why take notes? There are some tasks you just don't want to miss where a diary note is crucial. Leave shearing off the old hellebore or epimedium leaves too late and you will run the risk of cutting off the new growth with the old. February is the time to do this – early for the hellebores and late for the epimediums. Also in February, make a note to trim hedges before birds start nesting.

The catalogues thudding on the mat will leave you in no doubt when to order things! But when your seed order arrives it's useful to log when you need to plant which variety. You don't want to find them forgotten on the shelf at the end of the year.

Make a diary entry to check tree ties twice a year in November and May, and to get the mower serviced in December, which is often the cheapest time. A memo at the end of November to clear the *Clematis montana* out of the guttering, as it makes a bid for the chimney stack, will ensure you remove all the dead leaves at the same time.

Defining idea...

'*A garden is never so good as it will be next year.*'
THOMAS COOPER
(US photographer/teacher)

If you look at the herbaceous border when it's in full flow the gaps and mistakes will be obvious – to you if not to others. You imagine you'll easily remember to move that leggy phlox, or divide up the crowded crocosmia,

166

but you won't. Come the autumn, when all looks dead and brown, you'll be struggling to recognise the plants, let alone remember what you intended to do with them. So keep 'notes on the border' and, during the summer, jot down which plants to move, divide or keep for seed.

Idea 4, Don't pay the nurseryman, reminds you when to take which cuttings.

Try another idea...

A self-taught, enthusiastic and successful gardening friend was highly organised – too much so at times! But her 'order book' was worthy of publication. She recorded annually all the seeds, bulbs and plants she purchased – the supplier, the variety, quantity and price. This is a great way to avoid disappointment when you want to re-order and can't remember the name or the supplier.

Technology not only helps with lists and reminders but it simplifies keeping a photographic record of your garden too. A basic digital camera is an inexpensive way of recording the gardening year. The first snowdrop to appear, a planting combination that really worked, or the hosta, planted for its bold blue leaves, putting on an unexpected golden autumn show.

Some people are born list makers. Whether this is you or not, two lists are especially recommended. One for gardening items you would like to receive as presents – should anyone ask. The other, an immediate 'to do' list for the coming week or month. And, if it's not too daunting, start a 'major projects' list as well.

'The man around the corner keeps experimenting with new flowers every year, and now has quite an extensive list of things he can't grow.'
WILLIAM VAUGHAN, writing in the 16th Century

Defining idea...

How did
it go?

Q **How can I keep an account of the names of my plants as well as my trees?**

A *It's difficult to keep plants labelled in the garden and fancy markers are expensive. So keep a written or computer list with a page for each section of the garden; fruit and veg patch, border, shrub bed, etc. List plants as you purchase them, with a description and position. This task alone will help you remember the names!*

Q **What can I use as a prompt to set up my first diary?**

A *Start reading and watching. TV gardening programmes, newspaper columns and magazines contain detailed 'action needed' sections, covering when to prune what, when to take cuttings and care for your lawn, together with timely reminders for your border, vegetables and fruit plots, under glass and in the pond. Find a writer or presenter who shares your gardening philosophy and stick with them.*

39

Your own little powerhouse part II

As well as bulbs and corms, there's a range of other bulbous plants that can bring life to your borders. Welcome to the world of tubers and rhizomes.

Many, although certainly not all, of this wide range of plants form part of that loose collection of bloomers, summer flowering bulbs. It's also a group that happens to contain some of our most popular and colourful plants, although only a few are hardy, so they'll need bringing in over winter.

A quick word on definitions for all the lexicographers out there. A tuber is a swollen underground stem base which, unlike a bulb, has roots growing from the sides as well as the bottom. There are also lots of growth points scattered over its upper surface, perhaps best seen on the most common tuber of them all, the humble spud. In the herbaceous border you're more likely to recognise the good old dahlia (although this is actually a tuberous root, but let's not split hairs!).

Here's an
idea for
you...

Let's face it, even to the trained eye, one end of a begonia looks much the same as the other. Obviously this is a problem when it comes to planting so, if you're not sure which is which, put the tuber in a plastic bag of damp compost or perlite for a couple of weeks. Shoots will form and you'll be able to plant them outside, the right way up.

An individual tuber can last for years, with some, like the cyclamen, getting bigger and bigger rather than producing offsets, while others, like the dahlia, are soon crying out to be divided.

Rhizomes are thickened underground stems that have chosen to grow horizontally rather than vertically. Roots grow directly from the underside and the main growing point is at one end, although there may be additional buds along its sides. Irises and cannas are good examples, although quite different in appearance.

TUBULAR SWELLS

Dahlias are among the easiest garden plants to grow, with a colour for everyone, and a range of different flower forms from the simple single to the blousy pompon. Plant in late spring with the eyes about 10cm below the surface. They thrive in well-drained, rich soil and need full sun to reach their maximum potential. They generally bloom from midsummer until the first frost but with so many varieties (around 20,000 at the last count), each responding to slightly different conditions, it pays to pick one or two you like the look of, and then read up on them.

Defining
idea...

'No other flower sucks in light so voluptuously and returns it with such velvet intensity of pigment as an iris.'
MONTY DON

The tuberous begonia is the only one of the begonia family that you can treat as a perennial to be grown outdoors. Plant out (just below the surface as they're prone to rotting) in May, in

well-drained soil with some shade. But make sure there's plenty of room between the plants – perhaps as much as 50–60cm – to allow the air to circulate, and give them space to grow.

IRIS EYES ARE SMILING

Irises, which grow from fleshy, creeping rhizomes, are divided into three groups: bearded, beardless and crested. Once again some further reading will be required as some like acid soils, others alkaline; some open position with their rhizomes partly exposed, others dappled shade. Bearded irises are the most common type, and have wonderfully extravagant blooms. There are cultivars ranging from a miniature dwarf such as *Iris pumila*, with its white, purple or yellow flowers, to the taller *I. florentina*, with its blue-tinged, white flowers, and vanities that will flower from early to late spring. The name comes from the short hairs on the back of the petals just in case you were wondering! These unshaven beauties must be planted in gritty, sandy soil, with their rhizomes exposed on the surface, where they can be baked by the sun.

If your garden has heavy, badly drained soil, you'd be wise to consider some of the beardless irises which, although not as colourful as their 'hirsute' cousins, will put up with more moist soil. The bright blue flowered *I. sibirica* does very well in damp ground. Plant this type, with their more slender rhizomes, below the surface and allow them to spread.

For full details on how to store dahlias over winter see IDEA 5, *Indian summer*, and for more on bulbs and corms see IDEA 14, *Your own little powerhouse part 1.*

Try another idea...

'If you observe a really happy man you will find him building a boat, writing a symphony, educating his son, growing double dahlias in his garden, or looking for dinosaur eggs in the Gobi Desert.'
W. BERAN WOLFE (American psychiatrist)

Defining idea...

With cannas, it's a good idea to start them off indoors, in a propagator if you've got one. Cover with just a centimetre or so of compost and water sparingly. Pot them on when the shoots are about 5cm high.

Alternatively, they can be planted directly into the garden in about mid-May. Whichever method you choose, give them a spot that's got rich, sandy loam soil, preferably in full sun. They also need regular watering.

Finally, a quick mention for one of our favourite plants, Solomon's seal (*Polygonatum*). This is a woodland plant with various varieties that do well in different conditions. All are hardy and rhizomatous, and most have strong architectural foliage with fantastic greenish-white drooping flowers. Superb.

How did it go?

Q   Can I take root cuttings from my tubers?

A   *No, it's best to divide tubers with a sharp knife once they've started to regrow in early spring. Always making sure each part has at least one good bud. You can, though, take soft cuttings from the new growth that appears in spring, to swell your stocks.*

Q   My irises are doing well – too well in fact. Should I divide them?

A   *Definitely. Plants like irises grow in clumps which can easily get congested. Regular dividing (every three years or so) can breathe new life into them, and that means better blooms. You also get more plants to spread around the garden. Simply dig up the whole clump just after flowering and cut off the new rhizomes from the old woody centre, which you can chuck on the compost heap.*

Structurally sound

The familiar sound of splintering wood, the gentle crash of bricks, the air turning blue as you strike thumb, not nail. Oh, the joys of DIY.

For some, the pleasure of building something with their own hands is a complete anathema. Why, they reason, when the local garden centre has gazebos and arches stacked to the ceiling, should you even think about dragging out a box of tools that hasn't seen the light of day since you were forced to 'customise' a flat-pack wardrobe several years previously?

For others, it's a challenge and a chance to see how much of those woodwork lessons at school really sunk in.

Timber, ideally hardwood, is likely to be your key garden material. Best bought from a timber merchant or sawmill, rather than a garden centre, you need to make

Here's an idea for you...

Do not dismiss out of hand using reconstituted stone or good old concrete. The advantage of these materials is that you can make things to the size and shape required – a concrete seat for instance. Make a wooden frame corresponding to the seat-top's dimensions and stand it on a plastic sheet, leaving any wrinkles or creases in place (these will give the seat an age-old look). Shovel in the concrete. When set, mortar the top on two similarly made pillars.

sure it's been treated or pressurized. This means it's been submerged in tanks with the preservative forced into the core of the timber.

Failing that, use an untreated hardwood. Beech is fairly common, relatively inexpensive and, if bought from a timber merchant, it should have been properly seasoned, although it will still need further protection from the elements. Apply at least two liberal coats of preservative. You won't need to re-apply it and you'll be rewarded with a structure that will fend off everything the weather can throw at it.

OK, that's the wood sorted, now you need to put it together. Whether you're contemplating a pergola, an arch, or rustic table, consider trying some basic joinery rather than slamming in nails to hold it together.

There is method in the madness because, while using nails is undeniably quicker, the vagaries of the weather and constant use will soon have your structure wobbling or even collapsing, as the nails loosen.

Much stronger is a simple cross-halving joint, which is also perfect for a standard pergola built from 10 × 10cm timber. (You can even inspect the construction method at any garden centre.) A piece is cut out of one strut to slot into another. The principal working tools you need are a tenon saw, broad chisel and a mallet. No need for glue.

The picture overleaf shows a bench and table made with round, treated beech posts and held together with cross-halving, some mortice and tenon joints, and a few screws. The rough timber means the joints aren't accurate to the millimetre but they've stood in all weathers for 15 years, and are as good as new.

If you're not a 'brickie' by trade it's probably safer for everyone that you confine any brickwork to say a retaining wall, or something nice and low!

Before you start, always make sure the bricks for your project match those of your house, lest you end up with an unsightly mishmash of a wall made of London stock running alongside a house built of multicoloured, handmade bricks. Less of an eyesore, but also important, is to match the bond or pattern of the house bricks.

Building a free-standing dry stone wall is an exceptional skill. And, if only for safety reasons, should be left to an expert. However, a low dry stone retaining wall is much easier, and the end result offers endless scope for growing aubrieta, alyssum, campanula, and many other rock-loving plants. Just two tips. Lay the first course at least partially buried to give the wall some stability and, as you build, lean the stones slightly into the material you are retaining.

Try another idea...

There's more fancy brickwork in IDEA 46, *Up the garden path*, and tips on where to put them in IDEA 6, *Design without the despair.*

Defining idea...

'*Most of us tend to be very timid in our selection of external features, with the result that they do not make a strong enough statement within the garden's design, or are swamped by plants.*'
JOHN BROOKES, garden designer

How did
it go?

Q   What about using screws instead of nails?

A   *Screws can be used as additional support, but not as a replacement for a joint. Don't forget, screw into the cross grain not the end grain or they'll soon work loose. Once you've mastered the cross-halving joint, the basic pergola doesn't need screws or nails. What's more, if a strut is damaged it can easily be replaced without having to wrestle with screws or, worse still, rusty nails.*

Q   What can I do to save a stone wall ravaged by ivy?

A   *Pull away the ivy and remove the loose stones temporarily, if it helps you reach any ivy rooted in the wall. It's a good idea to burn the ivy but bear in mind it's highly flammable. You also need to remove all the loose mortar. There are products you can spray into the wall to kill off the ivy but new mortar and good pointing will also prevent re-growth. The ivy will start again outside the wall, so just cut it off wherever it raises its head.*

41

How to get the most from your containers

Even the biggest gardens have pots and containers brightening up a terrace, bringing life to a plain brick wall, or even lurking in the borders, adding a bit of timely, seasonal colour.

'Gardening with pots and containers — not like the real thing is it?' a friend quipped when we mentioned this chapter in the book. Oh, such folly! Containers are not an easy way out. They depend on you for constant food and water more than anything you have growing in the borders.

Yet this is also the beauty of containers – you're in control. You can move them, replant them, and keep them out of the reach of slugs and snails. You can let your imagination run wild, moving plants round as they come into bloom. And you can even surreptitiously place a few in your borders if they need a bit of a lift.

Here's an idea for you...

To speed up that aging process on your terracotta or stone pots, a liberal coating of natural yoghurt will give the mosses and lichens a helping hand. Make sure you've soaked the pots in water first and once 'painted' put them somewhere cool, damp and shady to let the bacteria do its work.

GETTING KITTED OUT

Plants will grow in just about anything, from ceramic vases to old watering cans, wooden planters to your own 'mock' rock troughs. But, even in small gardens, bear in mind you'll always make more impact by using large containers.

Terracotta pots are the pot of choice for most people. They look natural, age beautifully and are heavy enough to stand up to blustery conditions. But they're also very porous and, unless you line them with something like a bin bag with a few drainage holes added, they will soak up water before the plants get a look in. And stopping this water leaching into the terracotta also means they're less likely to crack when it freezes (and that goes for the so-called frost-proof pots as well).

The first thing to check with any container is that it has drainage holes at the bottom – if it doesn't, get the drill out. Next add some crocks, stones or old bits of polystyrene from broken up seed trays, to stop those vital drainage holes clogging up. An old cloth over the crocks will filter the water and stop your compost washing away.

Now for the compost itself. Tempting as it may be, avoid using garden soil as you don't know what pests and disease could be lurking in it. Better to use a loam based compost such as John Innes No2, or a general potting or multipurpose compost – peat-free of course.

However, despite its impeccable green credentials, the downside of peat-free alternatives is that they dry out quicker than peat, so add a bit of leaf mould or garden compost, and some water-retentive crystals too.

For acid lovers like rhododendrons, you'll need to use lime-free ericaceous compost.

For tips on how to grow vegetables in containers see IDEA 15, *Small but perfectly formed*. IDEA 43, *Small trees for small gardens*, gives further ideas for trees in pots.

Try another idea...

MIX AND MATCH

If you're planting up a container with several different varieties of plant, make sure that they all enjoy the same growing conditions. Arrange the plants, in their pots, on top of the compost first, imagining how they will fill out as they grow.

Start planting with the plant in the tallest pot (and therefore the biggest root ball) first. Put this in place and then add more compost to achieve the correct planting height for the smaller plants. This will also stop them sinking and ensure that their roots are in contact with the compost.

Always try and keep as much of the root ball intact as possible, tapping the base of the pot rather than yanking the plant out by its stem. Keep firming them in as you go, making sure there are no gaps or air pockets. If the roots of your plants have wound themselves around the bottom of the pot (pot-bound), gently spread them out before planting.

'Plants in pots are like animals in a zoo – they're totally dependent on their keepers.'
JOHN VAN DE WATER (US gardening writer)

Defining idea...

Your compost should finish about 3cm below the rim to allow for ample watering, which should also be your next job. Finally, add a layer of gravel both for decorative and practical reasons – it helps to retain moisture.

Bulbs are perfect for pots and growing tulips in containers allows you to appreciate their magnificence close up, and increases the chance of a 100% success. But you can grow most plants in containers – annuals, perennials, grasses, shrubs, climbers, vegetables and herbs, even small trees will be quite happy – as long as you look after them. And that's the key.

CONSTANT CARE

Plants in containers need regular attention and regular watering – rain isn't enough to keep them going (even in the winter you need to keep an eye on the dryness of the compost). Pellets of slow-release fertiliser pressed into the soil are a good idea too, although the plants will also appreciate a fortnightly dose of tomato feed in summer.

Deadheading, replacing plants that are past their prime and checking pots for any pests, such as slugs or weevils, that have had the audacity to climb in, should all become part of your maintenance routine.

Q   **I fancy a herb garden but don't have the space. How will they fare in a pot?**

A   *Very well. Try using a strawberry pot. Add plenty of grit and plant up each hole with your favourite herbs. Put in both the curly and broad-leaved · parsleys near the bottom leaving the sun seekers, like thyme and sage, near the top. Then you can place it right outside the kitchen door or on the patio near the barbeque. Herbs do well in hanging baskets too.*

Q   **Trees in containers – you're joking aren't you?**

A   *Not at all. The ones to go for are those that are naturally dwarf or slow growing, or which won't mind regular pruning. It also means that you can grow trees that won't thrive in the rest of the garden, such as tender ones. Citrus fruit grows well in large pots and you can wheel them inside for winter. Among good container trees for sunny spots are the bay laurel (*Laurus nobilis*) and the common fig (*Ficus carica*), while for shade you could try the evergreen* Pittosporum tenuifolium.

How did it go?

The herb garden

Why choose freeze dried when you could be picking fresh herbs every time you need them?

The beauty of herbs is that they'll go anywhere — the corner of a mixed bed, a container or hanging basket, or just dotted around the vegetable patch, where they may even become important companion plants to other crops.

Choosing which herbs to grow is a matter of taste in more ways than one. Grow what you enjoy cooking with but consider colour, form and structure too. Many herbs are perennials that you can leave in the ground to do their bit year after year, with just a haircut in autumn. They're easily propagated from cuttings too.

Herbs also throw up some attractive flowers, although the effort they put into doing this does detract from their core business of producing tasty leaves. The best time to harvest herbs is in the early morning.

SUN WORSHIPPERS

Many herbs naturally grow on the sun-baked, well-drained soils of Mediterranean countries, so choose a bright spot – near to the kitchen door if you can.

Here's an idea for you... **Bay (*Laurus nobilis*) responds well to being clipped – right down to the ground if necessary. So why not train (or buy) one as a standard, leaving room for other herbs below. Or place two in pots at your house entrance for a noble effect! Each time you prune save the clippings for the kitchen.**

Thyme, marjoram, basil, sage, rosemary and bay all need sun, which helps to improve their flavour, although the last two also enjoy a bit of shelter. For shady spots try chives, parsley, mint and chervil.

Most herbs prefer light, fertile soil and if you garden on chalk you're laughing. Mint and parsley like moister conditions. They do well in containers too – arrange those that enjoy the same type of conditions together.

MINT CONDITIONS

Mint is worthy of special mention for its wide range of uses and varieties. Its familiar flavour is used in soups, chopped up for mint sauce, and no new potato should be cooked without it. Pouring boiling water over a few sprigs in a jug makes an effective digestive at the end of a meal.

Unlike many herbs, mint likes its soil rich and moist and it will cope with light shade or sun. Give it plenty of room but, as a rule, better flavoured mints are less rampant.

To choose a variety that you like, pick a bit and taste it. The one your granny used to grow was probably *M. spicata* 'Moroccan' or 'Tashkent', with many blue/mauve flowers much loved by bees. Apple mint, with distinctive furry leaves, has good flavour for mint sauce. For purely aromatic reasons – and you can cook with them too – grow Eau de Cologne, lime or chocolate mint on or near the terrace.

MIXED HERBS

Below are some to consider for your plot.

- Basil – annual herb much used in Italian and French cooking, and with tomatoes. It likes full sun but loses its flavour when frozen.
- Sage – as much a hardy evergreen shrub as a herb. A quick trim in spring and after flowering will keep it vigorous, but don't cut back into old wood. Has purple-blue flower spikes in early to mid-summer and grey or purple foliage.
- Thyme – a dwarf evergreen that you can harvest all-year round. It needs good drainage and will grow happily in cracks between paving slabs. There are green and gold forms.
- Rosemary – at its best in full sun, it will grow into a small shrub and makes a good, low-growing hedge around the front of a bed of herbs. There's also a cascading form to grow over a low wall or raised bed.
- Tarragon – not fully hardy so make sure you give it some winter protection from frost. For taste, grow the French variety.
- Parsley – actually classed as a hardy biennial but, for the best flavour, treat it as an annual. Low growing with curly or broad-leaved varieties. Start if off in early spring under a cloche. Pouring boiling water over the ground first can help the seeds on their way. Keep some seeds back to sow in July and September to take you through to the year end.
- Chervil – an annual with a parsley-like flavour that can be sown anytime between April and August. Likes moist but well-drained soil. Doesn't work as a dried herb.

To learn more about how herbs can help control pests in your garden see IDEA 32, *Alright mate.*

Try another idea...

'Herbs are the friend of the physician and the pride of cooks.'
CHARLEMAGNE

Defining idea...

185

- Chives – throw up their mauve balls of colour in early summer and are great for the front of a bed or along a path. Deadhead if you don't want it to self seed.
- Marjoram (or oregano) – beloved of pizza makers. A hardy perennial that has small mauve flowers in summer. Its bright golden-green leaves and clump-forming habit make it a good ground cover plant for the front of the shrub bed. Trim back in autumn and divide every three years.
- Fennel – a tall, striking plant with umbels of tiny yellow flowers and wispy bright green or bronze foliage.
- Dill – similar to fennel with feathery blue-green leaves on tall stems. Use fresh or dried.
- Coriander – you can eat the leaves and the ripe seeds of this low-growing annual.

Of the more unusual herbs, horseradish is good value because not only do you get to use its hot, fiery root for sauce, but the young leaves can be used in a salad. A pot may be ideal though, as once planted you will never get rid of the root.

How did it go?

Q   My mint's gone mad! Can you help?

A   *Mint is invasive and best grown in a pot, sunken into the soil. (Make sure there are some drainage holes.) For the best results, cut mint right back in autumn and watch out for mildew.*

Q   My fennel's done well but the seeds don't really taste of fennel. Why's that?

A   *Chances are you've planted it too close to either some dill or coriander and it's cross-pollinated. This has a dramatic and adverse affect on its flavour.*

Small trees for small gardens

Choosing the right tree for your garden is possibly the most important horticultural decision you can make. So it pays to pick the right one.

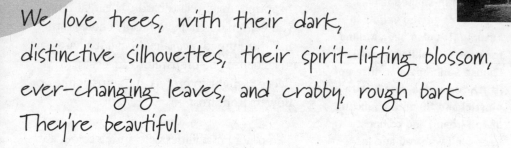

We love trees, with their dark, distinctive silhouettes, their spirit-lifting blossom, ever-changing leaves, and crabby, rough bark. They're beautiful.

So we were justifiably mortified when our neighbour explained that the roots of one of our sycamores was playing havoc with his garage door. He suggested it should come down. We were hesitant and phoned the council, hoping to find a tree preservation order had been slapped on it. It hadn't, and we were forced to call the tree surgeons in.

In retrospect, the neighbour was probably right. Some trees can outgrow their welcome, and the felling of the sycamore has let much more light into an already slightly gloomy north-facing plot.

We did our bit by replacing it with a silver birch and a simple holly, just two of a huge range of trees we could have chosen. For early blossom we could have plumped for a flowering cherry (*Prunus*), crab apple (*Malus*) or the delicate pink blossom of the

Here's an idea for you...

Still scared about what those roots could do to your foundations? Then how about growing a tree in a pot? The maidenhair tree (Ginkgo biloba) is a good choice, with its delightfully random habit and unusual fan-shaped leaves, which turn golden yellow in autumn (it's also been around for over 160 million years!) Choose a minimum 40-litre pot (if it's terracotta, line it with plastic) and fill with a mixture of soil (loam) and compost. Keep well watered and in spring top dress with fertiliser. Review the pot size every five years.

ornamental plum (*Prunus cerasifera* 'Nigra'), one of the first to appear, and with the flowers closely followed by deep purple leaves. A rose-pink flowered version of the wild hawthorn, *Crataegus laevigata* 'Paul's Scarlet', is also well worth considering for a small garden.

In spring, magnolia is hard to beat, although if you garden on chalk your only choice is the multi-stemmed *Magnolia stellata*. It's hardy but in cold areas be prepared to cover it with fleece at night to protect the starry white flowers from frost.

Two other possibilities with spring colour are lilac (*Syringa*), in its white, mauve and purple forms, and laburnum, which although poisonous is still a striking, slow-growing tree with graceful, yellow hanging flowers (racemes).

In summer a tree can be enjoyed close-up, so it needs to either complement surrounding plants or be a stunner in its own right, such as the variegated acer (*A. platanoides* 'Drummondii'), with its single straight stem and fabulous green, edged-white maple leaves.

The false acacia (*Robinia pseudoacacia* 'Frisia') has acid green foliage and looks good in a sheltered, sunny spot, and the honey locust (*Gleditsia triacanthos* 'Sunburst') has unusual, finely divided green and yellow leaves.

AUTUMN AND WINTER WONDERS

Autumn colour is a real boost as summer disappears. And the secret of those rusty reds and cheery yellows is all in the soil; the more acidic it is, the better the autumn colour.

See IDEA 10, *Support network*, for advice on staking your tree and why you should grow a small clump of hazel.

Try another idea…

Maples (*Acer*) are renowned for their autumnal colour but many grow into monsters so choose carefully. The Japanese maples are relatively small, and *A. japonicum* 'Vitifolium' or *A. palmatum* 'Atropurpureum' grow well if sheltered from the wind.

For a tough, uncomplicated little tree, with vibrant autumn colour, choose the Stag's horn sumach (*Rhus typhina* 'Laciniata'). or the crab apple (*Malus* 'Golden Hornet') that has both golden fruit and yellow leaves in autumn.

Trees in winter are a dramatic feature of the sky line but there's interest close up too. *Acer pensylvanicum* is not called the snake bark acer for nothing! The spindle tree (the deciduous *Euonymous*), on acid soil, turns flame red in autumn and its red berries, shaped like a cardinal's hat, are a favourite with robins in winter.

Some trees have it all and are interesting for most of the year. *Amelanchier lamarckii* is an easy-growing small tree, absolutely hardy, with pretty white spring blossom, black fruits in summer (again a meal ticket for the birds) and good autumn tints.

'**Except during the nine months before he draws breath, no man manages his affairs as well as a tree does.**'
GEORGE BERNARD SHAW

Defining idea…

Conifers are an extremely diverse group of trees: soft or spiky, with green, yellow,

bronze or blue foliage; upright and slim; spreading or weeping. Be sure to choose a slower growing type, such as the blue-grey *Chamaecyparis lawsoniana* 'Columnaris', the lace-bark pine *Pinus bungeana* or the golden cedar *Cedrus deodara* 'Aurea'.

TREAD CAREFULLY

Returning to the sycamore we now find that this is no more than a weed in most people's minds, so pull out all those little self-sown seedlings whilst they are small.

Unless your garden resembles a Capability Brown-style park, avoid planting potential giants. Leave beech, oak and ash to the countryside. But birch is a possibility. Plant three white-stemmed silver birches for a mini woodland glade, providing dappled shade for spring bulbs, foxgloves and hellebores.

Fascinating and popular once again, the monkey puzzle tree (*Araucaria araucaria*) is certainly different. It is hardy, will grow in any free-draining soil but may take ten years to reach 1.5m. After that, however, it will add 30cm a year! Bearing in mind it could last for 200 years, only plant it where there's plenty of room to grow.

Q   **I've got a couple of trees but there's room for one or two more –
     where should I get them from, and when?**

*How did
it go?*

A   *Go to a nursery, where you can check the root system and confirm its
      predicted height, spread and rate of growth with an expert. If you're buying
      a bare-rooted tree, plant it when it's dormant. Container-grown trees can
      be planted at any time, as long as it is not frosty or during a dry spell.*

Q   **I've bought the trees, now what?**

A   *Dig a hole large enough for the roots to spread out, loosen the soil on the
      sides and bottom, and add plenty of compost. Put the stake in first, and
      then place the tree so that, when the hole is filled in, the soil will be level
      with the old soil mark on the tree. Use a cane across the hole to check this.
      You can also add some slow-release fertiliser into the removed soil. Water
      well and keep the tree moist throughout its first couple of years. Keep an
      area of 1m around the tree free from weeds, and mulch in spring. As a
      general rule, tree roots are as long as the tree is tall so always plant them
      well away from buildings.*

191

Whispering grass don't tell the trees

Add movement and sound to your garden with the waving and rustling of ornamental grasses.

Visit a garden centre and it's hard to ignore the ranks of ornamental grasses. They seem the perfect filler for gappy borders, a ready-made solution for beds that need a bit of perking up.

Yet grasses are notoriously tricky to place, mainly because they're more informal than most garden plants, with features that can dramatically change as the seasons pass. What may start out as a low-growing tuft can suddenly explode into a riot of elegant spires. Some grasses need protection to flower well, and even then it may not happen until late summer or early autumn. And while some like moist, dappled shade others thrive in open sunny conditions.

SUPER GRASS

The list of grasses is long (and so are some of the names) but if you can get to know a handful and place them well, you'll have added a new dimension to your planting.

Here's an idea for you...

Be bold and brave and bring a little bit of the prairies to your garden by putting a whole area down to ornamental grasses. In this way you can overcome many of the difficulties of placing grasses by planting them together – perhaps where the garden becomes less formal, such as round a pond, or in a sunny, sheltered spot.

Bearing in mind the conditions they need, select a group of grasses of varying heights and try to group as many of one type together for maximum impact, such as seven plants of three varieties, rather than three each of seven different types.

To play to their strengths, marry grasses with contrasting plants. One winning combination we've come across is pairing the rust-coloured pheasant grass (*Stipa arundinacea*) with the erect shape and strong colour of red-hot pokers (*Kniphofia*); and the bold, flat leaves of hosta or bergenia complement the upright growth of *Calamagrostis*, with its fluffy flower heads that stiffen and cling on right through winter.

The sedges (*Carex*) love the damp, so here you can use their arching stems to soften the edges of a pond or pool – golden or striped leaves reflect best in the water, and *C. elata* 'Aurea' looks particularly good overhanging the water's edge. Other less fussy customers include hair grass (*Deschampsia cespitosa*), a tussocky evergreen with tall flower stalks that bear tiny shimmering flowers in June. It copes with sun or shade and thrives in moist soil. The variegated leaves of ribbon grass (*Phalaris*), commonly known as gardener's garters, are great for ground cover and it's quite happy with its feet in shallow water.

HIGH, WIDE AND HANDSOME

Some of the tallest grasses like the driest conditions. *Miscanthus sinensis* has banded, variegated or white-veined leaves. It's a well-behaved, medium-sized grass until late autumn, when it shoots up 2m-high flower stalks. These, of course, can be left on to catch the frost and enhance the winter garden. *Stipa gigantea*, as the name suggests,

is another tall, bulky plant with oat-like feathery flowers that appear in early summer.

IDEA 25, *Red alert – with a touch of orange, yellow, amber ...*, suggests other autumn plants to complement your grasses.

Try another idea...

But the daddy of them all is pampas grass (*Cortaderia*) reaching some 3m in height. Its late-flowering architectural plumes seem to be a resident feature in the front gardens of any house built in the 1970s. Used as specimen plants in the past, why not try placing it at the back of the border as a foil for other upright, more colourful plants? Protect the crown in winter and strim off the previous year's growth, dividing if necessary in early spring.

FULL FRONTAL

Not all grasses are leggy monsters and there's a good selection for the front of the border too. Quaking grass (*Briza*) has blue-green foliage and dainty flowers in June, it is hardy and favours a well-drained site in full sun. But bear in mind that it self-seeds like mad.

The small, soft bottle-brush flowers of *Pennisetum orientale* will only appear in July if given a hot, sunny, sheltered position, on light, sandy or chalky soil. Finicky maybe but it looks great flowering over the path or lawn edge.

Another candidate is *Hakonechloa macra* 'Aureola', which starts off with brilliant yellow leaves in April that later become striped with green, before a flush of red in autumn.

'At no time does it look so perfect as in the evening, before and after sunset, when the softened light imparts a mistiness to the crowding plumes, and the traveller cannot help fancying that the tints, which then seem richest, are caught from the level rays of the sun, or reflected from the coloured vapours of the after glow.'
CHRISTOPHER LLOYD on pampas grass

Defining idea...

195

Three other exceptional low-to-medium grasses, which can jazz up your planting, include the bright yellow-leaved *Milium effusum*, better known as Bowles' golden grass. It prefers semi-shade and acts as a perfect foil to blue-flowered plants such as forget-me-nots or bluebells.

In complete contrast there's the low-growing, black, grass-like *Ophiopogon planiscapus* 'Nigrescens'. Plant this where it will show up – in gravel or amongst plants with golden flowers or foliage. *Festuca glauca* is a bright blue grass, forming a low clump with slightly taller flower stalks. Don't give it too rich a soil and place it with grey or silver leafed plants, or on its own.

How did it go?

Q I never know when to move or cut down grasses. Any tips?

A *It depends upon the grass but as a rule only plant or divide grasses when they're active. This will mean leaving those that need warm temperatures to come into growth, until late spring/early summer. Cut down flower stalks and old growth on deciduous grasses in spring, at the very first sign of the new shoots appearing.*

Q Is it true that if my pampas grass gets too big I can set the centre on fire?

A *You can, but think about the mess you'll be left with! Instead, try digging it up and dividing it. Remember to do this when the plant is visibly growing, and wear gloves as protection against the sharp-edged leaves.*

The wow factor

Big, bold and quite often just a little bit frightening. Are you brave enough to let architectural plants into your garden?

Is your herbaceous border crying out for more? Even chilled out, informal planting sometimes needs a full stop, a punctuation mark to draw in the eye before leading you off to take in the surrounding plants. True, pergolas, pots and statues give interest but, whether pointed, prickly or broad-leaved, there's nothing like a good architectural plant to provide a much-needed exclamation mark!

Used in twos (or more) to flank steps, entrances or pathways, they entice you in; you want to know what's round the corner. And their geometrical shapes fit both traditional and modern designs. The green architecture of clipped hedges and topiary has been used for centuries to form walls and pillars, themselves containing softer, more decorative planting. But shaped and sculptured plants are equally at home in the contemporary garden. In fact, they're essential.

197

Here's an idea for you...

How about a bit of architectural lawn sculpture? By setting the mower blades at differing levels you can cut a low-level maze or pattern into your lawn. Hours of fun, effective to look at, and easy to do.

ON GUARD

Sword-like leaves, whether upright or arching, add drama to a garden. Take the strappy leaves of phormiums and yuccas – both striking on their own in pots, or shooting out of a bed of low growing plants. Try surrounding the bronze *Phormium tenax* with hellebores in spring and orange nasturtiums to trail through it in summer, and you'll create something altogether more exciting.

Equally arresting is a strategically placed *Yucca gloriosa* exploding out of a golden horizontal conifer (*Juniperus x media* 'Carberry Gold'). It's an effective contrast that increases the impact of the already striking yucca, which may, if it's in the mood, also decide to flower, producing a fantastic vertical spire of creamy bell-shaped blooms. Both phormiums and yuccas are hardy if sheltered. Much more tender is the weird, spiky foliage of aloe and agave. Their succulent rosettes, which can be up to 2m across, need temperatures of 5° or above and full sun to survive. You may have to wait 50 years for the agave to flower – on a 2m tall stem – but don't be too impatient as they die soon afterwards!

For a paved or gravel area that needs a bit of vertical interest try *Sisyrinchium striatum*. It's easy to grow and pushes up stalks of small creamy flowers, opening in the sun from amongst its iris-like leaves. A great self-seeder too.

A PRICKLY PRESENCE

Thistles, in the right place, can be an evocative sight, especially the ghostly grey, cobweb-strewn Scotch thistle (*Onopordum acanthium*). Its sculptured form fits best at

the back of a border, against a darker fence or hedge. A biennial, it will take two years to reach its 1.8m. The cardoon (*Cynara cardunculus*) is similar but slightly less ghostly. It's a perennial too, with purple thistle flowers that are a bit larger than its Scottish cousin.

Sea Holly (*Eryngium maritimum*) and the biennial Miss Willmott's Ghost (*Eryngium giganteum*) are prickly plants of more modest proportions, but nonetheless striking with their bristly leaves and blue flowers, which are loved by bees and hoverflies.

HAVE A BANANA

The banana (*Musa basjoo*) needs space to unfurl its wide, pale-green fringed leaves but it's winter-hardy if wrapped up against the frost. Cannas, with fabulous paddle-shaped leaves, takes less room but will need digging up and bringing inside over winter. For a taste of the Mediterranean, plant in groups with other hot-coloured perennials. The fan palm (*Trachycarpus fortunei*), which can grow to tree-like proportions with fans up to 1m wide, can stand temperatures down to –5°.

BROAD-LEAVED GIANTS

Apparently, during World War II, gunnera were grown on railway embankments to hide the tracks below from enemy bombers. This is a garden giant that means business and one of

IDEA 50, *Frills and fronds*, covers another striking group of plants, and IDEA 23, *Good enough for pandas*, talks you through the different bamboos.

Try another idea...

'One of the charms of today's designs is that there are fewer preconceptions as to how a garden should look, so native plants with strong forms as well as exotic-looking subjects from sub-tropical climates are frequently included in the layout to add an element of surprise and challenge.'
JILL BILLINGTON, garden designer, lecturer and author

Defining idea...

199

the best known is *Gunnera manicata*, a 2m-high giant, with leaves up to 1.8m wide. It likes the damp, but keep the crown protected in winter with old dried leaves.

Scaling things down a bit, but in the same wet conditions, try *Rodgersia pinnata* 'Superba', with its reddish star-shaped leaves, and *Hosta sieboldiana* var. *elegans* with its grey-blue textured leaves, arching 50cm off the ground.

How did it go?

Q   **It's all very well if you've got acres to garden but how can I use architectural plants in a small garden without them overwhelming everything else?**

A   Use them to increase the sense of space by playing tricks with perspective. Two lines of box balls can make the garden seem longer than it is. They look great topped with snow in winter and can be easily grown from cuttings (start them off in the veg plot and in a couple of years you can plant them in situ). They do well in pots and can be moved around for a different effect. To lengthen the garden use the Italian cypress (Cupressus sempervirens Stricta group), eventually reaching 10m, or the more modest 5m Juniperus communis 'Compressa', to provide tall, slim columns to draw the eye to the far part of the garden.

Q   **I have been given a cordyline. Will it perform like the phormiums and yuccas – it looks the same?**

A   Yes, it does have the same broad arching leaves but it is a little daintier and not so hardy. Why not get a second one and plant up two contrastingly curvaceous pots, to flank an entrance. This way you can move them into a light, frost-free place in winter.

Up the garden path

Paths provide your garden's arterial network, but think more winding B roads than motorways, with patios as the country pub.

Paths and patios are a mixture of taste and necessity, but even a small garden can benefit from some form of hard landscaping, whether it's a paved area by the back door, or some strategically placed slabs as stepping stones across the lawn.

What often puts people off is the cost, but with a bit of imagination and a spot of hard graft you can add structure and a touch of mystery to your garden.

ON THE RIGHT TRACK

There are no hard and fast rules when it comes to choosing a path. Use shingle, bricks, crazy-paving and, of course, grass. If you have a few zigzagging across your garden, think variety of materials in the context of the area they are passing through.

Here's an idea for you...

Acquire the reputation of a skip scavenger. A builder's skip is home to old bricks, pipes and every conceivable kind of timber. It's become something of a trait to heave perfectly usable items into skips and then spend hours in DIY stores buying something virtually identical. Keep your eyes skinned and you need never purchase a brick or piece of wood again.

Concrete, once laid, is easy to maintain and weed free but it does have a fearful permanency about it. A friend recently thought about extending a favourite border but was thwarted by a bed of concrete, and had no option but to scrap the plans or head off to the nearest hire and sale store for a pneumatic drill.

Crazy paving gets a bad press. Although it's another of those faddy ideas that smacks of the 1970s, like conifers and rockeries, it's actually pretty easy to lay and extremely versatile. You can simply bed it in grit or sand and only need to lay hardcore and mortar in exceptional circumstances, such as when it's earmarked as a driveway. Even for a patio, just bed them firmly in and grow rock-loving plants in the crevices. The sword-shaped leaves of sysirinchiums will give upright interest whilst the New Zealand burr (*Acaena*), the small flowered sedums (*S. acre* or *S. spathulifolium*) and houseleek (*Sempervivum*) are mat forming.

If the creative juices are really flowing, use the cracks to plant up a mini herb garden. Thyme and chives will take root in a little well-drained soil. And the occasional inadvertent kick will do them no harm, and give off a pleasant smell to boot.

For winding paths, it's hard to beat shingle, with its soft blend of beige and browns. As for laying it, just slash the bag and spread, but you will need to contain it otherwise it will disappear into the very border it's intended to show off. Choosing

the ideal side support is important, and while a metal strip is effective and lasts forever, pliable strips of treated timber are a bit more discrete. For the truly artistic, try bricks on their ends leaning at 45° like falling dominoes.

See IDEA 41, *How to get the most from your containers*, for how to dress up your patio.

Try another idea...

As for weeds, a plastic membrane will discourage the worst but the shingle on top does have a tendency to rut and slide. Otherwise, your path will never be totally weed free. You could spray with a weed killer but an alternative is to give it a thorough weeding and keep on top of it, picking out any new weeds that dare to appear.

Bricks are a personal favourite when it comes to paths. They obviously have an immediate link with a brick-built house (presuming they're the same colour) and, although individually they're a pretty basic geometric shape, they can be brought together to form some stunning swirling shapes.

However, before attempting to recreate an elaborate mosaic on the ground, consider a few simple brick paths to split up your vegetable plot, or as a hard area by the compost bins.

'I gave the four end beds a circular pattern, with paths running through so that you can walk right round and savour the scent of each plant on your way'
ROSEMARY VEREY

Defining idea...

If you go for a grass path, calculate the width and then add some more, lest you turn the air blue when you first try and run the mower over it, only to succeed in beheading your carefully planted summer bedding. You wouldn't be the first person to create a path that's too narrow to mow.

203

PATIO POWER

Unless you've got special building skills, try to treat the patio as a bigger, wider path, which uses the same materials as mentioned above. But remember that major construction tends to introduce formal lines, which can jar with the rest of your garden.

Just a few tips if you wish to lay your own patio. Make sure the ground is very firm – no need for hardcore. Set the slabs on blobs of mortar – five per paving slab. Press or tamp the slabs into place, making sure they are level. If laying a patio up to grass, set the slabs slightly below grass level to allow the mower to pass over easily.

Whatever materials you use, the size, quantity and placing of pots, troughs and ornaments make all the difference to a patio. And don't restrict planting to summer alone as the patio is the ideal spot for a bit of R&R at any time of the year.

Q **I've tried a brick path but many of them broke up or flaked after one winter. What's going on?**

A *Bricks will break if laid on uneven ground, so bed them firmly in sand. Some bricks are softer than others and are more likely to absorb water, freeze and flake. If your brick path is confined to the vegetable patch, the occasional scarred brick is fine and changing the odd one isn't too arduous. If you want a pristine path, use harder and therefore less porous bricks.*

Q **I have gone for mainly grass but those paths in constant use suffer from worn patches in the summer. Can it be helped?**

A *Many nurseries and some garden centres offer a variety of grass seed. Seek out the bin marked 'hard wearing suitable for children's play area'.*

Q **You mention using stone patio materials but I would prefer to lay decking. Is this as easy?**

A *Getting decking right depends on building a strong, level structure. This can be tricky and probably needs a professional touch. Large garden centres stock a wide variety of decking materials – including non-slip, easy-fix squares.*

How did it go?

205

Common diseases

Determined diseases will breach the best-laid defences if they put their minds to it. Here's how to lessen the impact of some of the most virulent.

Turn to the disease section of any decent gardening tome and the scale of the problem you're up against is monumental. From apple scab to tulip fire, neck rot to stem canker, it's a frightening list.

On the basis that prevention is better than cure, you can help stop diseases spreading round your garden with a few simple measures. Garden hygiene is crucial, so make sure that washing flower pots and seed trays before sowing becomes part of your annual routine. Likewise, your greenhouse needs disinfecting every winter, and tools that have come into contact with diseased vegetation should be scrubbed in boiling water.

Clearing up dead and diseased leaves as they fall is also vital. They should be bagged up immediately to stop the spores spreading, and then either binned or burnt.

Here's an idea for you... **Crop rotation can help prevent the build up of pests and diseases in the vegetable plot. When buying a new tree or fruit bush, check whether it's resistant to the common diseases that are likely to attack it.**

Of course, the more healthy and vigorous your plants, the more likely they are to successfully fight off a disease, so make sure you know what conditions they like before putting them in the ground. And keep checking them once they've become established, so that you can nip diseases and infestations in the bud.

A range of organic fungicides and pesticides is available, the difference being that they are derived from plants and other natural products that will break down quickly rather than linger in the ecosystem.

Bordeaux mixture is a finely ground concoction of copper sulphate and slaked lime, dissolved to form a fungicidal spray that controls fungus on fruits and blight on vegetables and perennials. Sulphur can be used to control powdery mildew. There are many proprietary and branded varieties too.

But, before you get trigger happy with your sprays and powders, these products can still have a harmful effect on the garden's beneficial insects. Instead, they're best used as a last resort, or alternatively as a quick blast when you first spot a problem, to stop it getting out of hand.

Here are some suggestions for coping with some of the most common diseases.

- *Grey mould*. Strawberries, and most other soft fruits, are a favourite of this rotting disease, which gets in through any bruised or damaged tissue. It thrives in cold, damp conditions and, although there's no organic cure, this is one of those diseases that can be prevented by good plant hygiene. Cut out infected growth as soon as you spot it and make sure there's a good airflow in and around the plant.

- *Rose black spot*. Sooty black marks begin to appear on rose leaves, turning them yellow and eventually causing them to fall prematurely. Worryingly, it can also spread to buds and stems. Remove and burn fallen leaves straight away, as this is where the fungi will overwinter. Over-feeding with nitrogen-rich fertilisers can also exacerbate the problem but there are plenty of resistant varieties, while shrub roses are naturally less susceptible. Curiously, polluted air will help control black spot.

- *Powdery mildew*. Many plants, including roses, apples and asters, are susceptible to this white powder, which is caused by a fungus and appears on leaves and shoots. It's caused by over-crowding and a lack of water getting to the roots, hence the fact that it thrives in dry, warm conditions. To cure it, cut out and burn all infected growth, and then give the plant a good water and dust with sulphur.

- *Blight*. This disease attacks potatoes and tomatoes. In damp conditions, brown and yellow patches begin to appear on the leaves. Spores can then be washed off into the soil and into contact with the tubers, or onto the fruit, causing them to rot. At the first sign of blight in potatoes, cut off all the haulms (stalks) about ten days before harvest. This should stop it spreading. In future years

For more on the pests that inhabit the garden see IDEA 51, Pests.

Try another idea...

'Now I'm not going to pretend that if you go "organic" your life will change overnight and all your troubles will disappear. That's unrealistic. But, by adopting organic techniques, you'll start creating a garden where nature can give a helping hand rather than appearing to get in the way all the time. 'Yes, you'll have leaves nibbled by slugs, and your garden will not be completely free of pests and diseases. But what garden ever is? It seems to me that the more chemical sprays you use, the more you have to keep on using them to help keep on top of the bugs and beasts.'
ALAN TITCHMARSH

Defining idea...

209

earthing up can protect potatoes. With tomatoes the picture isn't so hopeful but spraying with Bordeaux mixture may help.

■ *Clubroot*. This can take hold of your brassicas in the veg patch but will also set about wallflowers in the border, given half a chance. This disease is so easily spread that, if you own an allotment that's infected, using the same tools or boots in your own garden will spread it. In short, the roots become distorted, the plant withers and eventually dies. It can be eradicated over time through crop rotation, and liming the soil can help. As soon as you find an infected plant remove and destroy it, otherwise the roots will rot to a slimy mush, releasing millions of spores into the soil.

How did it go?

Q   Anything organic I can use to clean the greenhouse?

A   *Sulphur candles can be left to smoke out pests and diseases from the greenhouse during winter. There are also several organic, citrus-based disinfectants on the market that don't harm plants or wildlife.*

Q   Why is it that as soon as my seedlings poke their heads above the soil they seem to give up the ghost?

A   *Sounds like damping off. It's caused by a parasitic fungus that thrives in wet and overcrowded conditions. There's nothing you can do with the seedlings that have succumbed, but in future sow the seeds thinly into a sterilised seed compost (the fresher this is the more sterile it will be) and make sure there's good ventilation. Try watering the seed trays from below too.*

48

A place for everything, and everything in its place

From sun worshippers to shade lovers, the key to a blooming garden is giving your plants the conditions they love.

Some plants will grow just about anywhere, a band of tough, all-round performers such as lady's mantle (*Alchemilla mollis*), dead nettle (*Lamium*) and the frost-hardy *Tellima grandiflora* which, despite its insignificant flowers, has foliage that adds autumn colour to any garden.

Other plants are more choosy and will only flourish if you take the time and effort to plant them in the right position. Shoehorn them into a spot that's too sunny or too dark and at best they'll struggle, at worst they'll end up on the compost heap.

To get the best from your plants, and make the most of your money, you need to know the conditions they enjoy. Before embarking on a spending spree it helps if you have a particular spot of the garden in mind, then you know exactly the conditions you're buying for.

Here's an idea for you...

Always carry a notepad with you, whether you're visiting a garden or simply out walking. Note down plants you like the look of, and if you don't know the name ask, or write down a description. Record the conditions in which they're planted and the date, if they're in flower. Of course you may get lucky and persuade the gardener to give you a cutting!

If a particular plant has caught your eye, then try looking it up in a plant encyclopaedia before you set off to the nursery. The plant's label will also detail its requirements, listing its preferences when it comes to sun or shade, soil type, drainage and shelter.

Sometimes you can create a microclimate in your garden by introducing different soil, improving drainage, using other plants for shelter, or cutting them back to introduce more light. But it's best to force as little as possible and far better to go with a plant's natural flow.

SUN WORSHIPPERS

Just as we like to feel the sun on our backs, most plants enjoy the warming rays on their leaves. They need the sun to thrive. If their roots are kept moist (you can achieve this by making sure there are no gaps in your planting, which keeps evaporation to a minimum) most plants will stand quite high temperatures. After all, the classic herbaceous border is usually placed in full sun, because plants deprived of light will often lean, growing thin and straggly as they flop around in search of the sun.

Of course, it's not quite as straightforward as that. While large flowered clematis enjoy showing off their blooms in full sun, they insist on having their roots in the shade. If neighbouring plants can't supply this then rocks or slates at the base of the plant will do the job. Then there's the bulb *Nerine bowdenii*, which, you've guessed it, just loves to have its roots in the sun, at the bottom of a wall or fence, for example.

SHADE LOVERS

Plants suited to all-day-long shade are usually those with striking foliage – elephant's ears (*Bergenia cordifolia*) and hostas, with their broad leaves, the wide selection of ferns, and pulmonaria with its 'spilt milk' markings.

Fine dappled shade gives you a chance to grow flowering woodland plants like foxgloves, hellebores (*H. foetidus* and *H. orientalis*), violets, and Solomon's seal (*Polygonatum*) with its gracefully arching stems and white flowers.

The problem with shade under trees is that anything you plant has to compete for food and water with the tree itself. Early spring bulbs under a deciduous tree have a better chance, as they can bloom before the tree leaves deprive them of the light. Give them some extra feed (a sprinkle of bonemeal when the soil is not too dry) to swell the bulbs for next year.

If you have a problem area you could try the low-growing form of comfrey (*Symphytum grandiflorum*) as this is a 'thug' and seems to romp away in most conditions.

Two other plants with a particular liking for the shade are the climbing hydrangea (*Hydrangea petiolaris*), which has lush foliage and white blooms and is good at covering a north-facing wall, and the shrub *Philadelphus coronarius* 'Aureus'. This is a variation on the mock orange and, to keep its bright lime-green leaves, it needs to be grown in the shade.

Soil type also plays an important part in successful planting and IDEA 1, *Did the earth move?* takes you through the merits of an acid or alkaline soil.

Try another idea...

'**Odd as it may appear, a gardener does not grow from seed, shoot, bulb, rhizome or cutting but from experience, surroundings and natural conditions.**'
KAREL CAPEK

Defining idea...

213

FROST – UNPREDICTABLE BUT DEADLY

A late frost in April or May is the gardening equivalent of a crash on the stock exchange – it can do untold damage, destroying new shoots, fruit tree blossom and flower buds. And, although the plants will usually recover, you'll have to wait another twelve months for flowers or fruit. Winter frosts can reap even more havoc, leaving all but the most hardy plants dead to the roots.

So it pays to know where the frost pockets are in your garden. If you've got a cold, open site, or a plot on a low-lying valley bottom or exposed, windy hillside, then don't be seduced by shrubs that are not *fully* hardy. Plants such as rock rose (*Cistus*), convolvulus, and witch hazel (*Hamamelis mollis*), as well as daphnes and hebes, won't survive a heavy frost. Instead, try planting them in the lee of a wall or alongside the house, for some extra protection.

How did it go?

Q   How can I tell where the frost pockets are in my garden?

A   *Next time you have a frost make a note of those parts of the garden where it lies undisturbed, and those in which it gradually clears.*

Q   I planted some shrubs in the wrong place several years ago. Can I still move them?

A   *You can usually get away with moving shrubs in spring or autumn. Keep as much soil on the root ball as possible, move directly to the new, larger planting hole, and then water, feed and prune if necessary.*

49

Upwardly mobile

Climbers bring a dynamic element to the gardens, eagerly taking up the challenge to scramble over any natural and man-made structure you put in their way.

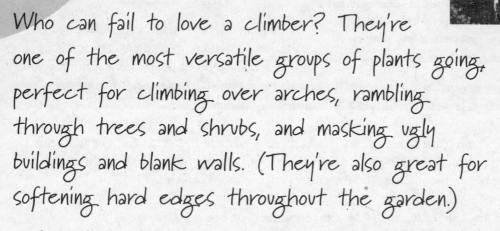

Who can fail to love a climber? They're one of the most versatile groups of plants going, perfect for climbing over arches, rambling through trees and shrubs, and masking ugly buildings and blank walls. (They're also great for softening hard edges throughout the garden.)

But despite their wanderlust and tearaway reputation, climbers also need a certain degree of TLC. Indulge their foibles and their fads with careful planting, regular food and water, and the correct pruning, and the social climbers of the plant world will pay you back with a stunning array of colours.

The best border in the world can be ruined by a backdrop of rotting fence panels, garage roof or uninspiring wall. Enter those rampant runners like Russian vine (*Polygonum baldschuanicum*), also known as 'mile-a-minute', whose sprays of snowy white flowers can cloak a shed overnight

Here's an
idea for
you...

If you've got a north-facing wall that needs brightening up, the climbing hydrangea (*Hydrangea petiolaris*) is the answer. It will thrive in the shade and rapidly clothe a dark wall with lush green foliage and lacy white flower heads in summer. What's more, after a little initial persuasion, it will cling on all by itself.

Ivy (*Hedera*) is another garden staple, yet often overlooked for more exotic climbing cousins. But with foliage that ranges from dark green to bright gold, and berries that veer from black to cream, it can clamber over anything from tree stumps to outhouses, adding a verdant and mystical air as it goes.

Virginia creeper (*Parthenocissus quinquefolia*) is another well-known and energetic climber, much loved for its magnificent autumn colour.

Well worth growing too is the crimson glory vine (*Vitis coignetiae*), its large plate-sized leaves also turning a brilliant red in autumn.

Two clematis that verge on the monstrous side, are the scented, spring-flowering *C. montana*, and the evergreen *C. armandii*. Both are vigorous, and while they need plenty of room, they'll do any screening job asked of them.

One word of warning – as with all climbers on houses, make sure they're kept away from gutters and roof tiles.

ROMANTIC RAMBLINGS

Slightly less invasive are the honeysuckle, rambling rose and jasmine. Try the purple and cream flowered honeysuckle (*Lonicera periclymenum*) or the evergreen honeysuckle (*Lonicera japonica* 'Halliana'). Both have a delicious, subtle perfume. *Rosa banksiae* 'Lutea', with its masses of small yellow flowers is vigorous and needs a strong structure – preferably a tree – to attack. *R.* 'Felicité Perpetué' has clusters of creamy pink flowers and

at 3.5m is more easily controlled. The climbing rose, R. 'Albertine', grows easily but within reason, with salmon buds opening to pale pink.

Idea 22, *It's been a good year for the roses*, introduces more climbing and rambling roses.

Try another idea...

At the turn of the year there's nothing so welcoming as the brave, bright yellow flowers of the winter flowering jasmine (*Jasminum nudiflorum*). The white flowered version (*J.officinale*), given a little shelter, will also romp away and scent the air in summer.

PRUNING FOR FLOWERS

Now people have devoted their lives to the clematis, and there are far more authoritative tomes on the plant than this one. But follow one basic rule and you're at least heading in the right direction. Clematis need to be pruned at the right time in order to encourage flowers.

'So when's the right time?', you may well ask. To which we can only reply: 'Read the label'.

Clematis come in three groups.

> **'A morning glory at my window satisfies me more than the metaphysics of books.'**
> WALT WITMAN

Defining idea...

- Group 1 includes *C. montana, C. macropetala, C. armandii, C. alpina* – those with small flowers that bloom in spring. These only require pruning when they get out of bounds. In which case be ruthless.
- Group 2 are the large-flowered beauties that perform in early to mid-summer. *C.* 'Nelly Moser', *C.* 'Marie Boisselot' and *C.* 'The President' for example. Prune these in early spring before new growth starts, remove any dead or damaged stems and cut the ends only, back to a strong pair of buds.

- Group 3 clematis flower towards the end of summer or in autumn on growth they have made during the year. Cut this group, including C. 'Jackmanii', C. *tangutica* and C. *viticella*, right down in January to the first pair of healthy buds.

Oh, and don't forget the wisteria, which also needs wooing, as well as pruning twice a year. In August cut back all the long, whippy shoots to six leaf buds, then in February cut these back further to just two. Drastic maybe, but as long as you keep the frost off, it will be well worth it.

FOR ONE YEAR ONLY

If you're worried about climbers getting triffid-like tendencies and taking over the whole show, grow some annuals. The cup and saucer vine (*Cobaea scandens*) provides quick cover and striking flowers from May to October, and Morning Glory (*Ipomoea*) – coming into flower in late summer – can be used to climb through and brighten up shrubs that have already done their bit.

Defining idea...

'**Climbers are invaluable in the small-space garden. Not only do they make it possible to enjoy plants for their own sake, without using up valuable ground space, but they can be used to soften visually hard structures or disguise ugly ones and, in conjunction with a pergola or openwork fencing, provide privacy, shade and shelter.'**
JOHN BROOKES

Plant a golden hop (*Humulus lupulus* 'Aureus') and it will cover an arch in a season with striking yellow foliage, plus a few hops as well. It's a perennial, dying back completely in winter but raring to go again the following spring. Grown with a dark red clematis (a group 3 type, by the way, which as you now know you prune in January) it makes a stunning combination.

Q **I now know how to prune my clematis but how do I prevent clematis wilt?**

How did it go?

A *The scourge of many a gardener but it can be quite easily beaten. Dig a deep hole at least 40cm away from the wall or fence. Fill with compost, sprinkle in some fertiliser and plant the clematis leaning towards its support. Sink the clematis so the point where the shoots emerge is below ground level. Then, should it succumb to clematis wilt, it will regrow happily from beneath the soil. Keep it well watered – better to apply six buckets of water in one go than one a day for six days – and shade its roots with other plants or stones.*

Q **What type of support should I use for vigorous climbers?**

A *The strongest you can find! Always make sure the supports are well grounded and, if wooden, use treated timbers sunk into met posts. Having to dismantle a tangled climber in order to replace its support is a nightmare.*

Frills and fronds

There's a lot more to ferns than unpronounceable Latin names.

Shade loving, slug resistant, maintenance free. Goodness, oh how we love ferns. The way their fronds unfurl, the way they filter the light, the way they gracefully cling to walls and rocks. It's enough to make even the most sceptical gardener go weak at the knees.

They even pre-date just about anything else you're likely to be growing in your garden, and the fact that they'll grow where others fear to tread makes them a virtually indispensable plant.

GREAT FOLIAGE, SHAME ABOUT THE FLOWERS

OK, that's quite enough hyperbole, especially given it's a plant that doesn't actually produce any fruit or flowers. What you see is what you get with ferns, green foliage and a plant that, to a greater or lesser extent, is happy in moist, light shade.

Not that it hasn't got a troublesome streak, and you need to get to grips with the fact that different types of the same species prefer different pH levels in the soil.

Here's an idea for you...

For the busy gardener on the lookout for all-year-round interest, plant bulbs in between the ferns. Choose varieties that die down in the winter, and mix in some early spring bulbs. The fronds will cover the bulbs as they die back. If you feel adventurous, add in some easy-care plants with different leaf types such as hosta, elephant's ears (*Bergenia*), or small shrubs like the slow-growing, glossy dark green Sweet box (*Sarcoccoca*) or dwarf azaleas.

The oak fern (*Gymnocarpium*), for instance, has a variety *G. dryopteris* which prefers acid ground, and another, *G. robertianum*, which is a native of that most alkaline of habitats, the limestone pavement. So, as with so many plants, you need to read up on them, rather then just lumping them all together and hoping for the best.

Woodland ferns that are at home in moist, humus-rich acid soil include the small and delicate maidenhair fern (*Adiantum pedatum*) with its bright green leaves and black stems, all species of lady fern (*Athyrium*), the soft-textured shield fern (*Polystichum*), and *Blechnum* with its glossy green leaves on upright fertile fronds.

There are fewer lime lovers for alkaline soil but the Hart's tongue (*Asplenium scolopendrium*) will happily colonise a stone wall, living off the lime in the mortar. *Polypodium vulgare* is not fussy about soil *and* will tolerate drier conditions but resist the temptation to cut its fronds back. Let them fade and shrivel, as the new growth takes time to develop (with most other ferns you can cut them back when the fronds die off in autumn).

MIMICKING THE WILD

As is often the case, nature shows us where plants like to grow best. If you see ferns by a woodland stream, or squeezed into a split in the rock, make a note of the type and try recreating the surroundings in your garden.

Waterside ferns include the upright shuttlecock fern (*Matteuccia orientalis*) and the royal fern (*Osmunda regalis*) with its ostrich-feather fronds. On moist soil both are quite capable of reaching over 1m in height. The Sensitive fern (*Onoclea sensibilis*) is hardy although its fronds will disappear at the first sign of frost. It too likes a wet site and the young fronds start off a pretty pink in spring.

The common but handsome male fern (*Dryopteris filix-mas*) is tough and undemanding, settling into shady north-facing cracks and crevices, growing to 1.5m. The variety (*D. filix-mas crispa-cristata*) is crested and smaller at 0.5m.

STICK IT WHERE THE SUN DON'T SHINE

The real beauty of ferns is that there's often a spot just right for them that's unsuitable for most other plants, such as a sheltered north-facing site at the bottom of a wall or hedge. Anywhere spring to mind? If so you could do a lot worse than dedicate it to the fern, and leave those feathery fronds to unfurl in peace. Just make sure it never gets waterlogged

To create a fernery, dig leaf mould, well-rotted compost or pine bark into the top layer of soil, along with some bonemeal. Avoid animal manure or artificial fertilisers as they're too rich.

On clay soil it may be necessary to improve the drainage by digging down two spits and adding rubble to the bottom. Mix grit into the top layer if necessary.

Try another idea...

IDEA 45, *The wow factor*, suggests other dramatic foliage to go with your ferns and IDEA 1, *Did the earth move?*, will help you determine your soil type.

Defining idea...

'Where the copse wood is the greenest
Where the fountain is the sheenest
Where the morning dew lies longest
There the Lady Fern grows strongest'
SIR WALTER SCOTT

Plant the ferns in spring or autumn. Once underway they need little attention, no staking and no deadheading! All will relish an annual mulch of compost in spring and, in the cold areas, be prepared to cover the crowns in winter with some bracken leaves.

How did it go?

Q   To add height to my fernery I would like to plant the tree fern (*Dicksonia antarctica*). Is it hardy?

A   *This fashionable and statuesque plant, with tree-like proportions, has lacy fronds growing out of a stout trunk. It will survive the winter in a sheltered spot if its crown is thoroughly wrapped up against the cold.*

Q   You have helped me choose ferns for my soil but which ferns are evergreen?

A   *Ferns that keep their fronds over winter are known as 'wintergreen'. In the spring new fresh growth will take the place of the old fronds so there's a succession of green. Wintergreens include* Asplenium, Polypodium vulgare, Polystichum, Blechnum, *and* Dryopteris affinis.

Q   You say ferns are the almost perfect plants but are they easy to propagate?

A   *Ferns reproduce through spores, the minute, dust-like particles that grow on the outside of the plant, usually the back of the leaves.* Athryium, Blechnum, Drypoteris, Matteuccia struthiopteris *and* Osmunda regalis *are relatively easy to grow from spores. It is a bit fiddly but quite possible if you read up on it.*

51

Pests

Chemical-free pest control has come a long way since the days of the fly swatter.

The late doyen of British gardening, Geoff Hamilton, once wrote: 'I firmly believe, and indeed have proved to my own satisfaction, that chemical pest control is counter-productive.'

Hamilton reasoned that, despite years of bombarding commercial crops with chemicals, pests were more prevalent then ever, something he put down to the indiscriminate nature of most sprays, which were killing friend as well as foe.

What is more, it was the fast-breeding pests that were re-establishing themselves a lot quicker than the predators that hunted them.

It was something Hamilton didn't want to replicate in his own garden. He knew there was no quick fix to the problem but with a mixture of healthy plants, good soil, vigilance and the patience to allow the garden's ecosystem to reset its own balance, the ordered garden could once again be harmonised with nature.

Here's an idea for you... **Although earwigs eat aphids, they can do more damage than greenfly, feeding at night on flowers and buds. To catch them, fill a small plastic flower pot with straw and place it on top of a cane. Chances are the earwigs will be attracted to the pot as a refuge during the day, handily gathering together so you can collect and destroy them.**

So, how can green gardeners protect their crops?

BIOLOGICAL WARFARE

Whilst spraying roses with washing-up liquid and picking off caterpillars may be effective, a range of biological predators is now available that will thrive in the warm conditions of a greenhouse or conservatory. You can buy small vials of parasitic wasps, ladybird larvae and other tiny bugs to let loose on your pest-infested vegetation.

The whitefly, for instance, destroys tomatoes and peppers by leaving a sticky trail that attracts sooty moulds. Well, a tiny wasp called *Encarsia formosa* lays its eggs inside the immature whitefly, killing them at the same time. Red spider mites suck the sap from a variety of plants, causing them to wilt, but they can be defeated by the introduction of another predatory mite, *Phytoseiulus*. In the same way you can introduce *Aphidius* and *Aphidoletes* into your greenhouse or conservatory to control aphids.

Yellow glue traps hung close to the plant are also effective but of course may trap some non-harmful insects too.

Defining idea... **'A blank helpless sort of face, rather like a rose just before you drench it with DDT.'**
Author JOHN CAREY

BEETLE DRIVE

Back outside, vine weevils are among the most destructive of pests. While the adult beetles will nibble at leaves, it's the grubs that do the real damage, devouring the roots until the

plant dies. But help is at hand in the form of a pathogenic nematode that can be watered into the soil to attack the milky white grubs.

Tackling slugs and snails is dealt with all on its own in IDEA 12, *Slugging it out*. Enjoy!

Try another idea...

Nematodes are also available to take on chafer grubs, leatherjackets and slugs. These biological controls are largely sold through mail order from the Internet, and to be effective you need to use them at exactly the correct time. But they are harmless to kids, pets and other wildlife.

There's little mistaking another destructive creature, the lily beetle, with its bright red body and black legs (the Cardinal beetle has the same colourings but is twice as big). Both the adult and grub feed on the leaves and flowers of lilies and fritillaries, and while they are one of those pests that are best picked off and destroyed, go carefully as the bugs are prone simply to drop off the leaves into the undergrowth as soon as they sense you coming. Lily beetles also overwinter as adults, so if you grow lilies in pots it pays to have a good rummage in the compost to hunt any out.

ALTERNATIVE REMEDIES

Hand picking is another simple way to keep on top of pests. Caterpillars on brassicas and nasturtiums can be dealt with in this way, while aphids are quite easily rubbed off buds and new shoots.

There's also a range of organic pesticides, most of which have been developed from plant extracts. Pyrethrum is effective against most insects, while Derris is effective on caterpillars. Neither is selective though, so should be used as a last resort.

'To hear some people talk of their garden you would think they were referring more to a battleground than to a place of peace and tranquility'
BERNARD SCHOFIELD, gardener, artist and writer

Defining idea...

227

Insecticidal soap kills the likes of aphids, whitefly, red spider mite, scale insects and mealy bugs. These soaps are harmless to humans, mammals, ladybirds and bees, but can damage some sensitive plants. A gentler alternative is soft soap, which can be used as a spray for aphids and red spider mite, but only hangs around for a day at most.

Add to these controls the likes of companion planting, encouraging more wildlife into your garden, making sure your plants aren't congested, and crop rotation, and suddenly the chemical-free gardener doesn't feel quite so alone.

How did it go?

Q **I've nothing against squirrels, apart from the fact that they dig up and eat my *@^% bulbs! What can I do?**

A *Firstly, plant them deep. Then sprinkle cayenne pepper on liberally, re-cover with earth, and lace the soil around them with more pepper. Sit back and watch their faces as they start digging! Alternatively, chicken wire secured over the pot or bulb site will prevent digging.*

Q **My fruit trees have taken a right beating. How can I protect them?**

A *Grease bands round the trunks of fruit trees, tied on in autumn, can help stop the winter moth from climbing up to lay its eggs. You can also use traps to take care of the codling moth. The caterpillars will eat into pears and apples but you can catch the adult males before they breed using pheromone traps hung in the tree from the end of May. The moths will get caught on a sticky pad inside.*

Currant thinking

Add a tang to summer with easy-to-grow currants and gooseberries.

For over 200 years we've been using the vitamin C in blackcurrants to protect against colds, while gooseberries have been around since the thirteenth century. They reached their peak through the popular Gooseberry Clubs of the 1740s, when there was talk of goosegogs the size of hen's eggs.

Both gooseberries and currants are related, and require similar conditions. They're all good croppers, respond well with minimum care and can be 'trained' to take up less room. Yet when was the last time you saw a punnet of gooseberries in the shops, or redcurrants that weren't priced as if they'd been imported from the moon?

Here's an idea for you... If you're really stuck for space, try planting a 'standard' gooseberry or redcurrant. Produced with bare stems to a height of about 1m, the tops are then pruned in the same way as the bush varieties. Standards look impressive and crop well, yet in a small garden allow other fruit or veg to be grown beneath. They do need strong and permanent staking though.

TURNING ON THE CURRANTS

With several different varieties of blackcurrant available, it pays to plant two or more bushes to ensure a good crop.

Blackcurrants relish an open, sunny site, sheltered from strong winds but where their roots can keep cool. Although hardy, the flowers can be damaged by frost so plant a late-flowering variety, like Ben Sarek or Baldwin, if you live in a frosty area. Where space is limited, try the compact-growing Blacksmith, while for an early crop there's the large fruited Laxton's Giant. Ben Hope is a mid-season variety that's resistant to big bud mite, the blackcurrant's main health risk.

For the best results plant two-year-old bushes between November and February, 1.5m apart, in a deep hole. Fill the bottom half with well-rotted manure and place the plant just below the original soil mark on the stems to encourage new shoots. After planting, trim existing shoots back to one bud and in January treat the bush to a high-nitrogen feed. A good mulch on top of damp, weed-free ground should ensure you can start picking in July.

COLOUR CHOICES

Mark's Dad had to take out a second mortgage to cope with his Mum's love of redcurrants. Of all the berries and currants these are the most acquired of tastes, as

well as the most expensive, and often the hardest to find in the shops. (White currants are a variation on the same theme.)

Plant as for blackcurrants but not as deep, as these currants fruit on branches off the main stems, so they don't need to keep producing new ones. Add a good helping of potash (use the bonfire ashes) when planting, and again in January, and mulch with grass cuttings in spring.

The early variety Jonkeer van Tets and the mid-season Laxton's No1 are both good croppers, as is White Versailles.

Have a look at IDEA 18, *Blow the raspberries*, to help you grow all the rest of the ingredients for a summer pudding.

Try another idea...

HARD AND HAIRY

The gooseberry can be one of the ultimate tastes in the garden. Pick the right one from the bush that is slightly softer, and slightly browner than other berries, and your taste buds will be dancing. Get it wrong, however, and they'll be quivering as the tart juices attack your palate.

These fruits are fully self-fertile, hardy and prolific. They come in shades of red, white, green or yellow and can be eaten raw from the bush, or used in sorbets, pies and crumbles, and to flavour savoury sauces.

The planting and care is similar to redcurrants. Get them in the ground between November and February, remove the lower branches to a height of 15cm – this makes picking easier and less painful – and cut back main stems by half. To create an open, airy bush you can also cut down the growth in the centre to just one bud,

'*These imaginary pictures
were of different kinds
according to the
advertisements which he
came across, but for some
reason in every one of them
he had always to have
gooseberries. He could not
imagine a homestead, he
could not picture an idyllic
nook, without gooseberries.*'
From *Gooseberries* by ANTON
CHEKHOV

which should help prevent mildew, a common
problem with gooseberries. Keep a lookout too
for gooseberry saw fly and pick off any tiny
larvae as soon as you spot them, before they
strip the bush of leaves.

You can start picking at the end of May/early
June, but to get both cooking and dessert fruit
from the same bush, simply pick alternate
berries, leaving the rest of the fruit to ripen
like grapes. Varieties such as 'Early sulphur'
and the yellow-fruited 'Leveller' have good
flavour cooked or eaten raw. 'White Lion' has
large whitish fruit, while for the novelty of a
red gooseberry, try 'Pax'.

PRUNING FOR PRODUCTION

On the bush form of blackcurrants prune out about a third of the plant to ground
level each year to encourage new stems. It's easiest to do this at the same time as
picking, so you can simply take the pruned branches into the kitchen and remove
the fruit.

Red and white currants, and gooseberries, need both summer and winter pruning.
In summer tidy up the plant, trimming side shoots to four or five leaves and taking
out any cross shoots. In winter take the side shoots back to two buds and cut the
lead shoots back by half.

Q   To save space can I grow my fruit bushes against the wall?

*A   Gooseberries and red and white currants can be trained against a fence or
wall on wires as 'fans' with their stems spread out, or on a single upright
stem as a 'cordon'. Trained fruit is easy to prune, protect and pick. Leave
5cm at least between the plant and its support, and refer to a pruning book
to find out how to encourage a good crop.*

**Q   Having planted, pruned and pampered my currants do I need to
protect the fruit from the birds?**

*A   Unless netted, your precious currants and any gooseberries left to ripen on
the bush will be devoured by the birds. Place four canes, with a small plant
pot on top, around each plant. Spread a net over the top and secure at the
bottom with bricks so no feathered or other 'friends' can creep inside.*

How did
it go?

The end...

Or is it a new beginning? We hope that this book has inspired you to transform your garden. Maybe you're trying some plant varieties you hadn't heard of before, or started a pond or a wildlife garden. When your friends visit we hope they're knocked sideways by your inspired use of shades and textures. Let us know if that's the case. We'd like to be as amazed and impressed as they are.

So tell us how you got on. What did it for you – what helped you to turn that old bed into something the Chelsea Flower Show would be proud of? Maybe you've got some tips of your own you want to share (see next page if so). And if you liked this book you may find we have even more brilliant ideas that could change other areas of your life for the better.

You'll find the Infinite Ideas crew waiting for you online at www.infideas.com.

Or if you prefer to write, then send your letters to:
Create your dream garden
The Infinite Ideas Company Ltd
36 St Giles, Oxford OX1 3LD, United Kingdom

We want to know what you think, because we're all working on making our lives better too. Give us your feedback and you could win a copy of another *52 Brilliant Ideas* book of your choice. Or maybe get a crack at writing your own.

Good luck. Be brilliant.

Offer one

CASH IN YOUR IDEAS

We hope you enjoy this book. We hope it inspires, amuses, educates and entertains you. But we don't assume that you're a novice, or that this is the first book that you've bought on the subject. You've got ideas of your own. Maybe our authors have missed an idea that you use successfully. If so, why not send it to info@infideas.com, and if we like it we'll post it on our bulletin board. Better still, if your idea makes it into print we'll send you £50 and you'll be fully credited so that everyone knows you've had another Brilliant Idea.

Offer two

HOW COULD YOU REFUSE?

Amazing discounts on bulk quantities of Infinite Ideas books are available to corporations, professional associations and other organizations.

For details call us on:
+44 (0)1865 514888
or e-mail: info@infideas.com

Where it's at...